THIS VERY READABLE BOOK takes a unique and fascinating approach as it applies Augustine's principles of a just war to consider what a Christian should do when being involved, when necessary, in a Just Divorce. The author begins by offering an excellent survey of the biblical teaching on divorce. What makes this book unique is that it then walks the reader through the legal issues involved in a divorce proceeding. The author brings together his decades of experience as an attorney alongside of his commitment to biblical principles. He encourages the person going through a divorce to do so Christianly – not vengefully trying to destroy the other party, pursuing peace biblically, and especially caring for the needs of the "non-combatants" – that is the children. When I started ministry nearly forty years ago I was unprepared for the number of Christians who would go through divorce and for the many challenges they would face. This book is a much-needed resource to help believers to navigate the legal process while seeking to honor God by following the principles in His Word.

DR. JIM NEWHEISER is the Director of the Christian Counseling program and Associate Professor of Practical Theology at Reformed Theological Seminary in Charlotte, NC. He is the author of *Marriage, Divorce, and Remarriage: Critical Questions and Answers.* Jim served in pastoral ministry for over thirty years and has been practicing biblical counseling since 1982.

THE SEVEN PRINCIPLES OF A JUST DIVORCE

BIBLICAL WISDOM AND LEGAL INSIGHT

JOHN S. WEAVER

JUST CONDUCT BOOKS
Mount Airy, Maryland

The Seven Principles of a Just Divorce

Biblical Wisdom and Legal Insight

ISBN-13: 978-1-7353496-0-2 (Paperback)
         978-1-7353496-2-6 (eBook)

Published by JUST CONDUCT BOOKS, Mount Airy, Maryland

ABBREVIATIONS:

AAML	American Academy of Matrimonial Lawyers
ABA	American Bar Association
ALI	American Law Institute
BATNA	Best Alternative to a Negotiated Agreement
BIA	Best Interest Attorney
FLQ	Family Law Quarterly
MNADV	Maryland Network Against Domestic Violence
NPNF[1]	Nicene and Post-Nicene Fathers, Series 1
PCA	Presbyterian Church in America
QDRO	Qualified Domestic Relations Order
UCCJEA	Uniform Child Custody Jurisdiction and Enforcement Act
UMDA	Uniform Marriage and Divorce Act
WCF	Westminster Confession of Faith

To MY SON, Rick, who is truly a blessing from God.
I am so thankful and proud to be your father and friend.
Your boundless curiosity and your passion for music,
art, and writing inspire me.

To TWO CHERISHED FRIENDS. I want this book to reflect
the spirit and heart of both of you.

Christa Wells, your songs, your creativity, and
your vulnerability touch my heart. For many years you
have been a significant encouragement, inspiration, and friend.

Anahita Norouzi, you are a devoted mother, dedicated
to your vocation, and a true friend who has enriched my life.
Your excellent character and your appreciation
of the simple things remind me what really matters.

CONTENTS

Preface   13
Acknowledgments   17
Introduction   19

PART ONE: The Just Decision to Divorce   24
When It Is OK to Divorce

PRINCIPLE 1: Just Cause: Biblical Grounds for Divorce

CHAPTER 1: Adultery and Other Serious Sexual Sin   25
    1. Adultery and Other Sexual Sin   27
    2. The Rise of No-Fault Divorces   28
    3. The One Who Hates and Divorces   28
    4. Jesus' Rejection of Divorce for "Any Cause"   29
    5. Summary   34

CHAPTER 2: Desertion/Abandonment   35
    1. Desertion Is Not an Option for Married Christians   35
    2. Desertion by an Unbelieving Spouse   36
    3. Summary   38

CHAPTER 3: Spousal Abuse and Other Grounds   41
    1. When Life Isn't Sacred and Families Aren't Safe   41
    2. The Widespread Tragedy of Family Violence   43
    3. Indicators of Abuse   45
    4. Choosing to Abuse Others   46
    5. Remaining with or Returning to the Abuser   46
    6. Abuse and the One-Flesh Bond: Desertion   48
    7. Divorce for Neglect of Marital Obligations   51
    8. Summary   52

PRINCIPLE 2: Right Intention   54

CHAPTER 4: Motives Matter   55
    1. Definition of Motive   55
    2. Improper Motives   56
      a. Hatred, Vengeance, and Enmity   57
      b. Material Gain, Economic Relief   60
    3. Valid Motives   62

a. Love and Restoration   62
b. Trust in God   63
c. Willingness to Risk   64
d. Humility and Regret   65
4. Summary   66

PRINCIPLE 3: *Last Resort* **and**   68
PRINCIPLE 4: *Legitimate Authority*

CHAPTER 5: **Divorce As the Last Resort**   69
and the Wronged Spouse's Divorce Decision
1. Reasonable Hope   70
2. Supporting and Protecting the Survivor of Abuse   72
3. Forgiveness and the Decision Whether to Divorce   75
4. Summary   76

PRINCIPLE 5: *Limited Objectives (Goals Matter)*   78

CHAPTER 6: **Reasonable Alimony**   79
1. Alimony: General Background   80
2. Pendente Lite   81
3. Fixed Term   81
4. Indefinite   82
5. In Solido   83
6. Nominal or Reserved   83
7. Reimbursement   84
8. A Court's Required Considerations   85
   a. Vocational or Employment Rehabilitation Factors   86
   b. Standard of Living   86
   c. Length of Marriage   86
   d. Monetary and Nonmonetary Contributions to the Family   87
   e. Marital Misconduct   87
   f. The Age and Health of the Parties   88
   g. Each Party's Financial Needs and Resources   88
   h. Monetary Award and Property Division   89
   i. Cost of Health Insurance Coverage   90
   j. Tax Consequences   90
   k. Any Previously Established Agreement Between the Parties   91
9. Alimony Guidelines   91
10. Modification, Extension, and Termination of Alimony   92
11. Summary   93

CHAPTER 7: Equitable Division of Property — 95
1. Community Property States — 95
2. Common Law and Equitable Distribution States — 96
3. Step 1: Classification of Property — 97
   a. Retirement Benefits — 98
   b. All Property vs. Marital Property Only — 98
   c. Source of Funds: Tracing and Comingling — 99
4. Protecting a Spouse from Financial Misconduct — 102
5. Step 2: Valuation of Property — 103
6. Step 3: Equitable Distribution — 105
   a. Marital Debt — 106
   b. Defined Benefit Plan (Pension) Benefits — 107
   c. Military Retirement Benefits — 108
   d. The Marital Residence — 109
   e. Contribution — 110
7. Interim Distribution and Modifying Orders — 110
8. Life Insurance — 111
9. Bankruptcy — 111
10. Attorneys' Fees, Suit Money, and Costs — 111
11. Summary — 112

PART TWO: The Just Process of Divorce: Just Conduct During the Proceedings — 114

PRINCIPLE 6: Proportionate Means — 114

CHAPTER 8: Effective Negotiation Strategies — 115
1. Prepare to Negotiate: Wise Planning — 117
   a. Prayer — 118
   b. Knowledge/Information — 118
   c. Understand the Problem — 119
   d. Understand Your Own Interests — 119
   e. Understand Your Settlement Objectives — 119
   f. Understand the Other Side — 120
   g. Understand Your and Your Spouse's BATNA — 121
2. Affirm Relationships — 122
3. Understand Interests — 125
4. Search for Creative Solutions — 126
5. Evaluate Options Objectively and Reasonably — 128
6. Closing the Deal — 130
7. Summary — 130

CHAPTER 9: Alternative Dispute Resolution 131
  1. The Mediation Process 131
  2. Collaborative Divorce 134
  3. Arbitration 138
  4. Christian Conciliation 141
  5. Summary 142

CHAPTER 10: Court Litigation 143
  1. Complaint and Summons 144
  2. The Answer or Response 145
  3. Financial Statements 146
  4. The Scheduling or Status Conference 146
  5. Discovery Process 147
    a. Interrogatories 148
    b. Requests for Production of Documents 149
    c. Depositions 154
    d. Requests for Admissions of Facts 155
    e. Court Enforcement of Discovery Obligations 156
    f. Self-Help, Cost-Saving Discovery Tips 156
  6. A Pretrial or Settlement Conference 158
  7. The Trial 159
  8. Summary 160

PRINCIPLE 7: Immunity of Noncombatants 162

CHAPTER 11: Child Security: Sheltering Children
from the Parents' Conflict 163
  1. Protect Children from Harmful Conflict 163
    a. Parental Conflict 165
    b. Authoritative Parenting 167
  2. Services to Protect Children from Harm 169
    a. Enhanced Access to Justice 169
    b. Court-Affiliated Parent Education Programs 171
    c. Custody Mediation 172
    d. Custody Evaluations 172
    e. Parenting Coordinators 174
    f. Best Interest Attorneys (or Guardians Ad Litem) 175
  3. Judicial Interviews of Children 176
  4. Restrictions on Custody and Visitation 177
  5. Child Abduction Preventive Measures 178
  6. What Does Custody Mean? 179

7. Strategic Parenting Plans   181
8. Summary   184

CHAPTER 12: Child Custody: How Courts Decide   187
What's in the Child's Best Interests
  1. Fundamental and Constitutional Parental Rights   188
  2. Common Legal Standard: "Best Interests of the Child"   189
  3. Factors Courts Consider   189
    a. Fitness to Care for Child   189
    b. Mental and Physical Health   190
    c. The Role as the "Friendly Parent"   191
    d. The Child's Preference   192
    e. The Parents' Preference   192
    f. The Ability to Reach Shared Decisions   193
    g. A History of Alcohol or Substance Abuse   193
    h. Incidents of Domestic Violence or Child Abuse   194
    i. The Child's Key Relationships   194
    j. The Ability to Meet the Child's Needs   195
    k. Age and Gender   196
    l. Stability and Continuity for the Child   196
    m. The Geographic Proximity of the Parents' Homes   196
    n. Primary Care Provider of the Child   197
    o. Religion   198
    p. Protecting the Child from Parental Conflict   199
    q. Military Deployment   199
    r. Relocation-Specific Considerations   200
  4. Which Courts Have Jurisdiction When Parents   202
    Live in Different States?
    a. Primacy of Home State Jurisdiction   202
    b. Continuing Exclusive Jurisdiction   203
  5. Enforcement of Custody and Visitation Orders   203
  6. Summary   204

CHAPTER 13: Child Support: Protecting Children   205
from Financial Harm
  1. Jurisdiction Over Obligor   205
  2. Age of Majority and Duration of Support   206
  3. Child Support Guidelines   206
  4. Income   208
  5. Health Insurance and Extraordinary Medical Expenses   209
  6. Child Care Expenses   210

7. Education Expenses   211
8. Determining Whether to Adjust the Calculated Amount   211
9. Impact of Shared Parenting Time   212
10. Split Custody   212
11. Income Exceeding the Guidelines Schedule   213
12. Retroactive Obligation to Pay Child Support   213
13. Modification of Child Support   213
14. Enforcement of Child Support   214
15. Summary   215

CHAPTER 14: The Way of Wisdom: Divorce that is Just, Fair, and Right   217

Bibliography   220
Endnotes   234

PREFACE

MANY BOOKS HAVE BEEN WRITTEN about divorce—some of them specifically addressing Christians—but *The Seven Principles of a Just Divorce* offers a different perspective. I will challenge you to think more biblically and broadly about what makes the decision to divorce just and what kind of conduct is just if you do decide to pursue divorce.

As a family law attorney and a Christian, I bring a unique background to this book. Having been an attorney for more than thirty years, I've represented hundreds of clients who were going through divorce and dealing with child custody matters, and for six years I presided over thousands of contested family law hearings as a magistrate.

I have dealt with divorce personally: I was divorced twenty-five years ago after a twenty-year relationship during which God blessed us with a child. As a church leader, I have taught classes about marriage and divorce, as well as wrestled through the issue of divorce with estranged couples in the church. My understanding of divorce and response to both situations was informed by my years of Bible study as well as the studying I did in pursuit of my master of arts in religion.

In seminary I had the privilege of studying under Dr. John M. Frame, who impressed upon me that Christian living is "the application of the Word of God by persons to all areas of life"[1] and that "ethical judgment involves the application of a *norm* to a *situation* by a *person*."[2] Ethics is a critical component of the decision to divorce and the pursuit of divorce. Ideally, we want to understand, apply, and obey God's Word.

13

PRINCIPLES OF A JUST WAR

The Seven Principles of a Just Divorce is my effort to integrate theology, life, faith, and practice. The catalyst for the book was an essay on divorce I wrote for the Pastoral and Social Ethics course taught by Dr. Mark Ross at Reformed Theological Seminary. As I was driving to the post office to submit "A Just Divorce or Just a Divorce?" before the mailing deadline, I suddenly realized that the principles a military leader considers when deciding whether a war is just—principles often credited to St. Augustine—could help an individual determine whether or not a divorce is just. My mind raced through the principles of Just War theory: (1) just cause; (2) just intention; (3) last resort; (4) legitimate authority; (5) limited objectives; (6) proportionate means; and (7) noncombatant immunity.[3]

I clearly saw that the Just War construct could facilitate the debate about divorce and remarriage, the analysis of pertinent biblical texts, and the identification of general biblical principles for conduct appropriate to the tragic circumstances of divorce. The Just War theory is not at all a forced metaphor or arbitrary analogy. The theory serves as a framework for applying both classical and biblical wisdom to an unfortunately all-too-common situation in order to achieve a righteous result in this fallen world.

Just War concepts may be applied to divorce because the questions asked in war have counterparts in divorce. To be specific, when deciding whether or not to divorce, we must consider not only (1) the biblical defense (just cause) but also the (2) motives (just intention); (3) alternatives to divorce (last resort); (4) the authority of the individual, church, and state in determining the validity of the divorce decision (legitimate authority); and the (5) goals of the divorce (limited objectives). Regarding the pursuit of divorce, we must consider (6) the means used to attain the goals as well as the consequences of the divorce and its process (proportionate means), including (7) the impact on civilians or noncombatants, specifically the minor children in the divorcing family (noncombatant immunity).

An interesting aspect of Just War considerations is that they address not only the decision of whether to go to war but also what constitutes the ethical execution of war. Significant in a Just Divorce is not only the biblical justification for pursuing that divorce, but also the morality of the manner in which it is pursued.

Although I was excited by the possible incorporation of this Just Divorce construct, my essay was due. I had no time at all to rework my paper. Later, though, my master's thesis provided an opportunity for me to use the Just War analogy to both summarize the biblical teaching on divorce and stimulate a discussion of what constitutes a Just Divorce.

My Hopes for This Book

Finally, I am well aware of my shortcomings as a spouse, parent, attorney, neighbor, writer, and person. These human failings too often lead to and even equate to sin, so I am grateful for God's grace in my life. I pray that by his grace the biblical wisdom and legal insight I lay out in this book will help you to apply his Word to this matter of divorce however it impacts your life, to grow in your faith, to navigate the difficulties and challenges you are facing, to learn what is "right and just and fair" (Proverbs 1:3), and to do justice, to love kindness, and to walk humbly with your God (Micah 6:8).

John S. Weaver
Mount Airy, Maryland

ACKNOWLEDGMENTS

I AM GRATEFUL for the many clients throughout the years who gave me the opportunity and privilege of representing them. Each of you helped me to become both a better attorney and person.

I am grateful to Dr. Howard Griffith, who recently went home to be with the Lord. As my thesis advisor at Reformed Theological Seminary, as well as after my graduation, he provided encouragement and cogent feedback.

In addition, Dr. John M. Frame and other seminary professors left their mark on my heart and mind.

I want to especially thank Natalie Nyquist, who was enthusiastic about the need for this book. She applied her exceptional professional editing skills to improve its quality and make it more readable in every way.

Finally, I much appreciate Lisa Guest's thorough copy editing and Bruce Barbour's guiding the manuscript through to publication.

INTRODUCTION

SEPARATION AND DIVORCE occur all too often, touching families of all religious faiths. In Christian circles the primary—and often sole—focus is whether biblically permissible grounds for divorce exist. But that discussion sometimes generates more heat than light. In this book I explain what constitutes a Just Divorce, and then I apply biblical wisdom and legal insight to both the decision and the pursuit of divorce.

A just *decision* to divorce involves more than a spouse's biblically defined misconduct. Proper motives for the divorce and the establishment of fair goals for the dissolution of the marriage are required, and the final decision to divorce should be made only as the last recourse after the two parties have weighed the realistic alternatives.

A just *pursuit* of divorce includes reasonable means and strategies for achieving a financially fair outcome and minimizing collateral damage, especially to children of the marriage.

Seven principles originally outlined as a tool for determining a Just War will guide both parts of *The Seven Principles of a Just Divorce*.

PART ONE: THE JUST DECISION TO DIVORCE

Principle 1: Just Cause: Biblical Grounds for Divorce
A Just Divorce requires that the divorce happens only in the case of just causes, specifically, substantial breaches of the marriage covenant. Principle 1 examines what the Bible teaches about the grounds for a Just

Divorce; divorce is not an option for every reason given by someone set on divorce. Willful misconduct (such as adultery and other serious sexual sin), desertion, and spousal abuse so strike at the essence of the marriage bond that divorce might be legitimate. Such misconduct involves unequivocal, intentional, and unilateral violation of the marriage vows, and the offending spouse is to be held morally responsible.

Principle 2: Right Intention: Motives Matter

Although a just cause may exist for a divorce, wrong motives—hatred, vengeance, and material greed—may invalidate that cause. Love for God and for neighbor (including love for an estranged spouse); the desire for peace; trusting God; and living with a spirit of humility are right intentions. During a divorce, however, shifting emotions like anger and hatred may surface. But if a person has the right motives for pursuing divorce—to promote good and to avoid evil—then the divorce is just in that respect.

Principle 3: Last Resort and
Principle 4: Legitimate Authority

Divorce is the last recourse when a husband and wife have no more resources to draw from, when—realistically—nothing can restore the marriage relationship. Even when a divorce is scripturally permissible due to one spouse's serious sexual sin, desertion, or abuse, the possibility of reconciliation should nevertheless be seriously and prayerfully considered.

Both church and state should be especially protective and supportive of abused spouses as well as their abused children. These individuals should seek out the guidance and input of their church or loving Christian community. However, when biblical grounds for divorce do exist, the decision to divorce is the decision of the wronged spouse. Only that spouse has the authority to make that call.

Forgiveness, however, does not remove all the consequences of a spouse's betrayal of marital vows. Divorce may in fact be the right path to take and a tough consequence for the betraying spouse to live with.

Principle 5: Limited Objectives: Goals Matter

A Just Divorce also involves pursuing objectives that are just, fair, and right. Equitable property division and reasonable spousal and child support require fair resolution. This principle is the lens through which I look at alimony awards and property division. A just financial outcome—whether through negotiation or litigation—is a crucial objective in promoting satisfactory peace.

PART TWO: THE JUST PURSUIT OF DIVORCE

Principle 6: Proportionate Means

Divorces often resemble wars in that battle tactics are frequently extreme. The means used in pursuit of divorce should be limited to what is reasonable and necessary to secure a just resolution.

Because couples usually resolve their issues before a contested trial begins, each individual's understanding of effective negotiation strategies may lead to more satisfying settlement. Mediation, where an impartial third party assists in reaching an agreement, is the most prevalent alternative dispute resolution process. Another option is collaborative divorce: a divorcing couple along with their attorneys and other professionals work to resolve issues. Third, in arbitration the parties appear before an impartial arbitrator who renders an award that may be binding. Finally, Christian conciliation is intended to be based on biblical principles, with attention to the spiritual dimension, and promote settlement in a conciliatory rather than adversarial manner. I will, however, provide guidance for navigating the adversarial litigation process, from the filing of the divorce action through the end of the trial. Litigation can be a reasonable and proportionate means to resolve divorce-related disputes.

Principle 7: The Immunity of Noncombatants

Children are neither the combatants in nor the spoils of a divorce. Yet many parents place their child in the crossfire of both their divorce war and custody battle when they actually have the moral duty to limit harm by reducing parental conflict. Authoritative parenting—that combines parental love with clear, firm, fair, and well-reasoned discipline—is also critical because it promotes the child's welfare. Finally, when necessary, courts can protect children with appropriate restrictions and conditions on parental access.

When parents can't agree on a parenting plan, the court will decide where the child will reside and allocate the decision-making responsibilities it deems to be in the child's best interest. A parent's obligation to support the minor child is both a moral duty and legal obligation, so in the last chapter we will examine child support guidelines.

Finally, valid biblical grounds for divorce do exist, but not every divorce is just even though it may be permissible. This book, however, provides a framework to help individuals wisely apply Just War principles to the end of their marriage. Doing so can help you determine whether a divorce may be biblically permissible and assure you that, in its commencement, execution, and outcome, yours will be a Just Divorce.

PART ONE

The Just Decision to Divorce
When It Is OK to Divorce

PRINCIPLE 1
Just Cause: Biblical Grounds for Divorce

CHAPTER 1

Adultery and Other Serious Sexual Sin

"THIS WAS EASIER than getting a driver's license!" my son exclaimed as the court clerk handed him his marriage license. I smiled as I recalled that Rick had to complete nearly 100 hours of a driver education course, do a good amount of parent-supervised driving, and pass both the written and the behind-the-wheel driving tests in order to get a merely provisional driver's license.

In contrast, to get their marriage license, Rick and his fiancée simply had to appear together at the county courthouse, fill out a one-page form, present their birth certificates and photo ID, and pay the $50 fee.

Marriage appears easy to enter into, but during the past several decades, it has become increasingly easy to exit as well. In fact, a then-married friend once suggested to me that a marriage license should be like a driver's license: renewable every few years. If you don't want to stay married, simply let the marriage license expire.

Others evaluate their marriage in light of their personal happiness and fulfillment. When feelings of love dissipate or dissatisfaction takes hold, the marriage contract should be terminable on demand—no questions asked. These views are founded on the idea that either spouse should be able to end the marriage for any reason—or for no reason at all.

A Christian considering divorce, however, must first determine whether the marital difficulties biblically warrant divorce. Our authoritative rule of faith and life is God's Word (2 Timothy 3:16),[1] and we are to humbly submit our will to God's. Yet doing so is complicated by the inconsistency between a legitimate scriptural basis for divorce and the court's grounds for divorce that are not scripturally supported. What, then, are the just causes that permit divorce?

According to Mennonite theologian and ethicist John Howard Yoder,[2] to justify going to war—or, in our case, to file for divorce—the offense must meet these standards:

- "Unequivocal..." "actual, not only possible"
- "Intentional, not inadvertent or unintended or an honest error"
- "Of substantial importance"
- "Objective, verifiable as to fact," and
- "Unilateral, not provoked"

As these criteria imply, no one begins a Just War because of trivial slights or offenses. Similarly, the just cause for divorce should be an actual offense of substantial importance, an offense that materially breaches the marriage covenant. These criteria provide a more objective basis than relying solely on an offended spouse's disappointment, hurt, or rage. Wise counsel is also helpful in assessing the nature and extent of the offense as well as the appropriate response.

The intentional violation of marital vows is a significant factor when deciding just cause. Yoder explains the moral responsibility: "The enemy must have responsibility for committing it; the offense must be something for which we can blame them, hold them accountable. It must not be something they slipped into inadvertently or indirectly. . . . We must be sure that the enemy is consciously doing something wrong and doing it to us."[3]

Similarly, scriptural principles show disdain for divorce that is prompted by trifling matters. God's Word upholds the justness of divorce for intentional offenses of substantial importance, such as adultery, desertion, and abuse.

Adultery and Other Sexual Sin

Scripture presents adultery as both a violation of God's commands for his children and a serious breach of the marriage covenant. The Ten Commandments, the laws of Deuteronomy, and the Holiness Code found in Leviticus clearly and consistently forbid adultery (see Exodus 20:14).

In fact, adultery was a capital offense for both parties (Deuteronomy 22:22) although no Old Testament passage reports an enforcement of the death penalty.[4] In New Testament times, the legal authority to implement the death penalty apparently did not exist under Roman rule. David Instone-Brewer observes that adultery was theoretically "still a capital offense in the first century CE, though there is no record of this ever being applied. The normal punishment was divorce without repayment of the *ketubah* [the Jewish marriage contract that had a financial component]."[5]

Further biblical evidence shows that certain sexual sins did not invariably result in the death penalty; at some point capital punishment for sexual offenses was either abolished or no longer enforced.[6]

In 1 Corinthians 5, Paul addressed an instance of incest where "a man ha[d] his father's wife" (v. 1). The penalty in Leviticus for such incest is the same as for adulterers: "both of them shall surely be put to death" (20:10). However, Paul directed the church at Corinth to excommunicate, not stone to death, the sexually immoral man.[7]

As God's law indicates, sexual immorality is a serious offense against God. It may also severely impact the marriage covenant as well as God's relationship with his people. Divorce and excommunication are, respectively, appropriate substitutes for the dissolution of marriage that would have occurred if the death penalty for adultery and other serious sexual sin were enforced.[8]

Despite the potential consequences, adultery continues to snare both men and women. Proverbs 7 is a cautionary tale about adultery's enticement, entrapment, and destruction. The speaker urges the son to not repeat the folly of the simpleminded, immature youth of the story;

the son must not become sexually involved with any woman other than his own wife. Accepting and living according to this wisdom will deliver the son from adultery's trap. The wise person will honor God by following his commands and protecting the sanctity of the marital bond.

Furthermore, Christians are called to "flee from sexual immorality" and "glorify God in your body" (1 Corinthians 6:18, 20). The writer of Hebrews also urged that marriage be honored by all "and let the marriage bed be undefiled, for God will judge the sexually immoral and adulterous" (Hebrews 13:4). Sexual unrighteousness and ungodliness provoke God's wrath, and a lifestyle of adultery and sexual promiscuity indicates the absence of an intimate relationship with God and can lead to a judgment that has eternal consequences.[9]

The Rise of No-Fault Divorces

In the United States, grounds for divorce are much broader and more permissive than the Bible's. Beginning in 1969, states have enacted liberalized, no-fault divorces that either supplant or supplement the traditional grounds for divorce that assigned responsibility, such as adultery and desertion. Forty-three states permit divorce on the grounds of a married couple's incompatibility, their irreconcilable differences, an irretrievably broken marriage, or some similar basis; a third of the jurisdictions have a no-fault option as the sole reason for divorce.[10]

The One Who Hates and Divorces

A spouse who lightly discards his marriage vows seriously displeases God. The action displays faithless covenant breaking, jeopardizes the raising of godly children (thereby diluting the covenant community), and often reveals personal hatred rather than covenant love.[11]

In the Old Testament the prophet Malachi wrote that God rejected his people's offerings because the husbands' breaking their marital covenants was so prevalent: "Because the LORD was witness between you and the wife of your youth, to whom you have been faithless, though she is your companion and your wife by covenant" (2:14).

Unfaithfulness in marriage is not only a sinful breach of the covenantal relationship of marriage to which God was a witness, but as a violation of the covenant God made with his people, this unfaithfulness is also a sin against God.[12]

While God hates divorce—that is, he hates the underlying marital sin, the breaking of vows that occasion divorce, and the grievous shattering of human hearts—the English Standard Version captures the proper sense of Malachi 2:16: "For the man who hates and divorces, says the LORD, the God of Israel, covers his garment with violence." The text condemns "what may be called 'unjustified divorce,' that is, divorce based on aversion."[13] Malachi's concern is "to condemn such divorces as unethical and, as an instance of infidelity . . . or covenant breaking (cf. 2:14), liable to divine judgment: 'Therefore, take heed to yourselves!'"[14]

Scripture does not approve of divorce on the grounds of generalized incompatibility, irreconcilable differences, or irretrievably broken relationships. Jesus' interpretation of Deuteronomy 24:1–4 reinforces this rejection of divorce for the reasons above, which is also referred to as "any cause."

Jesus' Rejection of Divorce for "Any Cause"

Divorcing a spouse for aversion or "any cause" is not supported by Scripture. Yet, despite the intended lifelong covenant of marriage that God had established from the beginning, Mosaic Law allowed divorce (Deuteronomy 24:1–4) because of—in Jesus' words—man's "hardness of heart" (Matthew 19:8). This Deuteronomic case law presupposed that divorce was permitted and regulated divorces and certain remarriages that might otherwise encourage casual and impetuous decisions.

Much of the debate about biblical grounds for divorce involves our interpretation of Deuteronomy 24:1, where a husband writes a certificate of divorce to his wife who "finds no favor in his eyes because he has found some indecency in her." This text recognizes the protection a certificate of divorce accords a woman by declaring her free to marry another man without further claim against her by the husband who divorced her.[15] The first husband, having given her a certificate of divorce, cannot then claim that her subsequent relationship with another man is adulterous. The text doesn't specify the grounds for divorce, and the meaning of "something indecent" is vague and unclear.

Vague yet broad, the phrase *some indecency* as grounds for divorce was a point of contention between two rival first-century Pharisees and their followers: the more conservative Rabbi Shammai and the more liberal Rabbi Hillel.[16] The Mishnah's collected rabbinic teaching includes the disagreements between these two rabbinic schools.

The school of Shammai emphasized the word *indecency* and narrowly defined it as some unspecified lewd or unchaste sexual offense or misconduct. In contrast, the school of Hillel stressed the meaning of *some* or *any* and broadly interpreted the phrase to include any matter. A wife's spoiling a meal was sufficient grounds for divorce. Along those same lines, the second-century Rabbi Aqiba even permitted divorce for the husband upon his finding someone he considered more attractive.[17]

This permissive divorce for any cause—for any reason whatsoever—was prevalent in first-century Judaism. A spouse could end the marriage for trivial reasons rather than genuine marital fault, making the divorce completely groundless.[18]

The Pharisees attempted to thrust Jesus into this rabbinical debate when they tested him by asking, "Is it lawful to divorce one's wife *for any cause*?" (Matthew 19:3, emphasis added). The Pharisees were not asking Jesus his view on whether divorce was ever lawful. After all, Rabbi Hillel and Rabbi Shammai agreed that divorce was lawful. Rather, the Pharisees were asking Jesus what he thought of the Hillelite "any cause" divorce and how he understood Deuteronomy 24:1.[19]

Jesus' response stressed that from the beginning God intended marriages to be lifelong (Matthew 19:4–6). This answer prompted the Pharisees to further test Jesus by inquiring, "Why then did Moses *command* one to give a certificate of divorce and to send her away?" (v. 7). Jesus replied that Moses *allowed* divorce due to man's "hardness of heart" (v. 8), but that "whoever divorces his wife, except for sexual immorality [*porneia*], and marries another, commits adultery" (v. 9).

In the Sermon on the Mount, Jesus taught that "everyone who divorces his wife, except on the ground of sexual immorality [*porneia*], makes her commit adultery. And whoever marries a divorced woman commits adultery" (Matthew 5:32). Jesus stressed that God did not command divorce, as the Pharisees had supposed, because divorce was completely contrary to God's original intention. Divorce was simply the concession and accommodation God made in light of humanity's hardhearted sinfulness, evident in their "stubborn unwillingness to be faithful to the marriage covenant."[20]

Jesus' teaching about Deuteronomy 24:1 was closer to Shammai's interpretation: Shammai saw the text limiting the grounds for divorce to sexual immorality while Hillel maintained that "any cause" was sufficient.[21] As Instone-Brewer concludes, in the context of responding to the question, Jesus (and the Shammaites) meant that there is only one valid type of divorce in Deuteronomy 24:1," but that he was not necessarily implying "that there is only one valid type of divorce *in the whole of Scripture.*"[22] Indeed, in 1 Corinthians 7, the apostle Paul addressed other circumstances—a spouse's desertion—when divorce is permissible.

Also note Jesus' teaching that divorce for sexual immorality was *permitted* whereas both rabbinical schools taught that divorce was *required* in those circumstances.[23] Thus, Jesus highlighted the opportunity and possibility of forgiveness and reconciliation rather than the mandatory dissolution of the marriage. Additionally, he applied this teaching to both men and women rather than to only men, as was the rabbinic tradition.[24]

Matthew 19:3–12 offers the perspective of the husband, but in view of the reciprocal teaching of 5:32 and Mark 10:11–12, Matthew 19 also seems applicable to both women and men. Just as a man may divorce his wife for her sexual immorality, so a woman may divorce her husband for that same reason.

Now, while the word *porneia* does mean adultery, it also refers to various kinds of sexual immorality, including homosexual conduct, incest, sexual abuse or molestation, indecent exposure, bestiality, and prostitution.[25]

Dr. John Frame, in agreement with a Presbyterian Church of America (PCA) report, asserts that when conduct such as habitual masturbation and obsessive use of pornography becomes so externalized as to "serve as substitutes for marital sex" and break the one-flesh marriage relationship, they may also be grounds for divorce.[26] All sexually immoral conduct of this gravity strikes at the sexually exclusive, one-flesh nature God intended for a husband and wife from the beginning.[27]

In light of God's original design for marriage, some Christians do argue that divorce is never permissible, and they base their case on Mark and Luke's omission of sexual immorality as grounds for divorce, the exception Jesus specified. Lacking any such exception clause, the Mark and Luke passages thereby seem to declare marriage to another after any divorce to be adultery[28]: a husband who divorces his wife and remarries commits adultery (Mark 10:11; Luke 16:18)[29]; a woman who divorces her husband and remarries commits adultery (Mark 10:11); and a man who marries a divorced woman commits adultery (Luke 16:18; Matthew 5:32).

Some scholars argue that the absence of an exception in Mark and Luke is due to the different audience: Matthew may have included it for his Jewish readers, while Mark and Luke may not have thought it necessary to include because their Gentile audience knew that sexual immorality was always a ground for divorce and they "took the clause for granted."[30]

While their audiences certainly may have influenced what the writers included in their gospel, an examination of the context of Matthew 5, Matthew 19, Mark 10, and Luke 16 will help clarify Jesus' teaching about divorce. In Matthew's account, Jesus taught about divorce in the Sermon on the Mount, "a discourse that gives the norms of the kingdom and the sanctity of marriage"[31]:

"It was also said, 'Whoever divorces his wife, let him give her a certificate of divorce.' But I say to you that everyone who divorces his wife, except on the ground of sexual immorality, makes her commit adultery. And whoever marries a divorced woman commits adultery." (Matthew 5:31–32)

Ancient Jews, Greeks, and Romans all held that lawful divorce granted a person the right to remarry, and the certificate of divorce given to a Jewish woman permitted her to remarry free of any future claim made by her former husband. Accordingly, Jesus' words "would almost certainly have been taken as permission for remarriage when divorce was permitted, i.e., after marital unfaithfulness."[32]

In contrast to tradition that was allowing husbands divorce for any reason, Jesus' point was the sanctity of marriage: Jesus sought "to prevent the betrayal of innocent spouses."[33]

In closing, know that this short discourse is hardly a comprehensive or definitive statement on what qualifies as grounds for divorce. So I encourage you to read this section in the greater context of the Sermon on the Mount's emphasis: individuals who are aware of their own spiritual need, who grieve for their own sin, who humbly submit to God, who seek righteousness, and who are also merciful, pure in heart, peacemakers, and willing to endure persecution (Matthew 5:2–10) will seek to preserve marriage rather than end an unpleasant one.

Also, Jesus' statement here should not be considered an absolute prohibition against divorce and remarriage, as will be shown in the upcoming discussion of Paul's allowing divorce on the basis of an unbeliever's desertion (1 Corinthians 7:12–16).[34]

Significant contextual matters regarding Matthew 19 are also worth noting. First, the Pharisees were trying to trap Jesus. Also, they asked Jesus specifically about a man who wanted to divorce his wife, not about a woman who desired to divorce her husband. Neither did the Pharisees raise such issues as physical abuse or desertion. It does not necessarily follow that because Jesus did not address any other basis for divorce, he was excluding all other grounds.[35] Despite arguments to the contrary, Jesus clearly taught that a person may divorce a spouse who has been sexually immoral, and Jesus implicitly permitted remarriage after that valid divorce.[36]

Summary

While every sin does not provide cause for divorce, adultery and other serious sexual sins that strike at the one-flesh nature and sexual exclusivity of the marriage bond qualify as biblically permissible just cause, and the wronged spouse may seek a divorce. The person who commits adultery not only abandons a spouse but also breaks a sacred covenant.

According to the Scriptures, divorce is expressly permitted on two grounds: a spouse's sexual immorality and an unbelieving spouse's desertion. Sexual immorality breaks the exclusive one-flesh intimacy of the marriage covenant, and desertion breaks the covenantal obligation to leave the parents' house and cleave to one's spouse[37] Both divorce and remarriage are allowed in these two cases.

CHAPTER 2

Desertion/Abandonment

APPARENTLY, in first-century Corinth an ascetic or pro-celibacy segment of the local church was urging believers to divorce if they could not live with their marriage partner in complete sexual abstinence.[1] In 1 Corinthians 7:1–7 the apostle Paul spoke forcefully against any insistence on celibate marriages. Then he addressed divorce when both spouses are Christians.

Desertion Is Not an Option for Married Christians

Paul clearly stated the Lord's authoritative charge: "the wife should not separate from her husband (but if she does, she should remain unmarried or else be reconciled to her husband), and the husband should not divorce his wife" (1 Corinthians 7:10–11).

The Greek words translated *separate* and *divorce* both commonly referred to divorce, and the two are used interchangeably throughout 1 Corinthians 7. Under Roman law, spouses who separated—whether a spouse left or was sent away—were legally divorced and free to remarry.[2] Adams observes that the word *separate* means "to separate by divorce."[3]

But the same principle underlying Jesus' disapproval of Jewish "any cause" divorces also condemns the equivalent Greco-Roman groundless divorce-by-separation. The general principle is that married believers should remain living together and not divorce.

If a Christian separates and persists in such desertion, it may be appropriate for this irremediable *de facto* divorce to be confirmed by a judicial divorce decree. At some point the deserting Christian's obstinate refusal to reconcile may result in his or her being treated as an unbeliever, permitting the offended spouse to obtain a scripturally legitimate divorce (Matthew 18:15–20).

Paul's apostolic teaching is consistent with what Jesus taught: Paul emphasized God's intended purpose of lifelong marriage and of believers avoiding adultery that results from divorce or divorce and remarriage (Romans 7:2–3). Paul's omission of the exception clause of Matthew 19:9 is likely because the fact that sexual immorality was grounds for divorce was taken for granted. Moreover, Paul was contrasting the situation of married believers (verses 10–11) with a marriage between a believer and an unbeliever (verses 12–16). Mentioning the exception allowing divorce on the basis of sexual immorality was neither pertinent nor necessary.[4]

Desertion by an Unbelieving Spouse

Due to the post-marriage conversion of a spouse, whether Jew or Gentile, mixed marriages arose as the gospel spread in Corinth. Some Corinthian believers seemed concerned that a mixed marriage somehow defiled the Christian and thereby required an end to the marriage. In Paul's authoritative judgment, though, a Christian being married to a non-Christian was not a sufficient basis for divorce. One reason a Christian should remain with an unbelieving spouse is that the Christian spouse sanctifies the divinely instituted marriage relationship as well as the marriage partner.[5] Their children are deemed "holy" or set apart, and they benefit from being educated spiritually and morally and nurtured in the Christian community.[6]

To believers who were married to unbelievers, Paul said, "If any brother has a wife who is an unbeliever, and she consents to live with him, he should not divorce her" and "If any woman has a husband who is an unbeliever, and he consents to live with her, she should not divorce him" (1 Corinthians 7:12–13), but "if the unbelieving partner separates, let it be so. In such cases the brother or sister is not enslaved. God has called you to peace" (v. 15).

God calls the believing spouse to live peaceably with the unbelieving spouse by maintaining the pre-conversion marital harmony. These new believers should not cause strife by initiating divorce against someone who has consented to continue in the marriage.[7] However, if the unbeliever chooses to end the marriage, the Christian is not bound to maintain it and is released from any obligations.[8]

Although Paul was not explicitly addressing remarriage in verse 15, the divorced Christian partner was completely free to do so. The divorce requested by an unbeliever would apparently give the believer freedom to remarry.[9] The Christian was not under any obligation to remain unmarried or to pursue reconciliation. Within Jewish, Roman, and Greek cultures of Paul's time, "divorce almost universally carried with it provisions for remarriage," and if Paul had intended to forbid remarriage, he would have expressly stated so in verse 15.[10] Christian counselor and author Jay Adams notes, however, that the believer could not remarry an unconverted partner. Doing so would violate the command that believers are to marry "only in the Lord" (1 Corinthians 7:39).[11]

The Westminster Confession of Faith also recognizes irremediable "willful desertion" as grounds for divorce.[12] Similarly, Adams states, "If the unbeliever is expressly desirous of separating (by divorce), the believer must not try to hinder him. . . . (Clearly) desertion would be an act evidencing a strong desire to separate. It would plainly imply lack of consent over continuing the marriage."[13]

This desertion—and even the mere desire to depart the marriage relationship—will be evident in the unbeliever's words or actions, including physically leaving the home; long-term unjustified refusal to engage in marital sexual relations; persistent verbal, emotional, or physical abuse (discussed in the next chapter); persistent and intentional withholding of financial support and living necessities; and such other serious, destructive, even cruel behaviors that constitute a deliberate renunciation of the deserter's marriage covenant vows and commitment.[14] A spouse's desertion can be a reality even when the marriage partners are living in the same physical residence. Clearly, the unbeliever's verbal consent to live with his spouse is not binding when his conduct belies his words.

Summary

The biblical grounds for divorce—adultery (a term that includes other serious sexual misconduct) and desertion—correspond with principles regarding a just cause to go to war: each offense is unequivocal, actual, intentional, verifiable, unilateral, and of substantial importance. The divorce exceptions of Jesus and Paul are similar in that they involve "the person whose marriage is ended against his or her will."[15] The bases for divorce are not trivial slights. Rather, they are intentional violations of marital vows, offenses of substantial magnitude for which the offender is morally responsible and provide just cause to hold the offending spouse accountable through divorce.

Consider what adultery and desertion—the biblically legitimate reasons for divorce—have in common. Both unfaithfulness and desertion destroy fundamental parts of the marriage covenant; both recognize the last-resort nature of divorce; and both "leave one party without any other options" when efforts to reconcile are rejected.[16] God does not intend unfaithfulness and desertion to give an easy out to spouses facing marital problems or inconveniences, but the presence of unfaithfulness and desertion may absolve from blame those individuals who tried unsuccessfully to keep their marriage together even as "their spouse's unrepentant adultery, abandonment, or abuse *de facto* destroyed the marriage bonds."[17]

Not only does physical abandonment destroy the marriage bond, but abuse and certain other egregious behaviors also communicate the deserter's deliberate renunciation of the marriage covenant. Ultimately, divorce may be just and biblically legitimate because it prevents even greater evil. Accordingly, other severe kinds of willful misconduct are not necessarily ruled out as grounds for divorce.[18]

Finally, the spouse who has an underlying biblical basis for divorce should not be faulted for obtaining a civil, no-fault divorce when that is the only option in the state of residence. No-fault divorce may also be practical in order to avoid the emotional and financial cost of a highly contentious and emotional divorce that assigns fault. Even when a state's divorce laws recognize the fault of one party, judges frequently grant the divorce on the available alternative no-fault basis. Finally, divorce decrees usually do not state the grounds for divorce. The important aspect of just cause is a biblically sound basis for divorce does exist whether or not a civil court bases its divorce decree on such a reason.

CHAPTER 3

Spouse Abuse and Other Grounds

DOMESTIC VIOLENCE is typically defined as "a pattern of coercive behavior characterized by the power and control of one person over another, usually an intimate partner, through physical, psychological, emotional, verbal, sexual, and/or economic abuse."[1] Coercive behavior may also involve spiritual abuse as well as attacks on children, property, and pets.

Family violence—whether between siblings, spouses, or parent and child—tends toward the destruction of life and dishonors God. Respect for human life is grounded in God's creation of man and woman in his own image (Genesis 1:26–27). Because men and women bear God's image, human life has God-given sanctity and dignity, qualities that are to be honored, preserved, and protected. Violence toward God's image bearers is ultimately an assault on God.

The sanctity of life therefore carries with it the responsibility to respect and protect life. Scripture recognizes the just defense of our own life—and the life of others—against violence (Exodus 22:2–3).

When Life Isn't Sacred and Families Aren't Safe

Jesus taught that everyone who hates his brother is a murderer, and John wrote that no murderer has eternal life (Matthew 5:21–26; 1 John 3:15). We often lose sight of the breadth of both the negative conduct and the life-affirming aspects of the sixth commandment,

"You shall not murder" (Exodus 20:10). The Westminster Larger Catechism expands that command, teaching that among the sins forbidden are "sinful anger, hatred, envy, desire of revenge; . . . provoking words, oppression, quarreling, striking, wounding, and whatsoever else tends to the destruction of the life of any."[2] Harsh, intemperate words and angry communication tend to stir up conflict and destroy relationships.[3]

What, then, does a positive response to Exodus 20:10 look like? The Westminster Larger Catechism says this:

> The affirmative pro-life duties required by the Sixth Commandment include, all careful studies, and lawful endeavors, to preserve the life of ourselves and others by resisting all thoughts and purposes, subduing all passions, and avoiding all occasions, temptations, and practices, which tend to the unjust taking away the life of any; by just defense thereof against violence . . . ; by charitable thoughts, love, compassion, meekness, gentleness, kindness, peaceable, mild and courteous speeches and behavior; . . . comforting and succoring the distressed and protecting and defending the innocent.[4]

God calls husbands to love and care for their wife in the same attentive way they care for their own body. Husbands are to nourish and cherish their wife in the same way that Christ loves, nourishes, and cherishes the church (Ephesians 5:28–33). Scripture warns that a husband who fails to live with his wife in an understanding way not only harms their marriage but may also hinder his own spiritual life and relationship with God (1 Peter 3:7).

Authors of *Battered into Submission: The Tragedy of Wife Abuse in the Christian Home*, James and Phyllis Alsdurf have learned a lot about husbands who don't honor, love, or care for their wife. The Alsdurfs therefore assert that for the church to be truly pro-life, it must advocate the battered women's cause:

Being pro-life . . . means taking a stance against all which stifles life and personhood. To be pro-life is to be *for* life. And violence by a husband toward his wife is one obvious offense to the integrity of human life. The life of any individual cannot be sustained—body, soul and spirit—when it is destroyed by violence, domination, fear and threat.[5]

The marriage relationship is one of intimate companionship, the utmost fidelity, and mutual respect. Never would Christ intimidate, demean, or abuse his bride, the Church. The same cannot be said of human husbands, and the resulting marital violence—whether isolated, mutual, or seemingly slight—tends to destroy rather than promote life.

The Widespread Tragedy of Family Violence

The existence of family violence, throughout the world, surely displeases God. Like child abuse, spousal abuse occurs at all levels of society and in every ethnic, racial, religious, and denominational group. Intimate partner violence (as spousal abuse is referred to) is no respecter of income level, socioeconomic class, occupation, age, gender, political, or geographic boundaries.[6] Furthermore, recent literature has sounded the alarm about the increased prevalence of both violence in teenage dating relationships and elder abuse by family members.

The victim—or the abuser—may be you or your spouse, neighbor, coworker, sibling, friend, casual acquaintance, or even a church leader, politician, celebrity, professional athlete, or other so-called role model. Tragically, spouse abuse exists in Christian and non-Christian marriages alike.

Although men are sometimes victims of abuse, it is estimated that women comprise at least 85 percent of the victims of intimate partner violence, and some reports indicate that men comprise only 5 percent.[7] About one-fourth of American women report that they have been physically abused by a husband or dating partner at some point in their lives, and at least 25 percent of female victims also report having been assaulted while they were pregnant.[8] The percentage of married women who have experienced physical abuse could even be as high as 30 to 50 percent.[9]

Although some women abuse their husbands, violence directed toward a male intimate partner often happens in the context of a woman's self-defense or effort to protect her children. Often men who abuse their female partners also abuse their children. Moreover, this abuse has generational consequences: children reared in a violent family are more likely to be violent or abusive in their future intimate relationships.[10]

Sometimes the woman's violent behavior is retaliation for prior violence against her or a desperate attempt to escape or end the abuse.[11] While some marital violence is mutual or directed by a woman against her husband, men commit substantially more physical abuse against their wives than wives do against their husbands, and the severity of the men's abuse of their wife is significantly greater.[12] Clearly—and not unexpectedly—women suffer greater adverse effects from domestic violence than men do. Women experience higher rates of physical injury, more severe injuries, greater need for medical attention, the resulting increase in health care costs, and more long-term psychological and emotional mental health effects such as depression, anxiety, and fear.[13]

Intimate partner violence is not limited to physical abuse alone. At the center of domestic violence is the desire for power and control. One prominent illustration is the Power and Control Wheel that shows power and control as the hub of a wheel. The various spokes extending from that hub link the "different behaviors that together form a pattern" of abuse and violence.[14]

These spokes include economic control, coercion and threats, intimidation, verbal attacks, isolation, minimizing, denying and blaming, using loved ones, and abusing authority. Each of these behaviors plays an important role in the abuser's general attempt to exert control over an intimate partner. A general distinctive of spouse abuse definitely is coercive behavior.

In contrast, the illustration of The Equality Wheel depicts a genuine partnership that has a nonviolent base. The spokes of this wheel include economic partnership, negotiation and fairness, respect, trust and support, honesty and accountability, responsible parenting, and shared responsibility.[15] The spokes on the two wheels are radically different.

Not every demeaning comment, heated word, or abusive action destroys the one-flesh marital bond to the degree that a divorce is justified, but even a single instance of physical abuse may cause serious injury, severely damage the one-flesh marital relation, and even warrant civil or criminal court intervention. Also, where a pattern of physical violence exists, other forms of abuse are typically present as well. But reference to a *pattern of abuse* is not meant to minimize or excuse other offensive and assaultive conduct that may impact the marriage. A look at characteristics and indicators of spouse abuse will help us better understand when abuse is indeed justified grounds for divorce.

Indicators of Abuse

An abuser's assaultive behavior takes many forms, varying in intensity, frequency, and degree, and often escalating over time. Physical abuse may include grabbing, hitting, slapping, pushing, punching, beating, choking, kicking, spitting, hair pulling, hurting pets, and threatening with weapons. Coerced or forced sex may occur. Some of my female divorce clients have reported being abruptly awakened by a spouse's sexual assault or rape.

Physical abuse is only part of a larger pattern, but sometimes no physical abuse occurs. Instead, the abuser will exert power and control in other ways, including psychological, emotional, spiritual, sexual, and economic abuse. One form of *psychological abuse* is threatening violence against self and others.

Emotional or verbal abuse includes humiliation, demeaning criticism, mocking, yelling, name-calling, and degradation.

An abuser often tries to isolate the victim from family and friends. This effort could involve monitoring or restricting phone calls, internet use, and emails/mail as well as controlling where the victim goes and what she does. The abuser may limit her ability to leave the house by taking away the car keys or hiding a passport. Sometimes in order to coerce and control, an abuser threatens to take away the children or create immigration/deportation issues.

Economic control may include not paying bills, refusing to give the victim money, not letting her work or interfering with her job, prohibiting her from going to school, or refusing to work to support the family. In religious households an abuser may distort Scripture to justify control of a spouse.[16]

Choosing to Abuse Others

Abusers choose to respond to a situation violently. They know what they are doing and what they want from their victims; they aren't acting purely out of anger, reacting to stress, or being rendered helpless under the control of drugs and alcohol. As the Reverend Al Miles points out, abusers abuse because they find it effective in "getting what they want when they want it," and they don't believe they will be held accountable for their actions.[17]

Abuse is not a side effect of merely losing one's cool in a temporary fit of anger. Abuse is the perpetrator's choice to engage in abusive conduct: the abuse is an "ongoing technique to enforce control through the use of fear, and it is part of a pattern of abuse."[18] While there appears to be a correlation between substance abuse and domestic violence, it is not a causal relationship. However, substance abuse lowers the abuser's inhibitions and may increase the frequency and severity of the abuse.[19]

Remaining with or Returning to the Abuser

The victim of abuse often stays with her abuser, or she returns to him after he says he won't use violence against her again, and she stays or returns for many reasons. Often she doesn't have the money, support system, or safety plan that would enable her to leave and not go back. Furthermore, victims believe that they don't have any viable options or anyplace to go where they will be safe from the abuser.[20] Kroeger and

Nason-Clark report that women essentially remain with their abuser "because they are fearful, . . . lack the economic or social resources to leave, and . . . cling tightly to the hope that someday their abuser will change."[21]

Religious women sometimes struggle with additional issues. Based on their religious background or biblical (mis)understanding, for example, they may question whether God permits them to leave. They may view marriage as a lifelong commitment regardless of how their spouse treats them, they may consider the abuse as their "cross to bear," or they may believe that God calls them to perpetual forgiveness for their spouse's recurring conduct. These women may also have difficulty sorting out the "difference between long-suffering in honor to Christ and their marriage vows and actively contributing to the danger of their own lives."[22]

Miles also observes that an abused spouse may feel pressure to uphold the sanctity of marriage. She may believe—wrongly—that a marriage must be saved at all costs or be concerned that divorce is a sin.[23] Miles rightly insists that we must "never put the sanctity of the marriage covenant before the safety of a woman and her children." He also explains that in domestic violence cases, "the marriage covenant is not broken by wives seeking safety (even if through separation or divorce), but by their husband's violence."[24]

Echoing much of what Miles says, Alsdurf notes that abused women generally remain with their abusive husbands "long after it is safe or reasonable to assume that change will come." He suggests they have a sort of missionary/rescuer mind-set, experience an "internal paralysis," and/or are ignorant of their legal rights.[25] Often an abused spouse is isolated from outside support and resources, subjected to threats if she even attempts to leave, and actually loves her spouse and wants the abuse, not the marriage, to end.[26]

Psychology also offers the explanation that battered women don't try to free themselves from their abuser because of their learned helplessness. After repeated abuse, the victim thinks that she cannot control the situation. Feeling utterly helpless, she becomes passive, submissive, and psychologically "paralyzed."[27]

Several years ago I was co-counsel for an abused wife in her successful challenge to an unfair property settlement agreement that we alleged she had been coerced to sign. After a contested trial regarding the validity of the agreement, the judge issued an opinion that was in line with our contentions, set aside the initial agreement, and made possible the pursuit of a more equitable resolution. Interestingly, the court's opinion suggested that the Stockholm Syndrome was a factor in her relationship with her abusive spouse.

The Stockholm Syndrome is the name of the unusual phenomenon in which a hostage begins to identify with and become sympathetic to the captor. At first the hostage identifies with the captor as a defense mechanism and out of an understandable fear of violence. The hostage magnifies the captor's acts of kindness—however small—and after several days the psychological shift has been made. Sympathy for the captor is the result.

The name *Stockholm Syndrome* derives from a 1973 failed bank robbery in Stockholm, Sweden. After six days of captivity, several hostages resisted rescue attempts, later raised money for their captors' legal defense, and even refused to testify against their captors. The trial judge in my client's case saw similarities between the survival behavior of the Stockholm bank captives and her response under the influence of her husband who kept her isolated, subjected her to emotional and physical duress, yet occasionally acted with kindness.

Finally, the reality that victims often tell no one about the abuse and repeatedly decide to either remain with or return to their abusive spouse indicates the situation's complex dynamics.

Abuse and the One-Flesh Bond: Desertion

When we speak of adultery as grounds for divorce, the term sometimes encompasses other serious sexual sins that may also break the one-flesh marital bond. Spouse abuse—such as sexual abuse or demanding/forcing a spouse to commit perverted sexual practices—could warrant divorce.[28] Nonsexual physical abuse, emotional abuse, and verbal abuse don't fit in the adultery/sexual immorality category. Abuse may, however, be a *moral equivalent* to adultery. Abuse is indeed a renunciation of the marriage vow as well as destruction of the marital bond, but abuse is not *identical* to adultery.

Family violence is more akin to desertion than adultery. This desire to leave the marriage relationship can be shown by words or actions. When John Jefferson Davis—a professor of Christian ethics at Gordon-Conwell Theological Seminary—points out that 1 Corinthians 7:10–16 discourages divorce and says that it may be "wiser" to define *desertion* in "the more narrow and literal sense," he actually presents a stronger argument for a broader understanding of desertion that would include spousal abuse:

> Behavior such as persistent physical abuse is a violation of the marriage covenant and is a prima facie indication that true consent is not being given to living in harmony with the believing spouse. Such persistent behavior could be construed as a *de facto* desertion of the marriage covenant. In such cases the believer who is being abused has the right to say to the unbelieving spouse, "If you intend to continue this marriage, then change your irresponsible behavior and fulfill your marriage vows." If the abusive spouse shows no willingness to change the irresponsible and destructive behavior, he or she is then in fact not demonstrating willingness to live in harmony (cf. v. 13).[29]

In a situation involving constructive desertion, though, the person leaving is not the deserting spouse. As a Maryland appellate court judge said, "A woman is not required to be a homicide victim before grounds for constructive desertion are established."[30] The judge then granted an absolute divorce to an abused wife on the grounds of constructive desertion.

The issue is whether the offending conduct is so intolerable that the complaining spouse is legally justified in leaving. When someone is compelled to leave because the spouse's offenses render it impossible to continue in the marriage safely, the spouse engaging in the egregious conduct is the responsible party. In *Is It My Fault?* Justin and Lindsey Holcomb write, "In an abusive relationship, there is every reason for a woman to flee and to see this as God's loving means of rescuing her from harm and harm to her children."[31]

David C. Jones views "a husband who habitually beats his wife or children" as committing a marriage covenant violation that is the "moral equal of adultery." Hear his conclusion:

> The adulterer, the deserter, and the inveterate abuser are alike guilty of gross betrayal of their marriage companion. By their actions they willfully repudiate the one-flesh relationship of the marriage covenant and so provide just cause for the dissolution of the marriage bond.[32]

Many grounds for divorce permitted by state courts are broader than biblically permissible just cause. However, sometimes state legislatures and courts recognize grounds for divorce that are consistent with biblical principles. When they do, these secular courts put to shame the church's tolerance of conduct that violates the marriage covenant. At times, society's response to family violence seems a step ahead of the church's response.

Courts have long applied, for instance, the principle of constructive desertion as grounds for divorce in spouse abuse cases. In response to family violence, including child abuse, courts have also recently been more willing to consider cruelty and excessively vicious conduct as grounds for divorce.

A brief return to our Just War construct helps explain the courts' position. An unjust attack on a third nation may justify a nation stepping in to prevent greater injustice or to rectify the wrong. That military involvement would indeed be a Just War. Similarly, in the context of divorce, a parent's abuse of a child in the family would permit the non-abusive parent to divorce on a charge of desertion/cruelty. In a case I handled, the appellate court agreed with our position to affirm the trial court's decision to grant a non-abusive parent a divorce on the grounds of desertion. During a two-year period that parent had witnessed again and again serious incidents of escalating verbal conflict and physical violence between the other parent and their teenager. Screaming, cursing, physical altercations, and obsessive monitoring of the teenager's activities on an almost-daily basis characterized the ongoing conflict. Furthermore, evidence the court found indicated a steady deterioration in the parents' marital relationship. The court deemed the abusive parent's conduct a justifiable reason for the other parent and the teenager to leave the marital home. The evidence supported the court's conclusion that the offending parent had deserted the other spouse by the abusive and destructive conduct that was completely counter to marriage vows.

Divorce for Neglect of Marital Obligations?

According to David Instone-Brewer's extensive review of the rabbinical tradition in the Mishnah, the law of Exodus 21:10–11—particularly the section addressing material neglect (i.e., food and clothing)—served as a reason for divorce in the first century.[33] He notes, too, that emotional neglect included the refusal of conjugal rights—which usually resulted in a fine—and that cruelty also fell in this category of neglect.[34]

R. J. Rushdoony argues that since the breach of obligation to provide the specified wife's rights was applicable to a captive woman (Deuteronomy 21:10–14) as well as a Hebrew slave or a bonded woman (Exodus 21:10), the implication is that "it is applicable as grounds for divorce for endowered wives."[35]

Instone-Brewer cautiously asserts that Jesus' silence regarding these additional grounds for divorce "is more likely to indicate that

Jesus agreed with the rest of Judaism that these grounds were acceptable."[36] Also, based on Paul's allusion to these marital obligations, Instone-Brewer considers them binding duties for both spouses (1 Corinthians 7:3–5, 32–35).[37]

However, Andreas Köstenberger finds such arguing from silence "precarious." He also asserts that one would have expected Jesus "to add marital neglect to [adultery] as a second exception for divorce if he had approved of neglect as a legitimate ground for divorce." Köstenberger maintains that Paul's allusion to Exodus 21:7-11 about marital obligations (1 Corinthians 7:3–5, 32–35) does not necessarily imply approval of divorce for marital neglect.[38]

Certainly, persistent neglect of obligations to one's spouse could suggest that the intentional abandonment of a spouse has begun. However, one has to be circumspect and cautious about broadening the grounds for divorce. Up to a point, neglect does not egregiously sever the essence of the marital bond. Yet the Westminster Confession of Faith (WCF) cautions against the sinful tendency to seek ways to circumvent what God's Word teaches in order to justify all manner of unbiblical grounds for divorce.[39] Thus, we have to be careful to not let lesser forms of neglectful behavior become just another unbiblical "any cause" divorce for minor and trifling offenses.

Summary

A significant problem in contemporary American society is what Robert Nisbet terms the large number of "loose individuals": these people are "loose from marriage and family, from the school, the church, the nation, job, and moral responsibility . . . playing fast and loose with other individuals in relationships of trust and responsibility."[40] We see this disloyalty and unfaithfulness in our culture's casual attitude toward the marriage commitment and the resulting frequency of the vow being disregarded and broken.

Divorce has become so prevalent not only in society in general but also among Christians that its occurrence seems rather commonplace.[41]

Divorce is now the culture's norm, and the church is not far behind. Couples who reach milestone anniversaries such as their silver twenty-fifth or golden fiftieth are rather extraordinary and definitely part of a shrinking minority.

Although hardness of heart prompted Moses to recognize and regulate divorce, the presumption in his day was that marriage vows should be kept. Scripture does not permit divorce for aversion, "any and every" reason, "incompatibility," "irreconcilable differences," or the pronouncement that the marriage is "irretrievably broken" as legitimate grounds for divorce.

As already discussed, divorce is warranted biblically in the cases of adultery (including other serious sexual sin) and desertion, including spouse and child abuse. These types of marital misconduct are unequivocal, actual, intentional, objective, and unilateral acts, and the offending spouse is morally responsible for violating marriage vows. That spouse's egregious behavior may indeed be just cause for divorce.

I'll close with this comment by Jay Adams: "[Since] God Himself became involved in divorce proceedings with Israel, it is surely wrong to condemn any and all divorce out of hand . . . It is certain that sometimes, in some ways, divorce, for some persons, under some circumstances is altogether proper and not the object of God's hatred."[42]

PRINCIPLE 2
Right Intention

CHAPTER 4

Motives Matter

AFTER INTRODUCING OURSELVES, Evelyn and I sat facing each other across my desk in my seventh-floor office.[1] I asked, "So, what brings you here?"

Looking intensely in my eyes, Evelyn pointed past me. "I want to see my husband hanging by his balls outside your window."

"I can't accomplish that," I said. "But let's talk about what I may be able to do for you."

Evelyn's bitter description of a loveless, lifeless marriage unfolded. She had kept thorough records of her husband's marital wrongs—whether large or small—but the couple had never tried to deal directly with their concerns. Sadly, it is common for a couple to allow their relationship to fester rather than trying—especially early on—to address, arrest, and resolve any underlying problems. Evelyn seemed to have been long planning a divorce—and plotting her revenge.

When considering the justness of the decision to divorce, what part do the instigator's motive and intention play?

Definition of *Motive*

A motive is "something (as a need or desire) that causes a person to act" and "implies an emotion or desire operating on the will and causing it to act: a *motive* for the crime."[2] It is difficult to discern and evaluate people's motives apart from what their actions and words reveal or

55

suggest (Matthew 12:34: "For out of the abundance of the heart the mouth speaks"). In this discussion of divorce, we consider the motive as something internal that incites behavior: *an intention to act.* We will emphasize intention in terms of a person's goals when we discuss the principle of limited objectives below.

Whether you are beginning a just war or wanting to pursue a just divorce, your intention must be to promote good and avoid evil. Only then will your divorce be just. Too often, though, the motive to divorce is a vindictive desire to avenge a perceived or an actual wrong rather than to uphold the integrity of marriage even through divorce.

The perceived need for biblical grounds for divorce—or equivalent civil grounds—may become the distorted longing for the spouse to commit a marital wrong. Then this offense could be used to escape a marriage that had withered for many years before the misconduct occurred. Furthermore, personal happiness or self-satisfaction has become an increasingly significant, if not determinative, factor in whether a person stays married or declares independence through separation and divorce. Lacking biblical just cause to divorce, Christians often adopt the prevalent notion that there is some unalienable right to be free from the shackles of an unfulfilling marriage and to pursue happiness in singleness or another relationship. That notion makes one's own desires preeminent, and the lifelong commitment to one's marriage partner is casually cast aside.

Improper Motives

In his discussion of just war, Yoder notes that right intention—in the subjective sense—has to do with "motivation, or attitude,"[3] with the "inward will of the actors. They must not hate people or enjoy beating them up. They must not use these hostilities in order to gain money. . . or personal vengeance. Nobody has the right to go to war simply out of a desire to get back at the enemy. That is not proper intention."[4]

Yoder lists some improper intentions, including two we will discuss: (1) hatred, vengefulness, enmity and (2) material gain. He concludes with the statement that "the cause may be justified, but participation may still be sinful if the intention is wrong in one of these ways."[5] Often, improper intentions like these are clearly driving the decision to divorce.

Hatred, Vengeance, and Enmity

Revenge is not a proper motive for ending a marriage. As John Stott observed, "Just causes are not served by unjust motives. So there must be no hatred, no animosity, no thirst for revenge."[6] While our spouse may at times seem to be the enemy, personal vengeance has no place in our relationship with an enemy whom we are called to love (Exodus 23:4–5).[7] God gives the power of the sword to civil government to maintain order and punish evil (Romans 13:1–7; 1 Peter 2:13–17), but it should not be an "instrument of vindictive and malicious hate."[8] While Scripture speaks of divine vengeance and justice, personal vengeance is different. Consider Peter's exhortation:

> Have unity of mind, sympathy, brotherly love, a tender heart, and a humble mind. Do not repay evil for evil or reviling for reviling, but on the contrary, bless, for to this you were called, that you may obtain a blessing. (1 Peter 3:8–9)

Murray notes, however, that "the demand of love . . . does not abrogate the demand of justice" as "they are really one" and are not contradictory.[9] Using "weapons of war" as "instruments of vindictive revenge, rather than instruments of retributive justice" desecrates "the dictates of both justice and love."[10] After all, "war in the protection and vindication of justice is not prompted by hate but by the love of justice, and such love never contradicts the love of our enemies which the Lord himself always and unequivocally demands."[11]

In deciding to divorce, we are to simultaneously uphold the demands of both love and justice; the lure of revenge must be avoided at all costs.

Up to this point, we have focused somewhat on the retaliatory side of motive, on those occasions of divorce when a spouse reacts to a wrong in a hateful, vindictive, or vengeful manner. But in other situations the spouse initiating divorce is not reacting to an offense but is instead the aggressor who wants out of the marriage for illegitimate reasons and despite the best efforts of their spouse. But sometimes an aggressive spouse, particularly an abusive one, uses the threat of divorce as a means of continuing to control and coerce behavior.

In a strained marriage relationship, spouses can struggle to "let the words of [their] mouth and the meditation of [their] heart be acceptable" in God's sight (Psalm 19:14). Yet in Ephesians 4, Paul issued a command along those same lines:

> Do not let any unwholesome talk come out of your mouths, but only what is helpful for building others up according to their needs, that it may benefit those who listen. . . . Get rid of all bitterness, rage and anger, brawling and slander, along with every form of malice. Be kind and compassionate to one another, forgiving each another, just as in Christ God forgave you (vv. 29, 31–32 NIV).[12]

James added that a "man's anger does not bring about the righteous life that God desires" (James 1:19–20). These verses are challenging, frustrating, and convicting to the person going through divorce. These verses also add stress: divorcing spouses are aware that some of their "unwholesome," bitter, and angry words will be exposed for all to see.

To that point, a significant change in how we communicate has occurred since I began practicing law almost forty years ago. In the past, communication between couples was primarily spoken, and what spouses said to each other essentially stayed within the walls of their home. Rarely were any adult witnesses present, so in court the testimonies were often a matter of he said/she said. Today, however, struggling couples frequently leave a digital trail of sarcastic, hateful, abusive, and even threatening messages. Once, when the court had appointed me to represent the children in a child custody case, I asked my son to summarize the hundreds of emails between the two parents. (Afterward, Rick said the assignment was the most depressing experience he had ever had.) Unable to tame their tongue—or computer keystrokes—these people spew curses on their spouse who is made in God's image.

Often an attorney bears the brunt of a client's charged emotions. We experience otherwise-civil people at the most awful moments in their lives—and usually it isn't pretty. But I've told clients, "It's OK for you to direct your anger toward me. I won't respond in anger. I won't drop your case. I'll be your lightning rod."

Sometimes such a comment defuses the client's anger, and we can focus on the issue at hand. And sometimes the fact that the client is finally expressing anger is huge. Both cases provide an opportunity to discuss with clients the benefits of seeing a counselor who can help them work through their emotions, learn effective coping mechanisms, and put that raw emotion to productive use. I am able to remind them how harmful it is to turn anger inward—doing so may lead to depression—or to simply suppress it only to have a more destructive outburst later.

Certainly, marital disharmony and disappointment, infidelity, and betrayal are all painful, and the decision to divorce is fraught with shifting and conflicting motives and intentions. Anger toward a spouse—and even toward God and others—and depression over the death of a marriage are natural parts of the grief process and can be overwhelming. The ripping apart of a one-flesh relationship is never painless.

Although divorce is always the result of some sin, the just cause discussion proves that *not all divorce is sinful*. However, it is important to guard our hearts against allowing an angry, bitter, or vindictive spirit to cloud our judgment and become the motive for divorce. Like an uncontrollable fire, unrestrained anger is destructive, and it can lead to all manner of sin and destruction (Proverbs 15:18; 19:19; James 3:5–5). It is possible to be angry and not sin (Ephesians 4:26).

Anger damages relationships. The risk of a hardened heart increases as that anger festers and bitterness take hold, leading to such severe spiritual consequences as falling out of fellowship with God. Christian friends can often help us both recognize what we're feeling and navigate the maze of shifting and even conflicting emotions.

Material Gain, Economic Relief

Other improper intentions in divorce involve money, specifically, these four basic financial aspects of a marriage (and divorce): (1) what you own (assets); (2) what and whom you owe (debts); (3) what you earn or the resources you have available to live on (income primarily); and (4) what you need to live (expenses). Issues that arise in one or more of these areas can put significant financial stress on a family.

But neither material gain nor relief from difficult financial circumstances is a just motive for divorce. Granted, as Regan observes, a Just War may "result, in some benefits that of themselves would not justify the war; right intention requires only that war should not be waged for the sake of such benefits."[13] This statement also holds true for divorce.

For example, you may be married to someone who is financially controlling and, although generous to others, miserly toward you and your children. While sharing financial decisions and goals may be important to marital harmony, partnership, and companionship, financial gain is not a permissible motive for seeking a divorce.

Sometimes divorce, however, exposes a person's greed and deception. In Maryland, for instance, divorce proceedings involving alimony require each party to file a detailed financial statement under oath, fully disclosing income, monthly expenses, assets, and liabilities. Early in my legal career, one of my clients completed a financial statement, and he signed it under penalty of perjury. Moments before the financial statement was to be filed, though, he asked me, "What if I forgot to include something?"

As I probed, I learned that he "forgot" to list an account holding $150,000. For fifteen years he had deposited his paycheck in the couple's joint bank account, but his wife did not know that before making those deposits, he had skimmed some of his wages off the top and diverted that money to his "forgotten" account. He kept the family on a tight budget, and they lived frugally on his deposited income with little spending on discretionary items. His family was completely unaware that he had squirrelled away money that he intended to keep hidden for his own use.

I counseled him that we were required to list the asset, that I would not file the false financial statement, and that I would have to terminate our relationship if he refused to disclose this asset. We filed the financial statement that disclosed this substantial asset—and he fired me shortly thereafter. One of his motives during marriage as well as in pursuing divorce had been financial greed. He wanted to retain family assets for himself, assets he had never intended to share with his spouse and family.

Sadly, some marriages are rife with financial stress. Your spouse may be a spendthrift who wastes the family's available funds, runs up debt, or makes excessive online purchases. You've become tired of that behavior and feeling like the family is on a financial treadmill.

Or perhaps you're a golf widow, or your spouse spends unreasonable time and money on other hobbies and interests. Maybe your spouse got a nice raise… only to gamble it away. Or maybe he is in and out of jobs, and this financial stress impacts the marriage. Financial difficulties certainly test the traditional marriage vow to take your spouse from that day forward "for better, for worse, for richer, for poorer." Even when finances are distressing and seem hopeless, we must examine whether the relief from such circumstances that we so desire is a just motive, a right reason to sever the marriage bond. The grass is not always financially greener on the other side of divorce. Divorce simply brings new challenges.

As a family magistrate I presided over more than 1,500 hearings involving the financial support issues of divorcing couples. Occasionally the family finances permitted the separated couple to maintain two households without much financial change or sacrifice. Frequently, however, the divorcing couple was already stretched beyond their means and had been unable to cover their expenses when they were all living under the same roof. This financial deficit increased with the expenses of now running two separate households.

Addressing this type of situation with a temporary order that met both parties' reasonable needs was difficult and, at times, impossible—until both adults made some sacrifices and some lifestyle changes. Just to meet their basic needs, the divorcing spouses would often have to forgo what used to be standard expenses—family vacations, dining out, entertainment, hobbies, gifts—and even charitable contributions.

No matter how fair any magistrate or judge sought to be, the court cannot magically create family resources to meet the needs of two households when the family could not meet their living expenses as one household.

Occasionally some economic benefits—such as obtaining a share of assets controlled by your stingy spouse, or escaping from your spouse's pattern of wasteful spending and excessive running up credit card debt—may flow naturally and fairly from the division of assets and monetary support responsibilities that are part of resolving financial issues in divorce. However, obtaining those benefits is not itself a sufficient reason to divorce.

Valid Motives

In contrast to invalid reasons to get a divorce are the valid motives. Yoder lists these valid Just War motives that can be applied to a Just Divorce: (1) love for the victims and for the enemy; (2) trust in God; (3) willingness to face risk or sacrifice; and (4) humility and regret at the needfulness of the evil of war.[14]

Love and Restoration

The two greatest commandments in the Bible are to love God with all your heart, soul, strength, and mind, and to love your neighbor as yourself.[15] Love, then, is the best motive we can have in any situation and every relationship. First Corinthians 13 stresses that love is essential in all we do, love "keeps no record of wrongs" (v. 4 NIV), and love is not "resentful" (v. 4 ESV). Love is never vindictive; it seeks restoration rather than destruction. Scripture is straightforward: "whoever loves God must also love his brother" (1 John 4:21).

As Christians we are called to look out for interests of others (Philippians 2:3–4). Appearing to put a spouse's interests first, though, can become a distorted pretense for leaving the marriage. For instance, one spouse tells the other, "I'm holding you back. It's best for you to move on with your life without me." Work problems, spiritual doubts, depression, too many commitments—a spouse might feel like a burden and be convinced that the partner would be better off without you. Perhaps this sentiment seems generous, humble, and selfless, but it's actually proud and selfish. One spouse presuming to know what's best for the other? That's not love. Furthermore, this line of thinking disregards the marriage vows and denies the being-left-behind spouse the opportunity to honor those vows.

In Micah 6:1–8, God calls his people to return to him in covenant loyalty: to do justice, to love mercy, and to walk humbly with their God (v. 8). This loving obedience is the true worship and sacrifice God desires from us. At the same time, loving obedience is the faithful response of a covenant servant grateful to the exalted King and Lord.[16]

Christians are also called to "strive for peace with everyone" (Hebrews 12:14). However, the dictates of peace may mean that—as Scripture says—a Christian deserted by an unbelieving spouse is not required to insist that the marriage stay intact (1 Corinthians 7:15). In fact, such insistence may actually be contrary to the rule of peace. Likewise, when a person faces persistent abuse from a spouse, seeking safety, refuge, and even divorce is the way of peace.

Trust in God

A Christian seeking to please God will trust him with every aspect of life, including—if not especially—the decision to divorce. God's wisdom is to guide all of our decisions. In his providence, he protects us and works all things to our ultimate good (Romans 8:28).

Proverbs 3:1–12 provides additional instruction. The person who trusts in God studies God's Word, has an obedient heart, holds fast to God's covenantal love and faithfulness, relies on God's Word as the authority in life, submits to God in heart and mind, fears the Lord, turns away from things that displease God, honors God as the provider of material needs, accepts God's loving chastisement, and relies on God's wisdom to make decisions that honor him.

We Christians are to sincerely trust God and obey his Word. Our decisions and actions are to proceed from a "heart purified by faith," "in a right manner, according to the Word," and "to a right end, the glory of God."[17] We are to "flee youthful passions and pursue righteousness, faith, love, and peace, along with those who call on the Lord from a pure heart" (2 Timothy 2:22).

We further show our trust in God when, willing to submit ourselves to his correction and direction, we invite Him to probe our innermost thoughts.[18] This kind of transparency is particularly important because we may be deceiving ourselves; we may not have an accurate view of our own motives (Jeremiah 31:33). God's living and active Word discerns "the thoughts and intentions of the heart. And no creature is hidden from his sight, but all are naked and exposed to the eyes of him to whom we must give account" (Hebrews 4:12–13). Acknowledging our heart motives is key in living a just life and pursuing a Just Divorce.

Willingness to Risk

Like the decision to go to war, the decision to divorce requires the willingness to take risks and/or make sacrifices, as the finances of a divorce illustrate.

Any financial burden a couple experienced while living together will only worsen during separation. The additional cost of attorneys' fees makes money even tighter, creating greater anxiety, uncertainty, and stress. A spouse motivated to divorce in order to escape financial stress or to become independent financially actually increases financial hardship and debt. That spouse may even have to liquidate assets to pay legal fees. Divorce does not create extra resources; it depletes them.

A couple pursuing divorce faces an uncertain financial future, both short-term and long-range. Also, they risk damaging relationships in the family and extended family, the community, and the church. We do well to count the cost—financially as well as relationally, emotionally, and spiritually—of the decision to divorce.

Humility and Regret

The decision to divorce—as Yoder notes regarding the decision to go to war—involves a humble spirit as well as "regret at the needfulness of the evil" of divorce. While divorce is permitted for just cause, it is generally not an occasion for celebration.

This fact particularly struck me one Valentine's Day. I was representing the wife in these divorce proceedings. She and her husband were in their late fifties, had been married more than thirty-five years, were Catholic, and had two adult children. We had settled all the property division and spousal support issues the evening before.

Once cases have reached that point, the now-uncontested divorce proceeding usually takes about ten minutes. This one took almost an hour because the trial judge himself was in his late fifties, had been married more than thirty-five years, was Catholic, and had two adult children.

Struggling to control his emotions, the judge spoke about it being Valentine's Day and how he would be going home that evening to celebrate with his wife. The preciousness of marriage and the solemn nature of divorce stood in sharp contrast, and an almost suffocating somberness fell over the entire proceeding and every person in the courtroom.

Immediately after the hearing ended, I took the elevator down to the first floor of the courthouse. The lobby was filled with joy and laughter: many couples had just been married or were waiting to have their Valentine's Day wedding in the courthouse's small chapel-like room.

Again, what a contrast between the heaviness of the divorce hearing and the joy of these wedding festivities.

Weddings are filled with anticipation, joy, and hope. Divorces—even divorces that are justified—are darkened by sadness and regret. Again, the decision to divorce is not one to be made casually or without careful consideration of the ramifications.

Summary

For the pursuit of divorce to be just, right intention and just cause are necessary—as are other considerations we will address in the coming chapters. This means that, "wrong intention may invalidate the justifiability of a war if . . . our war is intrinsically just, but we wage it with hatred in our heart, it is still a sin. The intent is not to give a blank check to moral vice on an individual level."[19]

Someone going through a divorce will undoubtedly experience anger and hatred and wish all kinds of bad things on a spouse, but God is not pleased when a vengeful spirit and an unjust motive are driving the divorce. If the decision is made with right intention and pure motives, then the divorce is just in that respect.

With a divorce, your family changes, the hopes of your wedding day are snuffed out, and the emotional and material suffering may be more painful than you ever could have imagined, but God will be there with his grace, his unconditional love for you, and the hope of both his healing and his redemption of this difficult season. He has given to us who don't deserve any of it so very much the benefits of his redemptive love and providential care that cannot be taken away by anyone, by anything. Not even by divorce.[20]

PRINCIPLE 3
Last Resort

and

PRINCIPLE 4
Legitimate Authority

CHAPTER 5

Divorce as a Last Resort and the Wronged Spouse's Divorce Decision

IN ORDER TO BE JUST, divorce should not be accepted as the automatic go-to option, considered the surefire and only path to take, or the easy way out—because nothing about divorce is easy. Instead, we Christians should always regard divorce "a measure of the last resort, to be accepted only when all reasonable attempts at reconciliation have been exhausted."[1]

Several years ago I attended the national conference of the Christian Legal Society, a nationwide fellowship of Christian attorneys and law students. After dinner one evening, an attorney I'll call Bill approached me and asked if I represented spouses in divorce proceedings.

After I responded affirmatively, Bill said, "It's wrong to represent someone who's seeking divorce. God hates divorce, and I will only represent a married client who's willing to solely pursue reconciliation. If a person wants a divorce, I tell them to go elsewhere. I won't represent someone who pursues divorce. And neither should you."

Bill went on to say that he had observed many remarkable instances of marital restoration, and he urged me to adopt his approach of talking to clients only about reconciliation. But I challenged Bill to look closer at how he views the person seeking his counsel.

"Have you considered that the one seeking your advice is a 'bruised reed that God will not break'?[2] She may have exhausted all paths of reconciliation, have a biblical basis for divorce, or need to respond to divorce proceedings she didn't initiate.

"By arbitrarily dismissing this Christian sister, you've abandoned her to someone who may not really care about her, and you may miss a chance to display God's lovingkindness to guide her through a difficult situation."

By the time the vast majority of my clients come to me for legal counsel, they have already made various attempts to reconcile, or one spouse has refused to even try. Bill's policy of turning people away can increase the helplessness, loneliness, and isolation of hurting people who may also lack the support of family, friends, or the church when they are struggling to decide whether to pursue a legitimate divorce.

Reasonable Hope

Just as, "nations are not justified in resorting to war as long as they have reasonable hope that means short of war can prevent or rectify wrong,"[3] so the decision to pursue divorce is only just when you have determined that no reasonable and available means can restore the marriage relationship.

Even when a divorce may be scripturally permissible due to a spouse's sexual sin, desertion, or abuse, both parties should consider the possibility of reconciliation.

Intervention, both informal and formal, may effectively identify the issues, address the conduct destructive to the relationship, and restore a deteriorating marriage before it ends in divorce. Interventions include individual or couples counseling with a mental health professional or a pastor; a Christian community's involvement; a church's redemptive discipline process; substance abuse treatment; abuser/batterer intervention programs with a coordinated community response to abuse; anger management programs; and emotional support and practical assistance from family, friends, and others.

Sometimes the initiation of divorce proceedings prompts the errant spouse to consider alternatives that might lead to reconciliation. The obligation to exhaust reasonable reconciliation efforts is particularly acute when just cause is not present or readily apparent.

Certainly, it would be appropriate to involve the church in efforts to protect an abused spouse, to prevent abandonment, to exhort a partner to fulfill financial responsibilities to the family, to uphold the sanctity of marriage where possible, and to determine the legitimacy of pursuing divorce when the couple's estrangement cannot be remedied.

For instance, a reconciliation/discipline dynamic addresses interpersonal wrongs according to Matthew 18:15-17 principles.[4] If the unrepentant spouse refuses reconciliation, then more formal church involvement and discipline might lead to the church's excommunication of the unrepentant spouse.[5] If that spouse continues being stubborn even after being removed from the church, that spouse would be treated as an unbeliever who is outside the Christian community. The innocent spouse would be permitted to divorce for desertion and would be free to remarry (1 Corinthians 7:15).[6]

Practical difficulties do arise when attempts are made to apply these principles to Christians in general and to married couples specifically. Often, for example, one of the spouses is not a committed Christian or formally connected to a church. Shared relationships may be few or even nonexistent. Or maybe neither spouse is a member of any church, or the two spouses belong to different churches that have disparate views of church discipline and handling estranged marriages.

Also, when held accountable by a church, a church member or attendee can simply leave and go to another church that may accept them without reservation. This newfound church neither judges nor honors the prior church's concerns or actions. Realistically, church involvement is no guarantee of a restored relationship. There may be no effective way of resolving the matter. On its own, the reconciliation/discipline dynamic is often impractical, and this approach may prove incapable of bringing about repentance, forgiveness, and reconciliation. Moreover, this approach may be especially problematic in an abuse situation where the victim's safety must be the highest priority.

Blomberg's suggested approach involves the Christian community in a less formal way than the reconciliation/discipline approach does. Divorce and remarriage would be permitted when "an individual, in agreement with a supportive Christian community of which that individual has been an intimate part, believes that he or she has no other choice or option in trying to avoid some greater evil. All known attempts at reconciliation have been exhausted."[7] For example, a greater evil than divorce would be suffering ongoing physical abuse by the spouse or the persistent desertion by a spouse who has moved in with a paramour.

Of course a disintegrating marriage is often accompanied by intense emotions. Grieving the loss of a marriage is similar to grieving the loss of a loved one through death. Feeling depressed and uninterested in things you previously enjoyed and being unable to fully function at work, home, or socially are common experiences during the grief process. More pronounced and persistent depression or depression-type symptoms may also occur, symptoms like impaired judgment and thought processes, sadness and hopelessness, and disrupted sleeping and eating patterns.

Your home church, or a church with a solid reputation for Bible teaching, or a mature Christian community may provide a helpful referral to counseling as well as valuable insight to help you avoid or at least not rush into a divorce. That said, when reasonable attempts at reconciliation have been unsuccessful your home church, a biblically solid church, or a mature Christian community may also be able to offer helpful guidance in sorting through the last-resort divorce options. A divorce, however, can honor God and may prevent a greater evil. Furthermore, getting the counsel of others provides you with significant spiritual advice so that you do not bear the entire burden of assessing the situation.

Supporting and Protecting the Survivor of Abuse

Know, however, that some of the ways that help many couples to reconcile—repentance and forgiveness, couples counseling, a supportive Christian community, anger management programs, substance abuse treatment, and mental health therapy—are insufficient when abuse has characterized the relationship. Even specific batterer intervention programs have varying and limited success in stopping abuse.[8] Furthermore, the hope of reconciliation often doesn't survive the harsh reality of the destructive patterns of behavior and the treatment-resistant nature of the abuser's attitudes and conduct. Most often an abused spouse does not have any reason to believe that these methods will lead to preventing or rectifying a marital wrong. On a more basic level, this abused spouse may legitimately wonder whether he/she would even be safe in the marriage.

Justin Holcomb, a seminary professor of mine, and Lindsey Holcomb, a counselor of domestic violence victims, make some pertinent comments regarding forgiveness and restoration in the context of an abusive relationship:

> It is important to be clear on this topic because abusers may cite Scripture to insist that their victims forgive them. A victim may then feel guilty if she cannot do so. Forgiveness, however, does not mean forgetting the abuse or pretending that it did not happen. Neither is possible, because sin has consequences and forgiveness does not remove those consequences. Forgiveness is *not* permission to repeat the abuse. Nor does it require restoring the relationship. As a matter of fact, it may be dangerous and life-threatening to restore the relationship. Rather, forgiveness means that the victim decides to let go of the experience in order for God to deal justly with her abuser. It is the decision to move on and refuse to tolerate abuse of any kind again.[9]

In addition, as Alsdurf notes, physical abuse "destroys something vital within a relationship. It is an attack on the essence of the woman. It is a concrete way of saying that she is worthless. The scars created from such a message run so deep that the restoration of that relationship is difficult indeed."[10] Kroeger and Nason-Clark point out that forgiveness involves "the idea of loosing or freeing ourselves from anger and resentment toward another" and "instead of holding something against another, we will be able to release it and thereby to be free of the grip that hatred, resentment and vindictiveness have had on us."[11] Abused women should not be pressured to immediately forgive the abuser or to stay in a marriage that has not been safe.

Alsdurf instructs the church regarding its responsibility when it may be appropriate for the victim to stay in the marriage:

> Unless the church is willing to enter into that situation of suffering with the woman—caring for her physical, emotional and spiritual needs and those of her children—it should not advise her to stay in a relationship where she is subject to degrading and inhuman treatment.[12]

Along those same lines, Jim Newheiser makes this bold statement: "Church leaders who send a woman back into a situation in which she is likely to be beaten have failed to fulfill their call to protect Christ's sheep (Acts 20:28) and are unworthy of their office (Ezekiel 34:1–10)."[13]

Finally, Justin and Lindsey Holcomb list eight ways the church can reflect Jesus' love for abused and at-risk women:

1. Know that God cares for those at risk and hates violence . . .
2. Stand with the vulnerable and powerless . . .
3. Believe the women; don't blame them . . .
4. Respond graciously, offering comfort, encouragement, and protection . .
5. Get informed and inform others of the prevalence of women at risk . . .
6. Learn about the effects of sexual assault, domestic violence, and other forms of abuse . . .
7. Clearly communicate the hope and healing for victims that is found in the person and work of Jesus Christ . . .
8. Get involved with the issue of violence against women.[14]

Clearly, the church has an opportunity to be an instrument of change and, in God's hand, a tool for transforming the culture of abuse. And when an abusive marriage is not reconciled, the church should wholeheartedly support the divorced survivor of abuse and her family.

Forgiveness and the Decision Whether to Divorce

When an innocent spouse grants forgiveness, does that action fully absolve the errant spouse or mandate reconciliation? Or will the errant spouse instead experience the just consequences—and one may be divorce—for seriously violating the marriage covenant?

Commenting on the matters of church discipline, repentance, forgiveness, reconciliation, and the right to divorce, Newheiser offers this opinion:

> [I do] not believe the innocent spouse can be compelled (e.g., under the threat of church discipline) not to exercise the right to divorce on the grounds of adultery, even if the adulterer claims to be repentant. Wronged spouses who refuse to fully forgive usually act this way because they are not convinced that the repentance is genuine... In addition, the [spouse's] sin might have been so serious (e.g., rape, molesting a child) that they do not wish to pursue reconciliation. Or [the betrayed spouses] may have decided that they no longer wish to remain married to a person who has callously broken the covenant or to live with the consequences of the sin (e.g., a sexually transmitted disease). Sometimes forgiven sin still has consequences (Gal. 6:6–7). The consequence could be the end of a marriage. Wronged spouses, however, must guard their hearts. Bitterness and hatred are always sinful (Eph. 4:31–32).[15]

Newheiser highlights the prominent role that should be sensitively granted to an innocent spouse who has suffered due to the errant spouse's unequivocal betrayal of marital vows. Newheiser also suggests appropriate limits for the church's use of discipline in bringing about reconciliation.

Next, Adams makes this assertion: "Divorce of a believing spouse who has committed fornication must, therefore, be restricted to those who refuse to repent of their sin."[16] Brauns says each time a repeatedly unfaithful spouse sincerely asks forgiveness, the faithful spouse must forgive the adulterer. Brauns views the question whether reconciliation must always occur as more complex:

> Forgiveness does not necessarily mean the elimination of consequences. In the case of marriage, there are times when the Bible allows for divorce (Matt. 19:1–12; 1 Cor. 7:10–16). So, in the situation described here, the wife might say to an unfaithful husband, "I do forgive you. But you have broken our marriage covenant repeatedly. I can't live any longer with someone I can't trust, so we can no longer be married." . . . Deciding what to do when a spouse repeatedly commits a grave offense is a matter of spiritual wisdom and discernment that should be made only by a growing Christian in close interaction with a pastor and other spiritual leaders.

Brauns's conclusion echoes Blomberg's suggestion that the guidance of a spiritual community is essential to a person's last-resort decision to divorce be made. Frame offers this guideline: "When a person has biblical grounds for divorce, he is not obligated to remain in the marriage. To divorce in this case is not sin."[17]

Summary

Instone-Brewer addresses the very essence of the issue when he clearly states the individual's role in determining the appropriateness of pursuing a divorce:

> Only the Lord really knows the heart; as Jesus said, evil comes

from within and loves the dark. We cannot leave it up to a minister or a church leadership team to decide when a marriage ends; it is up to the individual victim, in prayer before the Lord. Only they and the Lord know what their life is really like. Only they know if their partner has expressed repentance, and only they will have to live with the consequences of the decision.[18]

While divorce even on biblical grounds is to be the last resort, the decision to divorce on those grounds of adultery, desertion, and abuse is fundamentally the decision of the wronged partner.

PRINCIPLE 5
Limited Objectives:
Goals Matter

CHAPTER 6

Reasonable Alimony

"I'M NOT INTERESTED in alimony," my client Dan told me—again. He repeated these words like a mantra every time we discussed the financial settlement of his divorce case. I knew he had no interest in *paying* alimony and was hoping for me to change what was my consistent answer: "I know you're not interested in alimony, but you'll have to pay it whether or not you're interested in doing so."

According to vocational experts, Dan's business income was five times what his homemaker spouse, Sue, would earn when she reentered the job market. In their early forties, the couple had been married for about fifteen years, and their children were in elementary school. So in Dan's situation, an alimony award to his wife was certain; it was simply a matter of the amount and the duration of payments. In most cases, though, alimony won't be as obviously the appropriate financial option, so it is important to understand the financial aspect of divorce.

A Just Divorce involves pursuing objectives that are just, fair, and right. Often, though, when people decide to divorce, they give little thought to what would be a fair resolution. If both parties have not determined their desired outcome and therefore have not proposed any realistic terms to the other side, a peaceful resolution will be elusive. Just goals are essential, and clearly communicating those goals to your spouse is critical.

In a divorce the goal of the personal or financial destruction of the other spouse is the antithesis of a just peace. Here we are talking about *objective goals*—specifically, the financial outcome you are seeking as part of the divorce settlement. The overarching financial issues that require resolution are *property division*, *alimony* (also called maintenance or spousal support), and—if the couple has any minor children—*child support*.

Arriving at a divorce settlement means battles being waged, further costs being incurred, and additional resources being expended. The absence of clearly defined proper and specific objectives will delay a satisfactory conclusion or keep it unattainable.

Alimony: General Background

Because most divorcing couples do not have substantial assets, alimony may be the only means a court has to address the spouses' imbalance in earnings ability, the inequity of current income, and the lifestyle each wants to have. Some of this imbalance may be the result of marital roles the couple chose, such as one spouse remained home to care for the couple's children. This choice adversely impacts the primary caregiver's career opportunities and advancement, income, earning ability, accumulation of retirement benefits, and availability of other employment fringe benefits.

Determining alimony is rarely easy. Further complicating the decision is the great divergence between states and between courtrooms in the same state regarding appropriate alimony. The lack of certainty, consistency, and predictability is also due to the broad discretion vested in trial judges and rationale that varies from state to state. Generally, if the court has both subject matter jurisdiction[1] and personal jurisdiction over the other spouse, that court may award alimony when granting a divorce.[2]

Every state permits an alimony award to either spouse, and the recipient's marital fault usually does not preclude an award. Worth noting, however, is the movement away from needs-based alimony. Instead, courts look to provide rehabilitative or short-term support while the dependent spouse moves toward self-sufficiency. Long-term support may be available in exceptional circumstances.

The types and duration of support available reflect each state's public policy. Forms of alimony include:

1. *pendente lite* (temporary);
2. transitional (rehabilitative and short-term);
3. indefinite (permanent);
4. *in solido* (lump sum); and
5. reimbursement (compensatory).

Generally, the court awards alimony for a period beginning from the date of the filing of the pleading that requests alimony.[3] While most states permit more than one form, no state allows all of them, and the state's reasons for choosing or not choosing a particular form may vary. It is important to become knowledgeable about the types available in your state.

Pendente Lite

Most states permit a court to award either spouse *pendente lite* alimony that the other party pays during the divorce litigation period. Judges base this temporary award primarily on balancing the reasonable needs of the recipient spouse with the other spouse's ability to pay.[4] In seeking this difficult, if not impossible, economic balance, the court reviews the financial profile of a fractured family that may have had difficulty making ends meet as one household and now tries to satisfy the needs of two.

The court considers the parties' financial resources—namely, income and assets. The court usually looks at liabilities as part of the spouses' respective needs and ability to pay. Some states have adopted guidelines for use in alimony *pendente lite* awards.

Fixed Term

Again, in many states, the determination of alimony for the dependent spouse has shifted from a needs basis—maintaining a certain living standard—to rehabilitation.[5] This general trend favors fixed-term awards rather than indefinite alimony. Therefore, in practical terms, the dependent spouse needs a specific vocational plan for either updating prior skills or gaining additional skills through education and training—in order to be financially independent in a reasonable time period.[6] The expenses for skills testing, abilities and goals assessment, career guidance and job placement, and education are part of that spouse's need.[7]

The amount and duration of this short-term alimony should allow sufficient time for the recipient to increase earning capacity and obtain appropriate employment.[8] Some states have durational limits on rehabilitative alimony, such as three years from the date of divorce.[9] The recipient should make reasonable efforts to follow the rehabilitative plan.[10]

A court is usually able to modify and, under appropriate circumstances, extend fixed term alimony. Those circumstances would be, for instance, a substantial material change that, without an extension, would create a harsh and inequitable result. Or unforeseen events may create "compelling circumstances" that prevent the recipient from being self-supporting despite her or his best efforts, and the payer is able to continue to pay alimony without undue burden.[11]

Transitional alimony shares the purpose of rehabilitative support to provide for "short-term needs resulting from financial dislocations associated with dissolution of the marriage."[12] Transitional alimony provides assistance "to allow the party to make a transition from being married to being single."[13] This purpose is broader than merely a rehabilitative intention. A person may, for example, be self-sufficient yet still need assistance establishing a household apart from the other spouse. Depending on the state, this transitional form of alimony is for a definite and nonmodifiable time period.

Indefinite

Although the current trend in alimony payments is toward short-term rehabilitative alimony, many states permit awards for an *indefinite* term when appropriate.[14] But the term *permanent* is a misnomer because among the several possible terminating events are the remarriage of the recipient or the deaths of either the payer or the recipient.

Much less common today, indefinite alimony is generally only awarded in extraordinary circumstances. Case in point, Maryland recognizes two situations when a trial court may award alimony for an indefinite period: (1) "due to age, illness, infirmity, or disability, the party seeking alimony cannot reasonably be expected to make substantial progress toward becoming self-supporting" or (2) "even after the party seeking alimony will have made as much progress toward becoming self-supporting as can reasonably be expected, the respective standards of living of the parties will be unconscionably disparate."[15]

In Solido

A form of long-term support, alimony *in solido* ("as a whole") means the total amount is established on the date of the divorce decree and either paid in a lump sum or in installments over a set period of time.

Although its primary purpose is financial support, alimony *in solido* may also include paying attorney fees or effecting an equitable division of marital property. An award of alimony *in solido* is not modifiable by the court and is not terminable upon either party's death or remarriage.[16]

Nominal or Reserved

Now consider this important but sometimes overlooked fact: "If at the time of the divorce the court fails to either award alimony or reserve the right to award alimony at a later date, it is forever barred from ordering it."[17] An award of *nominal* support, though, will "preserve the court's authority to grant spousal support in the future."[18] Nominal support is similar to the reservation of alimony found in some states. Reservation may be appropriate when the trial court finds that the party requesting alimony "in the reasonably foreseeable future, will be in circumstances that would justify an award of rehabilitative or indefinite alimony."[19]

Reservation requires more than some vague future circumstance—such as the possibility a spouse's business may improve financially—or the mere possibility of some future financial need; it must be highly likely that in the near future the claimant's situation would present a substantial basis for an alimony award – such as the claimant's prospective loss of disability benefits.

Reimbursement

Reimbursement alimony applies in situations where the recipient has made significant financial or other contributions to the other spouse's "education, training, vocational skills, career or earning capacity."[20] Perhaps that spouse benefited from "the support of the other spouse while obtaining a professional degree or license."[21]

A compensating adjustment through alimony or property division may be appropriate when a lengthy marriage "dissolves on the threshold of a major change in the income of one of the spouses due to the collective efforts of both" or when the efforts of both spouses greatly enhanced one spouse's earning capacity.[22] Further, a spouse's economic missteps may warrant reimbursement alimony in order to achieve an equitable financial resolution; a property division order alone may not be able to accomplish that.[23]

Now let's hear from the American Legal Institute (ALI). The ALI *Principles* characterizes alimony's purpose as *"compensation for loss* rather than *relief of need."*[24] Underlying the *Principles* is the fact that financial losses are typical in divorce proceedings. The most significant kinds of compensable loss are these: (1) the spouse with less wealth or earning capacity loses the living standard experienced during the marriage and (2) a spouse who spends a disproportionate amount of time taking care of the children loses earning capacity during the marriage that will persist post-divorce.[25]

As a baseline, ALI uses the standard of living in longer marriages and, in shorter marriages, each spouse's premarital standard of living. In a short-term marriage an award may correct, for instance, a disparity due to one spouse's sacrifices for the other's benefit, and those sacrifices resulted in a standard of living lower than his or her premarital standard.[26] The court can award greater loss protection based on the marriage's duration[27] and the "child-care durational period," that time when the claimant provided significantly more care of the parties' children.[28]

Further, the *Principles* recognizes that assuming primary caregiving responsibilities for the children often limits employment opportunities and "typically results . . . in a residual loss in earning capacity that continues after the children no longer require close parental supervision."[29] The court should equitably allocate those losses in earning capacity that are reflected in the spouses' income disparity at the time of divorce[30] "without regard to marital misconduct."[31]

ALI proposes the statewide application of a formula based on the spouses' post-divorce income disparity and the length of the marriage.[32] The calculation is straightforward: multiply the disparity in the spouses' incomes at divorce by a percentage of the marriage duration or the child-care period in marriage.

A Court's Required Considerations

Courts are to determine the amount and duration of alimony payments. The goal is to arrive at fair and equitable awards. To guide the broad discretion that is accorded judges, forty-two states and the District of Columbia have adopted non-exhaustive lists of factors that a court must consider in making its award.[33] Case law may list other states' requisite factors. However, the factors are neither prioritized nor weighted in any particular manner.

Maryland's statutory list of nonexclusive factors includes eleven that are representative of the kinds that courts review, and it provides a useful outline.[34] The pertinent factors listed in other states' statutes and case law cover criteria similar to the considerations in this discussion.[35] These factors often reflect a particular state's preference for certain forms of alimony.

Vocational or Employment Rehabilitation Factors

1. The ability of the party seeking alimony to be wholly or partly self-supporting

2. The time necessary for the party seeking alimony to gain education or training to enable that party to find suitable employment

During a lengthy absence from employment, a spouse's past education, skills, or experience may have become outdated and her or his earning capacity permanently reduced. Most states also take into account a spouse's status as custodial parent:[36] they consider the supported party's ability to be gainfully employed "without unduly interfering with the interests of dependent children in the custody of the party."[37] The earning ability of the spouse seeking support is an important consideration.

Standard of Living

3. The standard of living that the parties established during the marriage

The parties' standard of living during marriage is a factor in all but a few states.[38] One state explains its public policy goal that the spouse who suffers "economic detriment for the benefit of the marriage" should have a post-divorce standard of living that is "reasonably comparable" to that "enjoyed during the marriage or to the post-divorce standard of living expected to be available to the other spouse."[39]

In Maryland, the second exceptional circumstance warranting indefinite alimony is when the party seeking alimony has made as much progress toward becoming self-supporting as can reasonably be expected, and the respective standards of living of the parties will still be unconscionably disparate.[40] A substantial disparity in income may also mean that the parties' respective standards of living will be unconscionably disparate.

Length of Marriage

4. The duration of the marriage

The duration of the marriage is especially important because awards for an extended period are more likely after longer marriages. While the length of marriage is generally calculated from the date the parties married[41] to the date of their divorce, some states may calculate to the date of separation[42] or to the date of filing the divorce action.[43] Several states put caps on the duration of alimony awards based on the length of marriage. Thus, the duration of the marriage is an important factor in the court's alimony determination, but it is even more significant in states with durational limits.

Monetary and Nonmonetary Contributions to the Family

5. The contributions, monetary and nonmonetary, of each party to the well-being of the family

The court recognizes that, along with the financial contributions both parties make to the marriage, the parties' respective nonfinancial contributions benefit the family and should be taken into account. These nonmonetary contributions may include "services rendered in home-making, childcare, education, and career building of the other party."[44] Ohio's statute considers each party to have "contributed equally to the production of marital income."[45] Some states emphasize the contribution made by the dependent spouse to the education, career, business, license, or earning ability of the other spouse.[46]

Marital Misconduct

6. The circumstances that contributed to the estrangement of the parties

Both the Uniform Marriage and Divorce Act (UMDA) model and ALI *Principles* attempt to eliminate marital fault from consideration in spousal support and property disposition awards.[47] But although no-fault divorces are available in all states—and is the sole grounds for divorce in one-fourth of the states—most still consider marital fault (e.g., adultery, spousal abuse, or child abuse) when determining an alimony award.[48] Most states have removed the automatic forfeiture of alimony penalty for those cases when the person seeking alimony has committed marital fault, but that rule remains the standard in a few states.[49]

Certainly, marital misconduct refers to domestic violence between the parties or toward a party's child.[50] Some states expressly include financial misconduct, such as any "unreasonable depletion of marital assets,"[51] a category that includes "excessive or abnormal expenditures, destruction, concealment or fraudulent disposition" of the parties' joint property.[52] All of these behaviors could contribute to marital estrangement and should be considered by a court.

The Age and Health of the Parties

7. *The age of each party*

8. *The physical and mental condition of each party*

The ages and the health of both spouses are significant factors in determining whether alimony is appropriate and, if so, its duration. One case, for instance, noted that the reentry into the job market by a 56-year-old, "even in excellent health, is problematic."[53] The job prospects of a 57-year-old married for 32 years and who has existing health concerns—are very different from those of a healthy 30-year-old who's been married four years.

In Maryland an exceptional circumstance under which the court may award alimony for an indefinite period is when, "due to age, illness, infirmity, or disability, the party seeking alimony cannot reasonably be expected to make substantial progress toward becoming self-supporting."[54] The connection between the health issue and the inability to be gainfully employed is significant. That said, though, someone could have medical, mental health, or disability issues yet still be capable of working and earning income.[55]

Each Party's Financial Needs and Resources

9. *The ability of the party from whom alimony is sought to meet personal needs while paying alimony*

10. *The financial needs and resources of each party*

In the determination of alimony, the parties' relative financial circumstances are a weighty consideration. In this context, *finances* refers to all the resources and all the needs of the parties—whether income, assets, liabilities, or other financial obligations, and even "the opportunity of each for future acquisition of capital assets and income."[56] Of course, the court has to be careful not to delve too deeply into matters that may be too speculative to quantify: being named the beneficiary of an estate by someone who's still alive is not at all a sure source of income.

Compulsory financial disclosure does assist courts: Maryland requires each party—under oath—to file a current financial statement that itemizes that party's monthly expenses, income, assets, and liabilities.[57] New York's compulsory financial disclosure statute requires the parties to file sworn statements of net worth listing all income and assets, including assets transferred in the past three years, and these statements "shall be accompanied by a current and representative paycheck stub and the most recently filed state and federal income tax returns."[58]

Chapter 10 will cover how to obtain pertinent financial information through both informal exchange and more formal discovery tools, and chapter 13 discusses non-exhaustive income items listed in child support statutes that are also useful in alimony cases. That same chapter addresses the issue of imputing income to a party who is underemployed or voluntarily impoverished. At this point, note some of the technical distinctions between child support and alimony awards.

Technically, "imputed income" is a child support concept predicated on a finding of voluntary impoverishment, which asks the court to consider several facts about a party's ability to work . . . Most, if not all, of the voluntary impoverishment factors will be relevant to alimony . . . , and so a finding of voluntary impoverishment would ordinarily entail a finding, for purposes of alimony, that the impoverished party *could* support him or herself, but *chooses* not to.[59]

Monetary Award and Property Division

When a married couple has considerable assets, the spouse who receives a substantial monetary award upon the equitable division of the parties' property may have a lesser need for alimony. Conversely, a dependent spouse who receives a smaller share of assets—or where there are few or no assets to be divided—may have a greater need for financial support.[60] Although an alimony award and a property disposition are separate matters with distinct purposes, a court should consider the impact of each in its effort to provide a fair financial resolution.

An equitable distribution of property may, however, provide assets that generate additional income. A house can be sold, and the proceeds, invested. In that case, a court needs to balance the fairness of including sales proceeds against a party's need for a down payment on a new residence as well as any other financial obligations.[61]

Cost of Health Insurance Coverage

In determining alimony, the court must also consider the significant cost of health care insurance.[62] Often, the employment-related health insurance policy of one of the spouses covers the family, and the employer pays a portion of the cost.

Upon a divorce or legal separation, COBRA requires most employers to offer temporary—usually thirty-six months—coverage to employees' former spouses, but the employer is not required to pay any part of the monthly premiums.[63]

A court may have authority to allocate the cost of the COBRA premium to one or both of the parties.[64] The court should also take into account the increased cost of health insurance for one spouse and the reduced cost for the other spouse who converts a family plan to employee-only health insurance.[65] Fairness matters. So does action because the lack of coverage places anyone at grave financial risk.

Tax Consequences

Courts consider "immediate and specific tax consequences to each party,"[66] again avoiding anything too speculative.

For 75 years -alimony—or any payments for the other spouse's maintenance that the court required—was taxable income for the recipient and tax deductible for the payer.[67] However, the Tax Cuts and

Jobs Act of 2017 terminated the deductibility of alimony to the payer and its treatment as income to the recipient for instruments (i.e., agreements, decrees, and orders) entered into after December 31, 2018. Those prior to January 1, 2019 are unaffected unless they were modified after that date with language expressly stating that the new law's treatment of alimony applies. Spouses may include a provision in their divorce or separation papers designating that otherwise qualifying payments are not alimony.

Understanding taxes enables the court to shape a fair resolution of both spousal support and property division awards and agreements.

Any Previously Established Agreement Between the Parties

11. Any agreement between the parties

A court will consider the terms of any valid written agreement between spouses. These agreements may even determine the outcome in states where parties are permitted to agree that alimony provisions are not subject to court modification.[68] Sometimes married couples used less formal agreements during their marriage, and those agreements may significantly impact the determination of spousal support. For example, couples often jointly decide their family's employment, education, and parenting structure, and those choices have financial consequences on the parent whose primary role is parenting rather than income production. It is therefore fair for the court to consider the parties' marital decisions and "their effect on present and future earning potential, including the length of time one or both of the parties have been absent from the job market."[69]

Alimony Guidelines

In attempting to address the unpredictability of spousal support, some states and local jurisdictions have recently adopted alimony guidelines.[70] These guidelines may address the amount of alimony, the duration of alimony, or both[71] as well as allow judicial discretion and the freedom to deviate from the calculated amount where it would be "unjust or inappropriate."[72] In states that have not adopted guidelines, trial judges may consult non-legislative guidelines issued by a neutral source that are consistent with the state's considerations so long as the guidelines do not control the trial court's decision.[73]

Here's an example of non-legislative guidelines that some courts find to be a helpful tool. The American Academy of Matrimonial Lawyers (AAML) proposes that the amount of an alimony award "should be calculated by taking 30% of the payer's gross income minus 20% of the payee's gross income."[74] However, the calculated alimony amount "when added to the gross income of the payee shall not result in the recipient receiving in excess of 40% of the combined gross income of the parties."[75]

The AAML recommends calculating the duration of the award "by multiplying the length of the marriage by the following factors: 0–3 years (.3); 3–10 years (.5); 10–20 years (.75), over 20 years, permanent alimony."[76]

Still, both parties have worries about alimony, and I hear these concerns regularly. One client fears receiving less alimony, the other client fears paying greater alimony, and all those fears reflect skewed thinking about both alimony and financial security.

Client #1: "I don't want to accept that promotion and make more money because it might reduce the amount of alimony I receive."

My response: "The salary increase is a higher base for years to come—and that raise is important for independence, self-esteem, and future financial stability."

Client #2: "I don't want to take that promotion—or receive that bonus or salary increase—because I may have to pay more alimony!"

My response: "I would rather earn a dollar and potentially give away ten cents than not earn the dollar."

Modification, Extension, and Termination of Alimony

A court may modify an alimony award as circumstances—especially a substantial or material change in financial circumstances—and justice require.[77] The Uniform Marriage and Divorce Act (UMDA) mandates that the person requesting a modification show "changed circumstances so substantial and continuing as to make the terms unconscionable."[78] This rule seeks to dissuade the filing of "repeated or insubstantial" requests for modification.[79]

Courts may also extend the period of an alimony award. For example, circumstances may arise during the period of a rehabilitative alimony award that would create a harsh and inequitable result without an extension.[80] The UMDA states the general rule regarding termination: "Unless otherwise agreed in writing or expressly provided in the decree, the obligation to pay future maintenance is terminated upon the death of either party or the remarriage of the party receiving maintenance."[81]

Also, many states—whether by statute or case law—provide for termination or modification of alimony upon the recipient spouse's cohabitation with a third party. In the case of cohabitation, the couple's finances—joint bank accounts, joint liabilities, sharing living expenses—are likely intertwined, and the living together indicates a mutually supportive, intimate relationship. Some states focus on the ongoing living situation, while others examine whether the new relationship will impact the need for financial support.

Finally, retirement is a common event that may warrant a court's determination of whether the alimony award should be modified or terminated. Some states codify the effect of retirement. Massachusetts, for instance, mandates that its indefinite alimony orders "shall terminate upon the payer attaining the full retirement age" unless the initial order provides a different date, and an award is subject to extension for good cause.[82] If the party who's paying alimony seeks to retire prior to attaining full retirement age, that party has the burden to demonstrate that the prospective or actual retirement is "reasonable and made in good faith."[83]

Summary

Alimony is the least predictable financial aspect of divorce. In addition to different rationales underlying the many forms of spousal support, no uniform standards regarding duration and amount exist. The factors that some courts consider when making the awards provide some general guidance for others, and several considerations may combine to be weightier in particular cases. There is no single right answer, but whether through negotiation or court determination, the goal should remain a fair and just result.

CHAPTER 7

Equitable Division of Property

HISTORICALLY, TWO MARITAL property regimes prevailed in the United States: common law and community property.[1] Now all states seek to equitably divide the married couple's property upon divorce. For a court to make a fair distribution of the property, it must have personal jurisdiction over the defendant spouse or jurisdiction over the marital assets physically located in the state hearing the action.

Just division of property depends on full disclosure. Parties must file not only sworn financial statements listing income, expenses, assets, and liabilities, but also property statements listing all property owned individually or jointly. The court may rely on these statements as judicial admissions.[2] Some states also require an exchange of recent paystubs and income tax returns, including related W-2s wage and tax statements.[3] A party who substantially and willfully fails to disclose this information may face financial and other sanctions, such as the court awarding a greater distributive share to the offended spouse.[4]

Community Property States

Eight states have community property—Arizona, California, Idaho, Louisiana, Nevada, New Mexico, Texas, and Washington.[5] Property acquired by either or both spouses during their marriage belongs to the marital community, not to either spouse individually. It is divided between the spouses when their marriage is dissolved. Some states require an equal division;[6] others apply equitable distribution principles.[7]

In contrast, separate property is owned or claimed before marriage; acquired by the spouse during marriage by gift or inheritance; and payment for personal injuries sustained during marriage (this does not include compensation for loss of earning capacity during marriage).[8] Some states, however, presume that all property acquired by either or both spouses during marriage is community property.[9]

Community property states generally build on the concept of title: property is acquired when title/ownership is taken. If title is taken prior to marriage, the property is separate; if title is taken during marriage, the property is community.

The community may be reimbursed for using community property to enhance separate property or pay separate debt; a spouse may be reimbursed for separate property used to acquire community property or to pay community debt.[10] Community property states differentiate between the parties' separate and community debt, designating which spouse is responsible to repay which debt;[11] the allocation does not affect creditor's rights.

Common Law and Equitable Distribution States

Equitable distribution has modified or replaced the title-based approach to property division in the forty-two common law states. This approach alleviates the inequities that can result from allocating property strictly by title. Some states assign property to the spouses in a manner that achieves an equitable result; other states may grant a monetary award to one spouse to achieve a "fair and equitable" property distribution. Know that in most states, however, *equitable* does not mean equal. Even states that presume an equal division is equitable may weigh relevant factors and thereby justify an unequal division.

Courts have broad discretion when it comes to determining whether to grant a monetary award. The courts rely on three elements: *Classification*–Identifying the property subject to division, usually distinguishing marital and non-marital/separate property; *Valuation*–Determining the value of marital property; *Equitable distribution*–Deciding any equitable allocation of property (including any permitted transfers of property) plus the monetary award and the method of payment.[12]

Step One: Classification of Property

The concept of property includes both tangible and intangible property. Most divorce courts would include the following in their determination of a couple's property:

- Real property—the parties' residence and any vacation or investment real estate or timeshare
- Vehicles, including motorcycles, recreational vehicles, and boats
- Household furniture and furnishings
- Bank accounts, stocks and bonds, investments, and cash
- A business or professional practice and its assets both tangible and intangible—though states differ in how they treat the intangible institutional goodwill and personal goodwill[13]
- Annuities, individual retirement accounts (IRA), a 401(k) account, and other deferred compensation plans, including related survivor annuity benefits[14]
- Valuables including jewelry and precious gems; gold and silver; coin, stamp, or gun collections; and sports, entertainment, or other memorabilia
- Promissory notes/loans receivable (money someone owes you or your spouse)
- Lottery winnings/annuities
- Unexecuted stock options
- Cash value of life insurance policies
- Intellectual property, including trademarks, patents, copyrights, trade secrets, royalty rights, and an internet domain name
- Permanent Seat License[15] and sports team season tickets
- Country club membership[16]
- Accumulated airline miles or hotel reward points
- Pets[17]

It varies whether a workers' compensation claim,[18] personal injury claim,[19] accrued holiday and vacation leave,[20] or a professional degree or license[21] is subject to division. Even when the value of a professional degree or license isn't subject to division, some states consider in alimony decisions the non-licensed spouse's support while the other spouse obtained the degree or license.

Retirement Benefits

Resolving retirement benefits issues requires knowledge of both federal and state law. The federal Employee Retirement Income Security Act of 1974 (ERISA) limited the rights of a spouse of a covered employee to share in the employee's pension upon divorce. The Retirement Equity Act of 1984 (REA) permits a state court to divide pension benefits as a marital asset and to pay benefits to someone other than the plan beneficiary.

Under REA, certain state domestic relations decrees—such as a "qualified domestic relations order" (QDRO)—are exceptions to the ERISA anti-alienation provision. Retirement plans constitute property, and the benefits acquired during marriage are marital or community property. Government, military, and other pension plans may also be transferred by a similar court order mechanism, although the appropriate orders will not be called a QDRO.

Federal law precludes courts from dividing certain property rights, including Railroad Retirement benefits (Tier I),[22] military disability, and VA disability.[23] Likewise, Social Security benefits may not be distributed due to the U.S. Constitution's Supremacy Clause (Article VI, Cause 2 gives priority to federal law over conflicting state laws). Federal law, however, does not preclude a court from including these benefits in tallying income for alimony and child support purposes.

All Property vs. Marital Property Only

During divorce proceedings, courts in many equitable distribution states may distribute *all* property owned by either or both parties, regardless of how or when it was acquired.[24] But most equitable distribution and community property states maintain the dual classification of property: marital (or community) *and* nonmarital (or separate).[25] In the dual classification jurisdictions, courts may only divide marital property.[26]

Distinguishing marital from separate property can be difficult. States differ on whether to apply these guidelines:

- *Inception of title*: The status of the property is fixed when the title is acquired.
- *Transmutation of property*: Contributing marital property to a separate asset by commingling may change the property's status.
- *Source of funds*: *Acquisition* means "the ongoing process of making payment for acquired property." The characterization as marital or nonmarital/separate would be based on the source of each payment when it is made.

Research attorney Brett R. Turner says, "There is no substantial difference in actual awards under both system . . . [but] the method by which that award is made differs substantially."[27]

Marital property generally includes property acquired during the marriage that was not inherited or received as a gift from a third person; separate property is property acquired before the marriage, received by gift or inheritance, or is directly traceable to these types of property. Spouses may also agree to exclude items of property from being considered marital.

Source of Funds: Tracing and Commingling
In a majority of equitable distribution states, it is important to identify the source of funds used to acquire an asset; directly tracing an asset to separate property could establish that the asset is at least partly separate.[28] The court might find property to be mixed, partially marital and partially separate.

Here is an example of this mixed property approach. Say you buy a townhouse and keep the title only in your name even after getting married.

Before Marriage (Separate Property)

Townhouse purchase:	$100,000
Mortgage:	$90,000
Down payment:	$10,000
Mortgage principal reduction by payments:	$10,000
Total Separate Investment:	$20,000

During Marriage (Marital Property)

Mortgage principal paid (marital investment):	$80,000
Total investment:	$100,000
Townhouse classification: 20% separate 80% marital	
Townhouse final value:	$150,000
Separate property interest:	$30,000 (20% x $150,000)
Marital property interest:	$120,000 (80% x $150,000)

This approach ensures that you—the owner spouse—get a fair and proportionate return on your initial premarital investment, and both parties receive the benefit of the contributions made during the marriage. Some states, however, only credit you the $20,000 premarital contribution and don't recognize any increased value of the asset.

Let's look at another example. Suppose the couple purchased the property while they were married, but they haven't paid off the mortgage. How is the source of funds formula applied in this scenario?

During Marriage

Property purchase:	$40,000
Mortgage:	$30,000
Down payment (wife's separate property):	$10,000
Mortgage principal paid (marital investment):	$10,000
Total investment:	$20,000

Property classification: 25% separate   75% marital

Property final value: $60,000

Separate property interest: $15,000 (25% x $60,000)

Marital property interest:

$25,000 (75% x $60,000 minus $20,000 unpaid mortgage)[29]

Also include in these calculations the source of funds for items such as property improvements (e.g., a deck, a new roof).

The next example addresses tracing and commingling aspects. Let's say that you receive a $20,000 inheritance and deposit all of it into an account titled solely in your name. You have never deposited into that account any funds that are from a marital source. Clearly, the funds in that account should be considered your separate property.

If, while you are married, you use that money to buy a $12,000 car, that car is separate: you exchanged your separate property funds for another asset. However, suppose you deposited that inherited $20,000 into a bank account—whether titled jointly or only in your name— and during your marriage, you deposit your paychecks into that account and pay living expenses from it. When you divorce years later, a few thousand dollars may be in the account, but all the funds have been *commingled.* As a result, your inherited funds may be impossible to trace; they are no longer distinctly identifiable. The $3,000 in the account would likely be deemed marital property.

In contrast to the source of funds approach, the transmutation principle applies a statutory preference to classify property as marital property – when you contribute marital property to a separate asset by commingling it may change the property's status to marital property in its entirety.

During divorce proceedings many courts also take into account anything the couple did while they were married that increased the value of a nonmarital asset. Often the emphasis is on any increase due to the efforts of a spouse, not simply passive appreciation.[30] In other states this increased value of a nonmarital asset remains separate property, but the marital unit might be reimbursed for the increased value due to marital efforts.

Protecting a Spouse from Financial Misconduct

In the context of divorce, the term *dissipation*—the waste of resources, intemperate spending—usually "requires financial misconduct involving marital assets, such as intentional waste or a selfish financial impropriety, coupled with a purpose unrelated to the marriage."[31] For example, taking an expensive vacation with a significant other or gambling away money that otherwise would be marital property could be considered dissipation.

The court may treat dissipated property as if it still exists and consider that property when determining its monetary award[32] or when making a property award to the spouse harmed by the misconduct.[33]

Not every poor business decision or wasteful management of funds, however, will be considered dissipation. After all, in marriage you take the good and the bad; you can't accept only the positive financial contributions of your spouse and expect recompense for all of the poor decisions made over the years. The timing of the financial misconduct, though, may be significant. Is one spouse wasting the parties' assets leading up to or during the separation or, perhaps, spending assets for personal benefit to harm the other spouse's ultimate property distribution? That situation is very different from making a poor investment fifteen years ago.[34]

As one divorce decision indicated, the court may consider evidence that a spouse dissipated marital assets before the couple's physical separation but during the contemplation of divorce or separation, or when the marriage was already in serious jeopardy.[35] Dissipation may also occur after separation or even while the divorce is pending.

When divorce papers are filed, several states automatically issue an order preventing each party from selling, transferring, or otherwise disposing of any property belonging to either or both parties without the other spouse's consent—except for the reasonable and necessary living expenses, or in the ordinary and usual course of business, or by order of the court.[36] The general equity jurisdiction in other states would allow similar orders when one party requests protection from the spouse's dissipation of property. In such cases, the reined-in spouse must give notice to the other party of an intended extraordinary expenditure and then account for the transactions. These statutes try to preserve assets and protect one spouse from the other's financial misconduct during the divorce proceedings.

Step Two: Valuation of Property

After identifying the marital property, the court determines its value as of a certain date. The most common dates are the date of final separation, of filing the dissolution, and of the divorce trial or the divorce itself. Consider the tools used in valuation:

- To determine the value of the couple's property, the court will rely on *fair market value*, defined as "the price at which the property would change hands between a willing buyer and a willing seller, neither being under any compulsion to buy or to sell and both having reasonable knowledge of relevant facts."[37]

- Sometimes, even though **appraisal** is not an exact science, an expert in the particular asset being considered will estimate or appraise the worth of an asset. For example, a real estate appraiser may provide an expert opinion regarding the market value of the parties' house. Knowledgeable owners may also express their opinion of the property's value.

- Buyers and sellers of **cars** often turn to Kelly Blue Book to establish a car's value.

- Stock market reports may be "trustworthy and reliable" sources of information about the value of **publicly traded stock**.[38]

- **Expert testimony** may be necessary, such as on the values of a business or annuity or pension benefit. A court may appoint an expert to value an asset and apportion the cost between the parties. Often, spouses agree on an expert to value property to save the added expense of hiring separate experts.

The court may also need a valuation of **retirement benefits,** and those benefits are also important in the equitable asset distribution. Two broad categories of retirement plans exist: defined contribution plans and defined benefit plans.

Typical **defined contribution plans** are IRAs, SEP/IRAs, 401(k)s (corporate employment plans), 403(b)s (public education entities and most nonprofit organizations), 457s (state/municipal employees and some nonprofit organizations), and Thrift Savings Plan (federal employers, including uniformed services members).

Defined contribution plans are the type most available through employment, and some employers provide matching contributions. The account balance is its value, and this value will increase and decrease based on the investment market.

Most states apply source of funds principles when classifying defined contribution plans. The marital property interest includes employee contributions from marital funds, the employer's contributions during the marriage, and any passive return on the investment itself. The separate interest includes employee contributions from separate funds, employer contributions made before marriage or for the employee's after-the-divorce efforts, and passive return on the investment.[39]

Suppose both the employee and the employer contributed $20,000 before the marriage and $60,000 during the marriage. In a basic analysis, the marital investment would be 75% ($60,000 divided by the $80,000 total contribution). So if the account value on the classification date is $130,000, then the marital interest would be $97,500 (0.75 x $130,000), and the separate interest would be $32,500. Some states require a more complex analysis to decide the marital and separate interests.

Now to the other category of retirement benefits: "'**Defined benefit plan**' means a retirement plan that is not a defined contribution plan and that usually provides benefits as a percentage of the participant's highest average salary, based on the plan's benefit formula and the participant's age and service credit at the time of retirement."[40] These plans are commonly referred to as *pensions*. Although it is possible to determine their present value, distributing a former spouse's share of future payments on an "as, if, and when" basis (i.e. at the time each monthly benefit payment is made) makes valuation unnecessary.[41] The formulas used to calculate the marital and separate shares of defined benefit plans is discussed in the next section.

Step Three: Equitable Distribution

Next, the court decides whether an award distributing marital property is necessary to make the property division equitable and fair. The award would include both the terms of any permitted property transfers (e.g., retirement benefits)[42] as well as the amount and method of payment of any monetary award from one spouse to the other. To guide its decision, the court must consider any relevant factors, including any listed in that state's statutes and case law. Although similar criteria apply to making reasonable alimony awards and equitable distribution awards, the criteria are considered separately and serve different purposes.

First, Professor Cynthia Starnes notes two conflicting principles that make an equitable distribution more difficult: "that property should be allocated according to spousal *contribution*, and . . . that property should be allocated according to spousal *need*. An emphasis on contribution will support a larger award for a primary wage-earner, while an emphasis on need will support a larger award for a primary caregiver."[43] The dichotomy may not be this pronounced because states also consider a spouse's nonfinancial contributions.

The Maryland factors discussed in the chapter on alimony also provide guidance here,[44] as well as two additional factors that are addressed in this chapter:

How and when property or an interest in property was acquired, including the effort expended in accumulating it; and the

contribution by either party of nonmarital property to the acquisition of real property owned by both parties. The list of Maryland factors is neither exclusive nor exhaustive. The contribution of each spouse—both financial and nonfinancial—in the acquisition, enhancement, depreciation, or appreciation of property is also considered. Other factors include financial support to an ex-spouse or to children from a prior marriage;[45] taxes on each party's share of the assets;[46] and the costs involved in the sale or liquidation of an asset, a step necessary for an equitable division of property.[47]

After considering the relevant factors, the court makes its property division. This decision may involve dividing retirement benefits, transferring ownership of real or personal property, and granting an award from one spouse to the other to adjust the parties' property interests. When the marital property is insufficient to produce a fair division, some states do allow the distribution of separate property in order to avoid hardship.[48] If a monetary award is made, the court determines the method of payment: lump sum or installments paid over a set period.[49]

Marital Debt

Most courts are authorized to allocate, "as between the parties, the responsibility for the payment of the debts of the parties whether community, joint, or separate."[50] The court's pronouncement does not limit the creditor's rights to pursue collection against either or both spouses.[51]

Brett Turner says the case law reflects a consistent understanding: "In most states, a marital debt is any debt incurred during the marriage for the joint benefit of the parties.[52] Conversely, a nonmarital debt is any debt incurred before or after the marriage, or any debt incurred during the marriage which is not for the parties' joint benefit."[53]

Some common marital debts include those incurred to purchase assets such as a house or car, to improve or maintain an asset, medical expenses, and supporting the parties' minor children.[54]

After the court classifies debts as marital or nonmarital, it values the debt (usually the current balance owed). This debt is subtracted from the fair market value of the marital property, and that net amount is subject to equitable distribution. Next, the court considers the debt as it settles on the division of property. Courts may allocate marital debts to one or both spouses. Some important factors in the court's allocation decision include: "(1) which party incurred the debt and the debt's purpose . . . ; (2) which party benefited from incurring the debt . . . ; and (3) which party is best able to repay the debt."[55]

Any debt, whether secured or unsecured, is offset by the purchased asset. An example will help. If you borrowed $10,000 from a friend to buy a car, the balance of that loan would be deducted from the car's value. However, suppose you purchased a $200,000 house, the mortgage balance is $180,000 when you divorce, and the house's fair market value has plummeted to $150,000. The house does not have a negative value for equitable distribution purposes; it has a zero value.[56]

Defined Benefit Plan (Pension) Benefits

The division of pension benefits can be based on the employed spouse's contributions to the fund plus interest; the present value of the benefits; a fixed monetary amount; a fixed percentage of the payment; or by applying some time-rule formula that will establish a percentage of benefits to be paid on an "as, if, and when" received basis.[57]

To calculate the former spouse's share of each payment, most states use the formula one-half (or whatever percentage the court has determined) of this fraction: the number of months credited toward retirement during the marriage (numerator) divided by the number of months credited to the date of retirement (denominator).[58]

Usually, the months of service credited toward retirement runs from the date employment begins. So, if the parties have been married fifteen years, during which one spouse worked 150 months (twelve-and-a-half years) that were credited toward retirement, the numerator would be 150. If the participant has 240 months (twenty years) at the time of retirement, the denominator would be 240. The marital share would be 0.625 (62.5%, or 150 divided by 240). If the former spouse receives one-half of the marital share, that would be 0.3125 (31.25%) of the monthly pension. If the retiree's monthly benefit payment is $5,000, then the former spouse's monthly share would be $1,562.50 (0.3125 x $5,000) and the retiree's share would be $3,437.50 (0.6875 x $5,000).

The terms of each pension plan are different, so the court must be clear what benefit amount the fractional share will be applied against—gross annuity, net annuity after certain deductions (such as the cost of survivor's benefits), self-only annuity, or some other terminology from that particular plan.[59] Because a former spouse's share of the pension terminates when the party who earned the pension dies, that spouse must be fully informed about any survivor's annuity that may be available. If a survivor's annuity is available, the court order must identify this benefit and outline how that payment will be allocated.[60] Usually, the retiree's monthly pension benefit is reduced by the amount that covers the cost of providing the survivor benefit.

Because pension benefits are often the parties' most substantial asset, both parties need a thorough understanding of the plan's terms and available options—pre-retirement death benefits, refund of employee contributions, survivor annuities, cost of living adjustments (COLAs), etc.

Most divisions of the pension benefits are initiated by a qualified domestic relations order (QDRO) or other qualified order that assigns benefits to the non-retiree spouse directly from the plan. Courts reserve jurisdiction to enter and amend these orders in whatever ways necessary for the plan administrators to accept them. Agreements and court orders regarding division of pensions must be carefully and properly drafted to ensure they correctly reflect the intended outcome and will be approved by the plan administrator.

Military Retirement Benefits

The Uniformed Services Former Spouses' Protection Act permits state courts to award former spouses a share of a service member's disposable retired pay, which is the member's gross retired pay less authorized deductions.[61] Some of the authorized deductions are the amount waived to receive VA disability benefits, disability retired pay, and premiums for the Survivor Benefit Plan. The amounts waived are not considered disposable retired pay.

Great care must be taken to address this determination of disposable retired pay. Former spouses who expect to receive a share of their military spouse's retired pay will receive substantially less than anticipated when a portion is waived so the service member can receive disability pay.[62] This possibility should be considered and addressed before it's too late. Perhaps that reduction in retired pay can be offset by a higher alimony award, a greater share of a Thrift Savings Plan, or a disproportionate share of property other than the military pension.

A state court's division of the military spouse's disposable retired pay may not be enforced by direct payment from Defense Finance and Accounting Service (DFAS) unless the service member performed ten or more years of creditable service while married to the spouse who is seeking the benefits (the 10/10 rule).[63] For those married less than ten years, a court may still award a share of the pension benefits—payable by the service member, not directly from the plan.

Awards must be expressed either as a fixed dollar amount (paid monthly), a percentage of pay, or a "hypothetical retired pay award."[64] A fixed dollar amount would preclude receiving COLAs. Expressed as a percentage, the COLAs are applied automatically to shares.

Often parties are divorced before the military spouse becomes eligible for retired pay. The National Defense Authorization Act for Fiscal Year 2017 (NDAA 17) significantly revised military pension division. Now when the divorce occurs before the service member's retirement, the division must be calculated as a "hypothetical retired pay award." It's also called "frozen benefit division" because, for calculation purposes, both the service member's rank and years of service are frozen at the date of divorce, not the date of retirement.[65] This new retirement plan applies to all who entered active duty on or after January 1, 2018.

The Marital Residence

The home is one of a couple's most substantial assets; it's also one of the most hotly contested items. Many courts have authority to transfer title either from one spouse to the other spouse or from both spouses to only one. The court may set the terms for one spouse to buy out the other spouse's interest. The court might also order a transfer of ownership, provided the receiving spouse obtains the other spouse's release from any lien on the property.[66]

Most courts are permitted to award the exclusive possession and use of the family house to a custodial parent for a limited period of time,[67] and some courts may award exclusive use even when no minor children are involved. Courts can also order the sale of the house and division of the proceeds. As their marriage ends, however, spouses have much greater flexibility and creativity than courts do in determining how to benefit most from this major asset, their house.

Contribution

A co-tenant who pays the mortgage, taxes, and other carrying charges of jointly owned property is entitled to contribution from the other co-tenant.[68] In the absence of an ouster of the nonpaying spouse, a married-but-separated co-tenant is entitled to contribution for those expenses they, as the paying spouse, paid to preserve the property.[69]

Some exceptions that may warrant denial of contribution include ouster of the nonpaying co-tenant; the parties' agreement concerning payment or division of house proceeds; payments made from marital property; the paying spouse residing at the property and receiving the income tax benefits of payment; or a court deciding that awarding contribution would undermine the equitable monetary award. Contribution is another factor that the court may consider in making a monetary award.[70]

Interim Distribution and Modifying Orders

If good cause or extraordinary circumstances exist, several states permit an interim, partial distribution of assets (and in some cases debt) during the divorce case—provided the partial distribution does not lead to inequity or prejudice to either party's claims for support or attorneys' fees.[71] A monetary credit or adjustment should be made in the ultimate equitable distribution at divorce to account for any interim property distribution.[72]

Generally, courts may not modify orders concerning property division or any distributive award.[73] Some states have exceptions, such as fraud, the parties' express written consent, the enforcement of the parties' "manifest intentions,"[74] or on remand following an appeal.[75]

Life Insurance

Some courts may require one party to maintain a life insurance policy designating the other spouse as beneficiary of the proceeds.[76] But in many states courts are not authorized to direct a party to provide life insurance coverage.[77] Spouses, however, could agree to require insurance coverage even though the court could not order such coverage on its own.

Bankruptcy

Federal bankruptcy law imposes an automatic stay on certain state court actions that are pending when a bankruptcy petition is filed.[78] This stay prevents the divorce court from distributing assets that are part of the bankruptcy estate.

The bankruptcy court has discretion to lift the stay if a spouse makes that motion. If the court lifts the stay, the divorce court may determine the debtor spouse's property rights and make an equitable distribution of property.[79] The bankruptcy court retains its exclusive authority to prioritize the respective rights of the spouse and the creditors.[80]

The automatic stay does not halt proceedings for domestic support obligations (spousal support and child support), child custody, or visitation proceedings.[81]

Attorney's Fees, Suit Money, and Costs

The American rule is that each party pays its own attorney's fees unless a contractual provision or a statute permits the court to require one party to pay all or part of the other party's attorney's fees. In family law cases, states typically have some provision permitting a court to award reasonable attorney's fees to the other party. These statutes permit the court to order either party to pay the other party an amount for the "reasonable and necessary expense" of prosecuting or defending the proceeding.

Suit money and costs may include counsel fees, expert witness fees, private investigator costs, vocational rehabilitation counselors' costs, deposition costs, litigation-related travel expenses, investigation expenses, and court costs where such expenses are "reasonable and necessary." Courts usually consider the parties' respective financial circumstances and whether the party had substantial justification for prosecuting or defending the proceeding.

To determine the reasonableness of requested attorney's fees, courts review such factors as the time and labor required; the novelty and the difficulty of the issues—and the skill required to perform the legal service properly; fees customarily charged in the locality for similar legal services; the experience, reputation, and ability of the attorney performing the services; and the results obtained and the benefit afforded the client.[82]

One way that attorney's fee awards may contribute to making divorce proceedings fair and equitable is that they can alleviate the expense incurred by the economically dependent spouse, can curb excessive litigation, and can level the playing field. Without an award, a party may not have the ability to obtain necessary experts. The court may order that the amount of the award be paid directly to the attorney, and the attorney may then enforce the order directly.

The court may also "impose counsel fees against one or more parties to the action" for the court-appointed child-advocate attorney or best-interest attorney for a minor child.[83]

Summary

The urge for victory—for conquest—often motivates people who are going through the difficult season of separation and divorce. A just financial outcome—one that equitably allocates the couple's assets to each of the two parties—is a crucial objective that ideally promotes some degree of peace despite the turmoil. Understanding how courts decide financial issues may provide you with reasonable and more realistic expectations as well as a greater likelihood that you'll understand and agree to a settlement. Whether the divorce court is in a community property state or an equitable distribution jurisdiction, the goal is similar: to achieve a fair, equitable, and just resolution by identifying the property subject to division, valuing it, and distributing it as appropriate.

Because multiple factors may weigh heavily on the side of one spouse, an equal division is not always an equitable one. Also, the division of retirement benefits is especially technical, and it is imperative to obtain competent advice. Dividing pensions appropriately, particularly military pensions, requires great care and understanding. The overall goal is that, when carefully and justly managed, the alimony, property division, and attorney's fee awards will, together, constitute an equitable financial resolution.

PART TWO

The Just Process of Divorce
Just Conduct During the Proceedings

PRINCIPLE 6
Proportionate Means

Chapter 8

Effective Negotiation Strategies

SADLY, DIVORCES OFTEN resemble wars, and the battle tactics are frequently extreme. Many spouses use severe measures or disproportionate means to reach the ends they desire. They employ scorched-earth tactics or get caught up in a passion that escalates the conflict to a mutually destructive end.

Understanding negotiation may help you achieve a more satisfying resolution of the dispute. After all, negotiating is a regular aspect of basic human interaction. Negotiation occurs whenever two or more parties communicate with each other to reach an agreement, and because most cases are settled prior to a contested trial, negotiation is integral to bringing a peaceful conclusion to the divorce process.

Many people view negotiation as a battle over limited resources: a pie will be divided, and each party is seeking a larger piece. Thus, as one party's portion increases, the other one's decreases. One person's gain necessitates the other's loss, encouraging a win-lose mentality. Another option exists, however.

Imagine negotiation that seeks to maximize the available resources, to explore many options, some of which do not conflict directly with one another, and therefore to provide an opportunity for creative solutions and win-win bargaining. Both parties create as much value as possible, which ultimately benefits both sides. Each person gives up less critical matters in order to get the things they value most.

115

The classic illustration of this is a tale of two siblings arguing over who gets the last orange.[1] The easy resolution would be to divide the orange in half, and that approach certainly *seems* fair. But one sibling wanted the orange to make juice, and the other wanted the orange rind for baking. Dividing the orange equally—cutting it into two same-size pieces—misses an opportunity for both siblings to get full use of the orange in a way that will exactly meet their needs. Had their real interests been communicated, understood, and addressed, one sibling could have squeezed twice as much juice, and the other would have twice as much rind for baking—clearly, a win-win settlement that is mutually satisfying and meets the interests of both parties. However, this value was never explored or considered by the siblings. Metaphorically speaking, merely cutting the pie—or the orange—in half does not necessarily result in a fair agreement or the best solution.[2]

Often, competitive bargaining exhibits a rights-based approach: the negotiators determine how to slice the pie so that their rights are not violated. However, a Christian's charge is not only to love and glorify God, but also to "love your neighbor as yourself" (Matthew 22:36–40). The Golden Rule— "whatever you wish that others would do to you, do also to them" (7:12)—offers further guidance. Rather than acting out of rivalry or pride, we are to humbly consider the good of other people. As the apostle Paul put it, each of us should "look not only to his own interests, but also to the interests of others" (Philippians 2:3–4).

Ken Sande, author of *The Peacemaker*, notes the downside to a strictly rights-based approach:

> When exercising a right allows you to avoid a moral responsibility or to take unfair advantage of others, you have not acted justly in the eyes of God, regardless of what a court might say. Therefore, always strive to exercise only those rights that would pass both a legal and a heavenly review.[3]

In contrast, an interests-based approach allows both parties to identify, address, and resolve their underlying interests for their mutual benefit. This approach often leads to the consideration of a range of possible outcomes that better address the concerns of both parties. The result is a more creative solution and greater satisfaction.

Leigh Thompson offers this observation: "The best state of affairs is to have a negotiator who is cooperative in working with the other party to understand and explore his issues and interests and competitive enough to claim valuable resources for himself."[4] The negotiator's challenge is to balance competitive, value-claiming strategy with cooperative, value-creating strategies that may result in mutually beneficial options.[5]

In their book *Negotiation Genius,* Deepak Malhotra and Max H. Bazerman propose seeking areas in which you can create value because "it is better to assume that you can enlarge the pie and later find out that you were wrong than to assume the pie is fixed and never find out you were wrong."[6] In his popular best-seller *Getting to Yes,* Roger Fisher defines a wise agreement as "one that meets the legitimate interests of each side to the extent possible, resolves conflicting interests fairly, is durable, and takes community interests into account."[7]

Every description of collaborative and cooperative interests-based negotiation highlights essential features like these, features that contribute to the formation of just and fair agreements:

- Plan wisely
- Affirm relationships
- Understand interests
- Search for creative solutions
- Evaluate the potential outcomes.[8]

Let's explore each of these elements of successful negotiation.

Prepare to Negotiate: Wise Planning

The book of Proverbs highlights the importance of wise planning, of having a virtuous goal and using fair and honest strategies (Proverbs 12:5). Also, a wise person seeks advice from other wise people (15:22; 20:18).

In the context of war, "the value of wisdom is not that it necessarily avoids war, but that it can provide the strategy through which strength can find its most efficient expression and thus lead to victory."[9] Those who plan good things receive good things both in their relationship with God and in their relationships with others (14:22). In all our planning we are to commit our plans to God (Psalm 37:5).[10]

Prayer

Prayer is not merely part of a Christian's preparation; prayer is to continue throughout the negotiations. When we seek God in prayer, we cultivate a dependent, humble, and grateful spirit, an attitude that contributes to calm and reasonable discussion. Also, as you prepare for and engage in negotiations, ask God to purify your motives, conform you to his will, and grant you humility, patience, wisdom, and discernment. God is concerned about every single one of your needs, and when you bring your concerns and anxieties before him, you can be assured of his goodness, providence, and peace.[11]

Knowledge/Information

Gathering information and gaining knowledge are essential aspects of effective negotiating. Think through the information exchange: determine what you plan to obtain from your spouse and what you are willing to disclose. Information helps you understand the other party's needs, interests, and goals; identify the range of a possible settlement; and minimize the effect of the other side's potential manipulation and deception.

Sound preparation makes significant strategic blunders less likely—and respect from the other side more likely. Your preparation may involve doing significant research and accumulating pertinent information, including looking for past precedents that may shape the outcome of your present situation.

Understand the Problem

If you do not fully understand the problem, you may end up expending your time, energy, and other resources solving the wrong problem. Be sure that your focus is not so narrow that you miss other possibilities and opportunities. Challenge yourself to understand the situation as thoroughly as possible.

Understand Your Own Interests

Ask yourself basic questions—*What are my needs?, How do I prioritize them?, Why do I want that?, Why is it important to me?*—so that you clearly identify what matters most to you. Charles Craver suggests prioritizing bargaining items in four broad categories:

1. *Essential* items include those that you must obtain to satisfy your fundamental interests and basic needs. If these key terms are not resolved to your satisfaction, you would prefer your nonsettlement alternatives.
2. *Important* items are those that you would very much like to obtain, but which you would forgo if the essential terms were resolved favorably.
3. *Desirable* items are those of secondary value that you would be pleased to have, but which you would be willing to exchange for essential or important things.
4. *Indifferent* items are those you would be perfectly willing to concede in order to achieve your other bargaining objectives.[12]

Prioritizing your interests like this will help you avoid trading away something significant for an item that actually means less to you. If at some point you find it necessary to make certain compromises or concessions, be sure to seek to compromise your wants rather than your needs.

Understand Your Settlement Objectives

After determining your primary interests, ask yourself, "What would be a good outcome for me?" Establish your desired outcome before negotiation begins. Seek high but realistic aspirations within the bounds of fairness and in consideration of both parties' best alternatives. In setting expectations, soberly estimate both sides' strengths and weaknesses.

If you overestimate your weaknesses and the other side's strengths, you may make unnecessary concessions and fail to preserve points that are truly significant to you. If you overestimate your strengths and underestimate your spouse's, you may be blind to both hazards and opportunities. If your expectations are unrealistic, negotiations may be undermined before you even begin because you may have unintentionally eliminated an area of possible agreement.

Be prepared to explain your thinking, to provide helpful information, and to explain why your expectations are reasonable. Awareness that your knowledge and assumptions are limited prepares you to make adjustments throughout the negotiations.

Understand the Other Side

One way to better understand your spouse's perspective is to put yourself in their shoes: consider what their interests and concerns may be and what a good outcome might look like from their point of view. Learning more about their real concerns and interests will equip you to navigate a seemingly entrenched demand because you will have recognized the underlying concerns that mean the most to your spouse.

Preparation also includes identifying areas of common ground, your spouse's basic interests, what aspects are of value to your spouse, and occasions for favorable compromise and trade-offs. Shapiro and Jankowski break down the negotiation process into Prepare, Probe, Propose with an emphasis on having good listening skills. They explain that these stages are not completely separate from one another: "You prepare for the negotiation *before* it occurs. You probe for information *before* and *during* the negotiation. You propose *after* preparing and probing. You *continue* preparing and probing as you respond to an offer."[13]

Understand Your and Your Spouse's BATNA

Your BATNA ("best alternative to a negotiated agreement") is your preferred course of action if negotiations do not result in the settlement you hope for. Your BATNA is the reality you will face if settlement discussions are unsuccessful, Clearly, it is not the result you hope to achieve in negotiations. If you do not have a good grasp of what you will do if no agreement is reached, then you will be more susceptible to the other side's tactics, which may press you into accepting what preparation would have shown to be an entirely unsatisfactory agreement.

Therefore, it is absolutely essential to determine your bottom line or walkaway point in advance. By "walkaway point" I mean the least favorable deal that you are still willing to accept rather than pursuing your BATNA. You would accept this agreement if it satisfies your interests at least slightly better than you think your BATNA could.

This walkaway point should serve as a warning light when you find yourself near to accepting an agreement: could it be worse for you than your BATNA? If you realize that your BATNA is weak, strengthen it—and you'll improve your negotiating position. As you define your BATNA and walkaway point and understand the other side's BATNA and walkaway point, you'll clearly see the negotiating space you have for a settlement that satisfies both parties.

So of course consider what would genuinely satisfy your concerns but be sure to address enough of your spouse's basic interests that the two of you might agree to a settlement. In what Shapiro and Jankowski have termed "WIN-win" negotiations, they say you should satisfy your interests well and satisfy their interests acceptably. In other words, the "best way to get most of what you want is to help the other side get some of what they want."[14] Indeed, it is prudent to develop a range of acceptable settlements for various issues, including in that range your desired settlement, your opening position, and your walkaway point.

Preparation also involves accepting the importance of flexibility in the negotiation process. Because negotiations do not follow a rigid and predictable course, don't let yourself be derailed by changes and unexpected developments. As you keep in mind your larger goal— a satisfactory settlement—you will be prepared to be flexible when you face the unexpected.

Affirm Relationships

Consider the wisdom of maintaining the relationship in the very negotiations prompted by the end of your marriage relationship:

> A strong relationship creates trust, which allows the parties to share information more freely, which in turn leads to more creative and valuable agreements and to a greater willingness to continue working together. But when a deal is struck that is not very attractive to one or both parties, chances are that they will invest less time and effort in working together, they will become more wary in communicating with each other, and their relationship will grow strained.[15]

Because disputes involve people and a problem, try to "separate the people from the problem."[16] After all, divorce negotiations often occur in the context of an ongoing relationship especially when the two parties will be sharing parenting responsibilities. Work to conduct negotiations in a way that will promote—rather than hinder—the relationship and the future negotiations.

Also, be mindful that, with the history you and your spouse share, simmering negative emotions may exist and, if they do, impact the ability of both parties to resolve the issues and to choose wisely the negotiation strategies they employ. Resist pushing those buttons that you know may provoke an angry or defensive response—and resist responding to unkind words with an unkind response. A tender or soft response helps create conditions that allow for constructive dialogue. A harsh and hurtful response may lead to further defensiveness and anger, both of which inhibit communication.

To avoid such landmines, decide in advance to show respect in negotiations. Good communication skills, for instance, will indicate your appreciation of the other side's perspective. Asking open-ended questions helps people distinguish between wants and needs. Ask, too, about the other side's needs, interests, concerns, and goals. Probe their willingness to trade one thing for another: "Do you care more about X or Y?"

Also, granting your spouse the benefit of the doubt—instead of interpreting every word or action in the worst possible light—can free you to see subtle position changes or come up with fresh ideas. A better understanding may lessen the conflict and increase awareness of self-interest. The wise will not only control their anger but also seek to minimize it in others (Proverbs 16:14).

Realize, too, that the positions you take in negotiations may hem in the other side. When that happens, your spouse may not see a way out that also permits him to avoid humiliation and embarrassment. Giving him an opportunity to save face is an act of respect and goodwill. That said, a party may find his or her own way to back away from the original claims—and to be able to justify doing so.[17]

Active listening skills also contribute greatly to successful problem-solving and reaching an acceptable outcome. Be deliberate about listening. When someone is speaking, we tend to focus on what we will say next instead of trying to understand the speaker's point, perspective, or concern. We regularly talk over or past each other. Fight that tendency when you're negotiating.

Related to that counsel is another integral aspect of constructive communication: exercise self-control. The wise and coolheaded person is careful in speech, thinking before answering. In sharp contrast, the impetuous person hastily blurts out whatever he wants to say without any thought about how the words will be heard or the damage they might do. Words are a reflection of our hearts, and they have the power to bring healing and blessing as well as the power to wound and destroy.[18] As pastor and counselor Jim Newheiser writes, "If our hearts are right, our speech will be wise."[19]

As part of good communication especially in negotiations like these, it is essential to strike a balance between empathy and assertiveness. It can be constructive to express empathy and respect for the other side's interests and to adjust your assumptions based on what you learn, but be sure to assert what you need, what you want, and the why behind items you mention.

Emotions often surface in negotiations, and when the divorce settlement is being debated, anger is common. The emotional intensity may increase as sensitive subjects are broached, legitimate concerns are belittled, and destructive patterns that contributed to the marital strife resurface.

Consider these strategies for increasing your ability to deal with angry negotiators so you can save both the deal and the relationship:

1. Seek to understand why the person is angry.
2. Acknowledge to them their anger: "I can see that you're angry, and I want to understand why that is. Please explain it."
3. Don't take personally the emotional outburst—and do consider whether it is genuine emotion or merely an intimidation tactic.
4. Help the person focus on the actual underlying interests: "What would you like to see happen now? What can help us put this behind us? Is there anything else you would like to discuss or clarify before we return to the substantive issues you highlighted earlier?" Be prepared to extend a symbolic gesture, perhaps an apology, where appropriate. [20]

Another way to preserve the relationship as well as the negotiations is to express appreciation. Efforts to build relationships can continue even after the negotiations have begun, and demonstrating empathy, respect, and courtesy will be helpful. A person who perceives no value in the relationship may get aggressive, but the other person offering affirmation can help moderate extreme behavior.

A relationship's value is more apparent when the spouses have minor children. These parents will be in contact for years to come, and at some point they may have to tackle together difficult matters involving their children. Aggressiveness in negotiations today may mean more difficult future interactions and transactions. In joint problem-solving be "soft on the people, hard on the problem."[21]

Understand Interests

When I discussed interests in the section on preparing to negotiate, I suggested differentiating between essential, important, desirable, and indifferent items to understand what is most significant for you and to consider the other side's interests as well.

Ken Sande says it is important to grasp the distinction between an issue, a position, and an interest. An *issue* is "an identifiable and concrete question that must be addressed in order to reach an agreement." A *position* is "a desired outcome or a definable perspective on an issue." An *interest* is "what motivates people. It is a concern, desire, need, limitation, or something a person values. Interests provide the basis for positions."[22] In other words, "Your position is something you have decided upon. Your interests are what caused you to so decide."[23]

To arrive at a wise solution, you will seek to reconcile the interests, not the positions. Leigh Thompson observes, "Many people falsely believe that the other party has preferences that are directly opposed to their own on all dimensions, when in fact this isn't true."[24] Although the parties' *positions* are frequently incompatible with each other and may even be in direct conflict, a party's underlying primary *interests*—needs, desires, concerns, fears, and values—may be compatible.[25]

As you better understand and address your spouse's interests, you'll be more persuasive and effective in negotiating a resolution. Also, it is important to be future-oriented: you want to avoid getting "caught up in a quarrel . . . [because] people are more likely to respond to what the other side has said or done than to act in pursuit of their own long-term interests."[26]

Know, too, that looking beneath opposing positions for the motivating interests often leads to the discovery of other positions that meet both spouses' interests. Some of the most significant interests are basic human needs, such as security, economic well-being, a sense of belonging, recognition, and control over one's life.[27] A case involving a request for alimony, for example, involves more than dollars. The person requesting alimony has other interests such as being psychologically secure, treated fairly or respected as an equal. Whether those needs are met may impact what is acceptable in terms of dollars.

Search for Creative Solutions

Certain mind-sets impede finding creative solutions:

- Perceiving issues with a "fixed pie" assumption
- Judging critically
- Seeking a single solution instead of being open to the possibilities of better solutions
- Concern with your immediate interests and position
- Failing to see that solving the other person's problem is also your own concern

Viewing negotiations as fixed-pie bargaining hinders negotiators because they fail to see the other issues that could expand the pie and provide for mutually beneficial exchanges.[28] Malhotra notes an interesting phenomenon related to the fixed-pie bias: *reactive devaluation*.[29] It's typical to devalue the spouse's proposals and concessions simply because they're being made by that person. You will view negatively something proposed by the other side even though the same proposal—if you made it—would seem to benefit both spouses. What's good for the other side isn't necessarily bad for you, so curb this instinctive reaction to dismiss the spouse's idea. You don't want to miss the real value or benefit to you in that proposal.

Another common mistake is to regard your initial position as the only acceptable solution. Whereas "initial positions act as anchors and affect each side's perception of what outcomes are possible,"[30] brainstorming results in numerous possible ideas for solving a problem, and criticism and assessment are deferred. Both sides are urged to suggest any and all ideas, and this proceeds without immediate critique.

In a brainstorming session, participants withhold judgment in order to avoid stifling the free flow of creative ideas, some of which may ultimately form the basis for an acceptable solution. Ury has observed the following:

> Criticism and evaluation, while important functions, interfere with your imagination. It is better to separate the two functions. Invent first, evaluate later. Suspend judgment for a few minutes and try to come up with as many ideas as possible. . . . After brainstorming a multitude of options, you can review them and evaluate how well they satisfy your interests—and the other side's too.[31]

Negotiators vary in how they want to address issues. Some prefer to begin with the easy ones and set a good tone, build momentum, and increase the parties' commitment to the process. Other negotiators first address the deal-breaker issues to gauge whether a tentative agreement can be reached before spending any time on less significant issues. The thinking is, those lesser matters may be readily resolved if the most difficult issue is settled at the outset. Still others choose to negotiate many issues simultaneously, an approach that can reveal respective priorities and potential trade-offs.[32]

Malhotra asserts, "The more issues there are available to play with, the more likely it is that each party will obtain what it values most and become willing to compromise on issues of relatively less importance."[33] Leigh Thompson discusses the concept of logrolling, which means "making mutually beneficial trade-offs between the issues on the table." Effective logrolling involves identifying and negotiating more than one issue, weighing the parties' different preferences, and managing to mix and match different alternatives.[34]

When issues are negotiated simultaneously, the parties wait until everything is discussed before reaching a final agreement on any one issue. Agreement on any part is merely tentative until there is a comprehensive agreement covering all aspects of the settlement.

Proposing a package deal—another approach to negotiating—presents your desired outcome regarding all the issues; a counterproposal would likely make some demands but also indicate flexibility on other matters.[35] These proposals make apparent which issues are most important and which are least important to the other side. When you know that your spouse highly values getting his way on a certain issue, you may be able to obtain concessions if you agree to be flexible on that highly valued aspect.

Another effective strategy is making simultaneous offers[36] that differ slightly but are *equally valuable* to you. If your spouse responds positively to one offer, you learn more about what they most value. Even if your spouse rejects both, you could ask follow-up questions to learn what is more acceptable. Then you could consider changes or prospective trade-offs.

At every point of the negotiations, pertinent information is important, and verification is key. While you may not believe everything your spouse says, you can make it clear that accurate and truthful representation, supported by documentation, is a prerequisite to finalizing a resolution. You may find it prudent to include in a settlement the enforcement mechanisms that you will use and the sanctions that will result in the event of any misrepresentation or noncompliance. Often one spouse is concerned about unilaterally providing information and, as a result, putting themselves at a disadvantage. Definitely require reciprocity in the exchange of information.

Evaluate Options Objectively and Reasonably

The consequences of some options may not be clear. Consider how well various alternatives address your specific needs and interests in the present and the future you anticipate. To negotiate for that goal on a basis other than the force of mere willpower, establish and follow objective criteria.

To be specific, fair standards are objective criteria that can help two parties reach the best possible agreement. One reason is disputes over each spouse's subjective, personal opinions may be settled by using objective criteria to evaluate the options.

Whenever possible, introduce fair standards like market value, pertinent precedent, professional standards, moral/biblical standards, efficiency, relevant facts, or professional reports. For example, a Kelley Blue Book vehicle valuation may help resolve a dispute over a car's worth, or an independent real estate appraisal may settle a disagreement over the value of the family residence.

Too often, parties pay their respective attorneys to argue over the value of some asset that could be determined independently for a lesser cost. Sometimes one party wants a certain disposition of an asset, such as a pension plan, that simply is not permissible under the retirement plan documents—or may be possible but only with severe income tax consequences.

Issues like these may be rather easily resolved with a careful review of retirement plan documents and/or applicable statutes. Advice from experts or other trusted advisors may be very helpful. If your spouse is persuaded that something is fair and reasonable, he is more likely to accept a proposal incorporating that standard. In fact, both parties may be more satisfied with an agreement supported by reasonable standards.

Sometimes impasses may also be resolved with such procedural solutions as taking turns, drawing lots, or designating someone else to decide. Other options include sealed bids, open bidding on a particular item that both parties want, and the "you cut; I choose" method.

Spouses, for example, often argue over household furniture, appliances, and even pots and pans. In one case the agreement divided certain personal property into categories, and within each category there was a selection process: the spouse who had first choice could choose one item, the spouse with second choice could choose two items, and then each took turns choosing one item. In the next category, the other spouse had first choice.

Closing the Deal

Once an agreement is reached, the terms should be written out. Doing so may prevent confusion and potential disputes; it will also bring closure. Sometimes the parties reach a tentative agreement that won't be formalized until later. This agreement should still clearly state whether it is binding or not in the event the more formal agreement is never signed. The terms sheet could at least provide a framework for the formal agreement and remind the spouses of the terms they anticipate being incorporated.

Summary

How each spouse—and any attorney representing either spouse—conducts negotiations impacts whether both the process and the resolution are just and fair. Attitudes, actions, and goals are all important. Identifying and understanding interests—both yours and your spouse's—is critical to searching for creative solutions, evaluating options, and reaching an agreement satisfactory to both sides. Divorce proceedings often require you to make crucial decisions, such as whether to negotiate, how to negotiate, whether to walk away, what to do if negotiations are unsuccessful, whether to accept a settlement proposal or pursue litigation, and whether to engage the services of a third-party mediator. When direct negotiations fail to resolve a dispute, a neutral third party—a mediator—may help, and we will explore that topic in the next chapter.

CHAPTER 9

Alternative Dispute Resolution

The Mediation Process

Mediation is an alternative dispute resolution process where an impartial and neutral third party—the mediator—helps the parties resolve their dispute to their mutual satisfaction. Simply put, "Mediation is facilitated negotiation."[1]

The mediator's role includes facilitating communication between the parties; assisting in the identification of the real issues of the dispute as well as the parties' interests; exploring the needs underlying their respective positions; and encouraging the brainstorming of options for the settlement. Wanting both parties to be able to make informed decisions, mediators get involved in information gathering and exchange so that both parties are aware of their current financial situation as well as any other relevant circumstances. A skilled mediator also helps parties process emotions, improve communication, appropriately address obstacles and unfair negotiation tactics, resolve any impasse they reach, preserve the relationship, and reach an agreement.

The goal of mediation is to enable the parties themselves to arrive at a mutually acceptable resolution. Through voluntary agreements, whether negotiated directly or with a mediator's help, spouses often reach creative and mutually satisfactory solutions in ways that the court could not.

Once the parties have reached an agreement, a written legal document is prepared. If the two are represented by counsel, one of those attorneys usually prepares the agreement. Upon request, the mediator will record the points of agreement and in some circumstances even prepare a comprehensive settlement agreement. When the parties privately mediate without counsel present, the mediator usually prepares a written document that the parties then take to their respective attorneys for review. *I strongly recommend that each spouse obtain an attorney* to advise them throughout the process and to review written documents before they are signed and become legally binding. The mediator must remain neutral and impartial and may not represent or offer legal advice to either or both parties.

The time needed to mediate varies depending on the extent of the issues, the degree of conflict between the parties, and their ability to engage in joint problem-solving. Often all of the issues may be mediated in several two- or three-hour sessions. Some court-ordered mediation requires participating in a session that lasts a minimum period of time (e.g., three hours).

Attorneys who serve as mediators are subject to their particular state's rules of professional conduct. States may set qualifications—particularly for court-designated mediators—including minimum age, completion of basic training, familiarity with the court's practices, and continuing education requirements.

Additionally, the American Bar Association (ABA) has adopted model standards of professional conduct that are explained in "Model Standards of Practice for Family and Divorce Mediation." The primary functions of the model are: "1. to serve as a guide for the conduct of family mediators; 2. to inform the mediating participants of what they can expect; and 3. to promote public confidence in mediation as a process for resolving family disputes." [2] The ABA promotes qualified mediators; advocates for the importance of structuring mediation so that the parties have sufficient information to make decisions; highlights the primacy of the parties' self-determination; emphasizes impartiality and confidentiality; and communicates the need to be sensitive to the impact of family abuse on the victim. Mediation may not be appropriate where there are safety, control, or intimidation concerns, but mediation is not always inappropriate where there was some domestic violence during the marriage. Where mediation proceeds, the mediator should structure the mediation process to provide for safety – proper security, holding separate sessions with each spouse, permitting a third-party to be present, encouraging participants to be represented by counsel, and so on. It is imperative that mediators screen for such family abuse issues both before and during mediation and remain sensitive to power-imbalance issues and the possibility of terminating mediation if deemed necessary. Court-based mediation programs typically screen for domestic violence and will not order mediation when physical or sexual abuse has occurred.

The traditional mediation model involved the mediator and all participants being present in the same room to discuss the ground rules and process, to exchange opening statements and information, to create an agenda, to explore interests, to brainstorm, and to seek creative solutions. The mediator would have breakout sessions ("caucus" – a meeting with one party (and counsel) in the absence of the other party (and that party's counsel) with one side or the other (or with the attorneys), then the group would either reconvene, or the mediator would shuttle back and forth.

The current trend in family mediation, however, keeps the parties apart, and the mediator goes back and forth between the two rooms to communicate requests and proposals. In many family law cases, the parties simply do not want to see each other, much less be in the same room, and their attorneys and mediators often accommodate this client preference.

While a truthful exchange of information, needs, and preferences may promote creative settlement alternatives, sometimes a party may be more open to sharing in confidence to the mediator, who then helps facilitate an agreement.[3] In a caucus with one party (and any attorney of the party) a mediator may help each party "privately to structure its own interests" and "separately and confidentially to find its BATNA," which provides a reality check on each option's reasonableness.[4] Parties often use the mediator as a sounding board, and mediators can also help confirm the parties' agreement on each issue.

A mediated settlement is less costly than trying a case to its conclusion in court, and usually both spouses are more satisfied with the process and the result than those couples who choose to let a judge decide the outcome. Satisfaction with the mediated agreement makes it more durable, and fewer enforcement issues arise.

The informal sharing of information, rather than the formal discovery process of litigation, may be sufficient to protect participants' interests, but make absolutely sure all the necessary information has been furnished. (Mediation often occurs in the context of ongoing litigation, and in that case adequate information may have already been exchanged.)

Collaborative Divorce

In 1990, divorce attorney Stuart G. Webb founded the Collaborative Law alternative method of resolving divorce-related issues, including alimony, property division, and other financial issues, as well as child custody and child support issues.[5] In a collaborative divorce, the divorcing couple and trained professionals work together to resolve issues in a non-adversarial, problem-solving process. Each spouse hires a different attorney who has been trained in the Collaborative resolution strategies.

The most basic form of Collaborative Law is the lawyer-only approach, where each spouse has an attorney and, together, the four attempt to resolve the issues. Any other professionals, such as accountants and mental health providers, are involved in the limited role of an expert or consultant as needed.

This lawyer-only approach may also have a referral aspect: at any stage of the process, one attorney will refer a client to additional professionals—such as a financial consultant, accountant, or mental health professional—to assist as necessary at any stage of the process. In both the basic Collaborative Law and the Collaborative Law Referral models, the team consists of the two lawyers and two clients.

Another approach, which has gained in popularity, is the Collaborative Divorce Team.[6] Selected by the spouses at the outset of the process, this interdisciplinary team consists of two Collaborative attorneys, a neutral financial specialist, two mental health coaches (each spouse selects her or his own coach), and a child specialist who advocates for the child(ren). In this interdisciplinary Collaborative approach, each party has an attorney who provides legal guidance and an interest-based focus in the settlement negotiations.

A neutral financial specialist—preferably trained as a Certified Financial Planner (CFP), Certified Public Accountant (CPA), or Certified Divorce Financial Analyst (CDFA)—assesses the family's financial circumstances, educates the two parties so they understand those circumstances, and provides guidance and training in budgeting, tax issues, the implications of proposed settlements, and using financial data to promote discussion and settlement.

A child specialist, who is a licensed mental health professional with specific training in child development and who has experience dealing with families in transition, is neutral regarding the parents but advocates for the child. This professional keeps the child's needs in the forefront, assesses the child's emotional and psychological state, helps the child to express feelings, thoughts, and concerns, and then communicates these to the child's parents. In addition to being a voice for the child, this specialist may also provide child-development education to the parents and help them formulate their parenting plan.

Mental health professionals serve as Collaborative or divorce coaches for each spouse, but do not act as the spouses' therapists. Aware that emotions and poor communication can inhibit the efforts to forge a constructive settlement, these specialists work with each other and the spouses to provide skills for more effective management of emotional issues as well as better communication patterns. Additional neutral experts—real estate appraisers, jewelry/personal property appraisers, vocational evaluators, business valuation experts, etc.—may be engaged in the process as necessary.

Serving as case manager, one of the Collaborative team members schedules meetings and follows up on task completion. The team members are co-equal and interdependent, and all are working toward the same goal of resolving the couple's divorce-related issues. The four-way meetings center on identifying issues, gathering information, developing settlement options, and negotiating solutions.[7]

The spouses and their attorneys sign a written agreement—usually called a Participation Agreement—that specifies the Collaborative ground rules. Some aspects ordinarily covered include agreements to do the following:

- While pursuing a Collaborative resolution, work in good faith toward a settlement without resorting to litigation
- Make full, complete, and accurate voluntary disclosure of all necessary and relevant information
- Avoid inappropriately communicating with the children about the divorce
- Identify the legal issues that need to be resolved (e.g., child support)
- Recognize that some present issues—such as financial support and parenting time—may require immediate attention
- Obtain any necessary neutral experts such as an accountant or child psychologist
- Recognize circumstances that may require both attorneys to withdraw from the process – e.g. if divorce papers are filed
- Respect the confidentiality of the Collaborative settlement proposals
- Acknowledge that the attorneys are obligated to withdraw from representing their respective clients if the Collaborative process does not result in settlement, and each spouse would then have to retain new counsel for representation in any contested litigation[8]

In mediation a neutral third party attempts to facilitate the couple's settlement. In a Collaborative process, the four-way meetings between the husband, the wife, their respective attorneys, and other involved professionals ordinarily take place without a mediator.

Ideally, Collaborative divorce is pursued before either spouse initiates divorce proceedings in court. However, sometimes a divorce action has begun before the parties are even aware of the Collaborative option or before they have jointly agreed to pursue a Collaborative resolution. As Collaborative divorce becomes more prevalent, courts will become more supportive of the process and will adapt and adjust dockets accordingly.

For example, upon written request some courts may "stay" (put on hold or suspend) pending divorce proceedings for a reasonable period of time to allow the parties to try to resolve the disputed issues through the Collaborative process. The Uniform Law Commission has adopted the Uniform Collaborative Law Rules and Act, which has become law in several states.[9]

Collaborative divorce has potential benefits, some of which are also evident in mediation:

- Rather than being subject to a court-imposed solution, the two parties have the freedom of self-determination and the opportunity to structure a personalized, interests-based settlement that meets the family's specific needs
- The Collaborative approach is potentially less expensive than litigation if the process leads to a full settlement—but the final cost could be considerably more if Collaborative efforts fail. In that case, all the professionals must withdraw, and they are not allowed to be involved in the divorce litigation
- The parties are required to be open and honest in the informal, transparent sharing of information
- The presence of attorneys facilitates the process as they provide advice in four-way meetings and contribute to more fully informed decisions

- This joint problem-solving, decision-making effort is rooted in the commitment to reach an agreement that meets both parties' needs. In contrast, litigation tends to establish an adversarial mind-set that fosters each party looking out for themselves
- Client satisfaction with both the collaborative process and the outcome is higher than client satisfaction with a court trial and outcome
- Privacy and informal setting as opposed to a public, formal court proceeding
- Pursuing settlement on a timeline shaped to the parties' schedules and pace that may take less time than a more fixed court timeline
- Built-in assistance handling emotions, improving communication, and addressing personal obstacles
- Preservation of relationships that litigation invariably damages

If this option seems worth pursuing, know that you might have to search for an experienced practitioner. Most family law attorneys are not trained in the collaborative process.

Finally, the collaborative model does have much to offer, but it is not a good fit for every couple or every situation.

Arbitration

Arbitration is an alternative dispute resolution process in which the two parties appear before one or more impartial arbitrators. Each presents evidence and arguments in support of their respective positions, and the arbitrator renders in writing a reasoned award that—depending on the parties' agreement—may or may not be binding.

Most jurisdictions provide for the enforcement of arbitration awards: upon request, the court will enter an order confirming, denying, or vacating the award. The grounds to vacate are generally limited to circumstances like these:

- The award was procured by corruption or the arbitrator was guilty of corruption
- The arbitrator acted with evident partiality or engaged in prejudicial misconduct
- The arbitrator refused to postpone the hearing upon sufficient cause
- The arbitrator refused to consider material evidence
- The arbitrator exceeded their powers
- There was no arbitration agreement
- The arbitration was conducted without proper notice, a factor that substantially impacts a party's rights[10]

The parties agree to the rules under which the arbitration will be conducted, and these rules are more relaxed than those of a courtroom. Following procedural requirements ensures that both parties have the same adequate notice of a hearing and a meaningful opportunity to participate. In addition to the option of being represented by their own retained counsel, both parties are able to present testimony and other evidence, obtain pretrial information, and subpoena witnesses to the hearing.

Among the potential benefits of arbitration are these:

- Private proceedings and nonpublic evidence
- Joint selection of the arbitrator, who may have unique, desirable experience or expertise
- Completed in a shorter time period than a fully litigated court case
- Flexible scheduling that is not determined by crowded court dockets
- A more client-friendly and comfortable setting than a formal courtroom
- Compared to a court decision, more limited grounds on which to appeal an arbitrator's decision (Arbitration may not be as protracted as contested court litigation.)

- The agreed-upon procedures and rules tailored to fit the parties' situation
- Possibly more economical even though the arbitrator will be paid while a judge's time costs the parties nothing
- Arbitrator possesses the same powers as a judge and must apply pertinent state laws
- Among the family law disputes that may be appropriate for arbitration are the division of property rights, claims for alimony, and interpretation of agreements between the spouses
- Sometimes parties pursue arbitration on limited issues such as the division of the household furniture and furnishings

Historically, binding arbitration has been problematic in child-related disputes due to public policy reasons, including the court's parent-like role to intervene on behalf of a child needing protection and its responsibility to promote what they determine is in the best interest of the children. Some states do permit these issues to be submitted to binding arbitration, but others do not. Even where the arbitration of child custody and child support matters is permitted, courts retain the ultimate authority over these matters, including over subsequent modification proceedings.

The American Academy of Matrimonial Lawyers (AAML) has adopted a Model Arbitration Act and Rules.[11] This document specifies an important reason for a court to vacate an arbitration award: "The court determines that an award for child support or child custody is not in the best interest of the child. The burden of proof at a hearing under this subsection is on the party seeking to vacate the arbitrator's award."[12]

The National Conference of Commissioners on Uniform State Laws adopted the Uniform Family Law Arbitration Act (UFLAA) in July 2016 and recommended it for enactment in all the states.[13] This act would govern arbitration of family law disputes, but any state could exclude from arbitration any child-related issues. Judicial review of child-related dispute decisions is meant to determine whether the decision complies with state law and is in a child's best interest. Court review of other arbitrated family law matters is more limited to circumstances (discussed above) regarding the authority to vacate an award.

Christian Conciliation

Christian Conciliation Service and Institute for Christian Conciliation both offer alternative dispute resolution intended to promote resolution in a conciliatory, rather than an adversarial, manner. They use biblical principles and includes the spiritual dimension that may be lacking in secular approaches.[14]

When a person initiates a request for conciliation, the organization "may provide the parties with individual biblical counseling/coaching or written resources designed to facilitate a private resolution."[15] If a case is accepted, the conciliation process commences only after the parties sign an agreement that lists the issues to be resolved.

Any party may withdraw from the mediation process at any time. However, a party may not withdraw from mediation/arbitration (agreement to arbitrate if mediation fails) or from arbitration unless all parties consent in writing. The parties have the right to independent legal counsel throughout the process.

To promote candid discussion and the admission of wrong in disputes, communications are treated as settlement discussions: strictly confidential and inadmissible in court except under certain specified circumstances. The parties agree to provide documents and other information that the conciliators need so they can understand and resolve the dispute. If one party "is unwilling to cooperate with the conciliation process or refuses to abide by an agreement reached during mediation, an advisory opinion, or an arbitration decision," the conciliator or the other party may enlist the leaders of the uncooperative party's church to become involved. Finally, the mediators prepare a written record of any agreement, but it "shall be legally binding if, and only if, the parties or their attorneys reduce it to a contract or stipulation that is signed by all parties."

Summary

These alternative dispute resolution methods provide reasonable and effective ways to attempt to resolve divorce-related disputes. Whenever the option is practical, the timely and effective use of mediation, collaborative divorce, or conciliation efforts—all undergirded by a solid grasp of interests-based negotiation principles and objectives—may be all that's necessary to secure a just peace.

CHAPTER 10

Court Litigation

LITIGATION REFERS TO settling a lawsuit by judicial process. Although parties may negotiate and mediate a resolution of their dispute during the course of litigation, those litigation proceedings remain adversarial. Spouses going through separation and divorce do not need that additional conflict which can intensify and even stimulate further disharmony. Clearly, court litigation would be the last course of action I would advise.

First, the court system is poorly suited to handling the highly personal matters intrinsic to a divorce case. The public process reveals some of the most private and personal affairs of life. It also tends to draw in others—including children—and, in doing so, inevitably perpetuates the strife.

Rather than expediting resolution, the nature of litigation itself sometimes carries the parties and their conflict along: "The psychology of litigation suggests that *litigation is dedicated to carrying on strife, not resolving it.* . . . Litigation lives only so long as strife is maintained."[1] No wonder litigation is usually not the best path to a peaceful resolution. Thus, in deciding how to arrive at a divorce settlement, you have to consider not only your objectives but also ways to defuse anger. Along the way you might find yourself exercising some forbearance rather than pressing all your rightful claims.

But perhaps you have been thrust into divorce proceedings you do not want. You're faced with what could even be termed the wicked conduct of a fool who scoffs at justice and the interests of others (Proverbs 28:5). There is no arguing calmly with someone who will try any approach except the quietly rational.[2]

Litigation, however, is often unavoidable. Perhaps one spouse is unwilling or unable to resolve the matter prior to initiating a legal proceeding, or you are compelled to respond to a legal action filed by your spouse, or the court's intervention may be necessary to either protect you and your children from physical harm or to prevent other harmful conduct by your spouse.

States have residency requirements that must be satisfied to file for divorce. This is usually some specified minimum time period—such as ninety days, six months, or one year—that either or both spouses have resided in the state, or you are both residents and the grounds for divorce occurred in the state.[3]

A spouse—the plaintiff or petitioner—initiates litigation by filing a complaint in the clerk's office of the appropriate court. The plaintiff also pays any statutory filing fee unless the court excuses advance payment for a compelling reason such as the party's indigence.

Complaint and Summons

The complaint must contain allegations that show entitlement to some relief and include a list of the requested relief, such as absolute divorce, alimony, property division and a monetary award based on marital property, joint/sole physical custody, joint/sole legal custody, or reasonable child support.

Some courts, such as those in California, provide statewide, uniform family law forms for parties to fill in and file.[4] Other courts provide forms for individuals who are not represented by an attorney but who need to file papers in divorce, custody, visitation, child support, alimony, or contempt actions.[5] These forms provide access to courts for those unfamiliar with the process.

Many jurisdictions also provide assistance in completing the forms for self-represented or *pro se* litigants, often on an income-eligibility basis. Local bar associations and legal aid offices may be resources for the financially needy, enabling them to obtain representation by an attorney on a *pro bono* or sliding scale basis.

The content of the filed pleadings is critical because the asserted issues limit the authority of a court to act.[6] A general request for relief —"for such other and further relief"—should be included, but such a request may not excuse the filer's failure to properly plead and request specific relief.

Once the complaint is filed, a summons is issued and—along with the complaint/petition and any other required papers such as case information forms—must be properly served on the other spouse (the defendant or respondent). It is improper service for a spouse to personally hand the summons, complaint, and other papers to their spouse. Another adult may serve the papers. Other alternative means are often permitted, such as leaving the papers at the spouse's residence with an adult who lives there or mailing by certified mail with restricted delivery. The service of the summons and complaint gives the defendant notification that an action has been filed against him/her and starts the clock running on the time period for responding to the complaint.

The Answer or Response

The defendant must file an answer or response within the time period prescribed by the court rules of the state where the case is filed. Certain challenges to the court's jurisdiction must be filed either separately in a motion before any answer is filed or may be included in the answer. When responding to a complaint, the defendant may also file a counterclaim that sets forth allegations and requests for relief, to which the plaintiff must file an answer/response.

When a party fails to answer or otherwise respond appropriately to the complaint or counterclaim, the court may treat that party as being in default of their obligation. Upon the written request of the party who did not receive the court-mandated response, the clerk of the court may then formally enter an order declaring the non-responsive party in default. If the defaulting party does not cure the default after proper notice, a judgment may be entered awarding the other party the relief sought in their complaint or counterclaim. The court would hold a hearing as necessary to determine what relief is appropriate.

Financial Statements

The court may require the two parties to file sworn financial statements disclosing their respective income, expenses, assets, and liabilities. According to the rules of a particular jurisdiction, the court may also require other financial information such as recent pay stubs.

The Scheduling or Status Conference

After the answer or proof of service is filed, the court will typically hold a conference to identify the issues, schedule various hearing dates, and direct the parties to participate in certain services. For example, at a scheduling hearing or initial status conference, the court may set the following:

- A *pendente lite* hearing on
  - alimony
  - parenting time (residential schedule/visitation)
  - child support
  - attorney's fees and suit money (e.g., costs for experts, appraisals, deposition transcripts)
  - use of the family residence
- Settlement conferences with the court
- Trial dates for
  - child custody matters and the divorce
  - spousal support
  - property division determination

Services that may be available during the litigation and that courts may require the parties to participate in include custody mediation; mediation of property, support, and other financial issues; co-parenting education and skills classes; and a court custody assessment, evaluation, or home visit. Courts sometimes appoint a Best Interest Attorney (BIA), also known as a guardian *ad litem*, to represent the minor children's best interests and to determine whether a child's therapist/patient privilege should be waived so that the therapist may testify in court.

Discovery Process

While parties may informally and voluntarily exchange information in litigation, court rules also permit obtaining information formally through the discovery process. The scope of discovery is broad regarding nonprivileged relevant matters, and grounds for objection are limited.

The privileges and limitations vary from state to state. Certain privileges permit a person to prevent the release of records, communications, and information. For example, a psychiatrist–patient or psychologist–patient privilege may grant a "privilege to refuse to disclose, and to prevent a witness from disclosing: (1) communications relating to diagnosis or treatment of the patient; or (2) any information that by its nature would show the existence of a medical record of the diagnosis or treatment."[7]

Other typical privileges include attorney–client, public accountant–client, and minister/clergyman/priest–penitent,[8] and some courts have extended the mental health provider–patient privileges to include communications with a licensed certified social worker (LCSW)[9] or other mental health specialist. Additionally, HIPAA (Health Insurance Portability and Accountability Act of 1996) establishes national standards to protect individuals' medical records and other personal health information from disclosure except under limited permitted circumstances.[10]

A state's statute may also preclude a spouse's testimony from disclosing "any confidential communications between the spouses occurring during their marriage."[11] You also have the constitutional right to not be compelled to testify in self-incrimination; however, a court may make inferences if you exercise this privilege.[12] Generally, attorney work product (their impressions, conclusions, opinions, or legal theories) is protected from discovery, as are documents prepared in anticipation of litigation.

The primary discovery forms are interrogatories, requests for production of documents, depositions, and requests for admissions.[13]

Interrogatories

Interrogatories are written questions directed to the other party, and they must be answered under oath within a court-prescribed time period such as thirty days. Court rules usually limit the number of interrogatories (e.g., twenty-five or thirty) that may be submitted to the other side. Interrogatories may cover many areas relevant to issues in the litigation, such as employment, income, assets, liabilities, medical and mental health care, expert witnesses, persons who have personal knowledge of the pertinent facts, the grounds for divorce, and child custody arrangements.

The following samples are representative of an interrogatory form and substance:[14]

> *Employment.* "If you are currently employed in any capacity, identify each current employer and, for each employment, state: (a) your job title, (b) your duties, (c) the number of hours in your average work week, (d) your regular pay period, (e) your gross wages per pay period, and (f) the deductions per pay period made by your employer from your wages. If overtime work was available to you during the past twelve months, state: (a) the number of overtime hours you worked during the twelve months and your rate of pay for those hours and (b) the number of overtime hours that were available to you during the twelve months but that you did not work and the rate of pay you would have received if you had worked those hours" (No. 3).

Income. "Identify the sources and amounts of all taxable and nontaxable income you received during the past five years" (No. 8).

Property/Assets. "List each item of property in which you have any interest. For each item listed, state how it is titled, its value, the amount of any present lien or mortgage on the property, the date of acquisition of the property, and the identity of any other person with an interest in the property. If you claim that any property listed is not marital property, state the facts upon which you base your claim, including all sources of funds used for the acquisition of the property and identify all persons with personal knowledge of those facts" (No. 10).

A party represented by counsel will usually provide preliminary responses to the attorney, who will edit them into their final form. This heavy attorney involvement in drafting and finalizing answers substantially filters the information, in contrast to a party's testimony in a deposition.

Requests for Production of Documents

Parties may serve requests for inspecting or copying documents or electronically stored information. The party must describe each requested item and category with reasonable particularity and state a reasonable time, place, and manner for the documents to be submitted.

States generally do not limit the number of document requests in the same manner interrogatories are limited. Requests may also cover inspection of tangible things and entering land to inspect and photograph it. This may be necessary when the other side resists an appraisal of personal or real property.

The court may require a written response in addition to the documents, which should be organized and labeled either to correspond with the categories in the request or as they are kept in the usual course of business. A party must provide all itemized documents in its "possession, custody or control," a phrase that is broadly interpreted.[15] The reasons for any objections to providing the requested information must be specified.

Electronically stored information is an increasingly important part of discovery. Emails, text messages, smartphone photos, Facebook and Instagram accounts, other social media pages, blogs, online dating profile pages, and similar information is subject to discovery by the other side. So, in addition to wanting to review your social media pages and total online footprint, your attorney will request that you be circumspect about what you post. Additionally, you should change your passwords on all accounts so your spouse cannot easily guess them.

Online banking and credit card websites make documents accessible to download and submit to the other side. Also, many banks, credit card companies, financial institutions, and businesses—in and out of state—will accept a subpoena by fax. Call first and find out if they will. The use of a fax can save a lot of time and money as well as reduce service of process problems.

Courts may sanction parties for spoliation—the intentional destruction, mutilation, alteration, or concealment—of evidence. Spoliation may be used to establish that the material was unfavorable to the party responsible for its destruction. Attorneys typically send letters to their client and to the other side reminding them of the obligation to take every reasonable step to preserve electronically stored evidences. This letter would include the obligation to cease all data destruction and backup-tape recycling; to preserve hardware unless an exact mirror image is made; and to maintain all pertinent information and tools necessary to access, view, and reconstruct all requested or potentially relevant electronic data.

The following samples represent the categories of documents you may want to request:

Communications between the parties. All documents, including but not limited to text messages, e-mails, cards, notes, letters, and other correspondence between the parties since January 1, _____.

Electronically stored data. All correspondence, email, and any electronically recorded information produced electronically in its native format, relating to your claims or defenses including, but not limited to, _____.

Employment/self-employment income. All documents relating to your compensation from your employment, independent contractor work, consulting, or self-employment including, but not limited to salary, bonuses, deferred compensation, commission, profit sharing, benefits, and any other types of compensation and/or benefit for the period of January 1, _____ to the date of any trial or hearing in this matter.

Pay stubs. Your employment-related salary stubs or wage statements since January 1, _____.

Income tax returns. Copies of your five most recent calendar year state and federal income tax returns, and additional returns through the date of the trial, including your W-2 forms, 1099 forms, K-1 statements, and supporting schedules.

Bank statements. Copies of monthly statements on all savings, checking, investment, and retirement accounts in which you have or have had a direct or indirect interest, since January 1, _____.

Retirement benefits. All documentary evidence of profit sharing, pension, or retirement funds, in which you have or have had a direct or indirect interest since January 1, _____, including a copy of the latest benefit statement; a copy of the plan, all amendments, and the summary plan description; a copy of the latest actuarial report; and a copy of the latest form 5500.

Property purchases. Copies of all documents relating to the purchase of any other asset, including but not limited to automobiles, either solely or jointly, since January 1, _____, including but not limited to the receipt, bill of sale, financing documents, and related insurance coverage.

Credit card statements. All monthly and year-end credit card, debit card, and charge or store account statements for each and every card to which you (whether solely or jointly with any third party) have had access or on which you (whether solely or jointly with any third party) have or have had signatory authority at any time since January 1, _____.

Current debt. Documents evidencing your current debts.

Loans. Evidence of any transaction in which you are involved wherein money was loaned by you to an individual or entity, and any evidence of any loan made to you (whether business or personal) for the past five (5) years.

Health insurance coverage. All documents relating to your current health insurance coverage and documents identifying those individuals covered under the policy.

Health. Any and all documents referring or relating to any diagnosis or prognosis made by any professional or health care provider of you for any mental or physical condition or problem for the period January 1, _____ to the date of any trial or hearing in this matter.

Assets: marital or nonmarital property. (A) All documents supporting your claim that certain assets are not marital property. (B) All documents supporting your claim that certain assets are marital property. (C) All documents or records that support your contention that any existing property in which you have an ownership interest is directly traceable to an inheritance or gift from a third party received by you during marriage. (D) All documents or records that support your contention that any existing property in which you have an ownership interest is directly traceable to property acquired by you before marriage to your spouse. (E) If you contend that any property you have acquired during the marriage is non-marital as defined by statute, provide copies of any documents that would support your contention. (F) If you contend that any property you have acquired during the marriage is 'marital' as defined by statute, provide copies of any documents that would support your contention.

Child custody. (A) All documents upon which you rely in support of your contention that it is in the best interests of the parties' minor children that you be granted custody. (B) All documents upon which you rely in support of your contention that it is not in the children's best interests that the other parent be granted custody.

Subpoenaed documents. Any and all documents received by you or your agent in response to subpoena, subpoena *duces tecum*, and/or a trial subpoena issued in this case.

Life insurance. All existing insurance policies on your life that have a cash surrender value or any policies that covered your life from January 1, _____ through the date of trial.

Expert witness report. Any written report made by any expert hired by you or any agent for you, whom you propose to call as a witness.

The quantity of documents exchanged in divorce cases has increased dramatically over the past thirty years. Although generally exchanged digitally (on CDs, thumb drives, or file-sharing through a service such as Dropbox), the pages printed out for trial use now fill many boxes. Although it would seem that in most cases you could limit the time period of requested documents and save considerable time and expense gathering and reviewing them, distrust and efforts to prevent legal malpractice drive the demand for more documents than are usually necessary.

Depositions

Court rules permit a party to take a deposition—out-of-court testimony—of the other party or third-party witnesses for discovery and/or evidence.

A notice of deposition must be served a certain time period before the deposition (e.g., ten days) and further in advance (e.g., thirty days) if you want the deponent (the person being deposed) to bring documents. The notice and any necessary subpoena must include a list of the requested documents. The notice also specifies the place, date, and time of the deposition and the officer (usually a court reporter who is a notary) taking the deposition.

Sometimes depositions are taken by audio or video; video depositions of an expert witness are often taken for use at the trial. If the parties agree, depositions may be taken by telephone, and I've been involved in cases where the deposition took place over Skype. In a divorce action, deposing a person by written questions is permissible but unusual. The ordinary manner is spoken questioning that provides an opportunity for immediate follow-up questions.

The deponent is sworn in before testifying, and the oral testimony under oath may later be transcribed—usually at a set cost per transcribed page. Court rules often limit the duration of a deposition, such as to one seven-hour day.[16]

If an attorney represents you, she will prepare you so that you know both what to expect and how to respond to questions. I ask my clients to watch a 20-minute deposition preparation DVD that provides practical guidance that I reinforce and expand on when we meet to discuss substantive preparation. This preparation is critical because a poor performance at a deposition could have serious consequences for the case. Depositions may be used for contradiction and impeachment, by an adverse party for any purpose, or by any party for any purpose where the witness is not available or exceptional circumstances exist.

Depositions of third parties, such as banks, investment companies, and other financial institutions, are often scheduled for the sole purpose of obtaining relevant documents. The company usually provides the documents prior to the scheduled date, accompanied by a business records certification by the company's custodian of records. Often also scheduled are depositions of third parties, such as employers, who designate someone to testify on the employer's behalf and to provide certain documents.

Requests for Admissions of Facts

Although not as popular as the other main discovery tools, requests for admissions can be effective. These request the admission of the truth of any relevant matter of fact or of the genuineness of any relevant document or electronically stored information. The matter may be deemed conclusively established if a party fails to deny it within a specified time. When a party fails to admit something that is later proven true or genuine, the court may award the party forced to prove the matter the reasonable expenses incurred in making the proof.

Court Enforcement of Discovery Obligations

Courts are often called upon to enforce a party's discovery obligations and may enter appropriate sanctions for failure to comply with discovery rules and orders. These three are some of the available sanctions:

"1. An order that the matters sought to be discovered, or any other designated facts shall be taken to be established for the purpose of the action in accordance with the claim of the party obtaining the order;

2. An order refusing to allow the failing party to support or oppose designated claims or defenses, or prohibiting that party from introducing designated matters in evidence; or

3. An order striking out pleadings or parts thereof, or staying further proceeding until the discovery is provided, or dismissing the action or any part thereof, or entering a judgment by default that includes a determination as to liability and all relief sought by the moving party against the failing party if the court is satisfied that it has personal jurisdiction over that party."[17]

The court will schedule any required hearing to take testimony or receive other evidence. Another sanction may be requiring the failing party to pay the other party's attorney's fees incurred by the failure.

Self-Help, Cost-Saving Discovery Tips

Inexpensive self-help steps can be taken to obtain information outside the formal discovery process:

1. *Mortgage, refinance, and home equity lines of credit applications.* Loan applications are usually signed under oath and contain statements of the individual's assets, liabilities, and net worth. Backup documentation may also be helpful:

- An appraisal of the real property
- Personal and business tax returns
- W-2 statements
- Recent bank statements for all personal and business accounts
- Profit and loss statements and balance sheets for any business in which the borrower has an interest
- Recent credit card statements
- Statements verifying retirement assets
- Recent pay stubs
- HUD-1 settlement statements
- Gift letters

Rental applications, car lease applications, and credit applications may also contain important information.

2. *Income tax returns.* By submitting Form 4506 to the IRS, you can request copies of your filed individual or joint income tax returns, supporting schedules, and W-2 and 1099 forms. Returns are generally available for a seven-year period before they are destroyed. The IRS charges a fee for each return supplied, and it may take up to sixty days to process the request.

You could also file a Form 4506-T to obtain a free tax return transcript that provides most of the line entries from the filed tax return.[18] Return transcripts are available for the current and prior three years. Most requests will be processed within ten business days.

3. *Bank statements and canceled checks.* To subpoena records from a bank is costly because they charge both for research time and a copy of each item. You can obtain statements as well as related personal and joint account documents either directly from the bank or online.

State laws generally prohibit informally obtaining a spouse's separate account information, and when you use a formal subpoena, notice may have to be provided to the account holder. Seeking someone else's financial or other personal information should be done only in compliance with the applicable laws.

4. *Credit and charge card statements.* Obtain statements directly or online from the credit card company, store, or other charge card company.

5. *Court records.* You may be able to obtain directly from the court records of court proceedings your spouse was involved in—such as civil suits, traffic offenses, criminal proceedings, and protective order or peace order proceedings.[19]

6. *Real property land records.* Land records may reveal whether your spouse owns any real property—or liens on any real property—that are not already disclosed.[20] Private companies will do these searches for you for a modest fee.

7. *Motor vehicle administration records.* You may be able to obtain a certified copy of your spouse's driving record for the past three years and any motor vehicle ownership records.

8. *School records.* In custody cases, school records may provide helpful information about whether a child is doing well. Report cards, attendance records, and teacher comments may be indicative of how well the child is coping with and adjusting to the separation.

Whether you are preparing for an alternative dispute resolution approach or are already in the midst of litigation, appropriate self-help information-gathering may ultimately save on the expense of formal discovery. At the same time, you will be gathering significant information necessary for making an informed settlement decision.

A Pretrial or Settlement Conference

The court may also schedule a pretrial or settlement conference with the parties and counsel. Conducted after discovery has been concluded, this conference focuses on the trial issues, the evidence that will be used at the trial, and settlement possibilities.

Parties may be required to submit pretrial statements that provide the following:

- The disputed issues
- Prospective witnesses
- Trial exhibits
- Any required forms/statements identifying the property owned by either or both spouses
- Each party's assertion concerning the ownership, marital or nonmarital nature, and the value of each item listed
- The amount of any liens against the property

The Trial

At the trial the parties formally present their case. They offer testimony and documentary evidence in support of their allegations and positions. They also make oral arguments.

Generally, self-represented spouses are held to the same standards as an attorney representing a party. Some judges may offer certain practical, technical assistance, and some may even interject questions to a witness, usually for clarification or to get essential information (e.g., the amount of work-related childcare expense, information necessary for calculating child support pursuant to the state's child support guidelines). The self-represented party is responsible for complying with the applicable evidentiary and procedural rules.

Judges or magistrates conduct family law trials in most states, but a handful of states have a jury trial for some or all of the issues. At the end of the trial, the court enters a judgment stating the results of the proceeding as well as the specific relief granted to the respective parties. Sometimes parties may have to wait several weeks or months after trial for the judge's or magistrate's decision to be issued. A dissatisfied party may appeal by filing a notice of appeal with the court clerk within a prescribed number of days after the judgment is entered. Courts also permit certain post-judgment motions within a specified period.

Summary

The judicial system attempts to provide an orderly process with judges who are fair, impartial, and just (Deut. 16:18–20).[21] Litigation can be a reasonable way to resolve divorce-related disputes, particularly when alternative methods have been unsuccessful. If you have no choice but to go to court, do your best to avoid getting caught up in a destructive and escalating litigation battle. Be aware of the great potential for aggressive tactics, increased financial cost, damaged relationships, and a less satisfying outcome. Too often a settlement is reached on the eve of a trial and only after a bruising period of litigation. Other times the post-trial outcome pronounced by judicial fiat brings anger and disappointment. Both scenarios leave more wounds and fewer resources for the divorced couple than the successful use of other available alternatives would have.

PRINCIPLE 7
Immunity of Noncombatants

CHAPTER 11

Child Security: Sheltering Children from the Parent's Conflict

FOR THE PAST twenty-five years, I have led a legal education seminar that provides free family law training for attorneys who agree to represent a client *pro bono* in contested child custody proceedings. One year the person speaking before me mentioned an American Academy of Matrimonial Lawyers (AAML) goal: "An attorney representing a parent should consider the welfare of, and seek to minimize the adverse impact of the divorce on, the minor children."[1]

Moments later, he leaned forward, paused, and told the seventy attentive trainees, "Sometimes you have to destroy the child in order to win custody." He said this without apology and seemingly without any twinge of conscience. In his mind, harming children was simply a means to an end. He wasn't cautioning that children, regrettably, are collateral damage in some divorces, so we need to be careful to prevent or mitigate such damage. This attorney was promoting targeting children as a winning litigation strategy! Beware of the advice you receive from anyone that disregards the welfare of your children.

Protect Children from Harmful Conflict

It is critical for parents to consider the effect of their attitudes, actions, and words on their children, whom they have the privilege and responsibility to protect and nurture.[2] This statement is true for life in general, and living out its truth becomes even more critical in the pursuit of a Just Divorce.

Slightly reworded to apply to divorce, the applicable Just War principle says, "If parents either willfully do not consider the effects of their action on their children or act with reckless disregard of those effects, the parents violate the principle of discrimination just as much as if they were deliberately to target their innocent children." In their mind and heart, each parent absolutely must separate their relationship with the other parent and the related adult issues in their marital break-up from the needs of their children, who are innocent bystanders still counting on their parents' protection.

As Robert Emery notes, the absence of conflict is more important to children's mental well-being "than having a good relationship with both parents."[3] Children raised in "low-conflict divorced families have far fewer emotional problems than children in high-conflict divorces (or high-conflict marriages)."[4] Andrew Schepard concludes that "most children of divorce are better off if they are placed in a demilitarized zone between their parents" and "they are also better off if, consistent with safety, they have a meaningful relationship with both parents."[5]

Parents must manage their own emotions, work through their fractured marital relationship, and endeavor to establish and maintain an effective co-parenting relationship. Their spousal relationship may be over, but their relationship as parents continues.

Janet R. Johnson, Vivienne Roseby, and Kathryn Kuehnle write this about what characterizes a "successful" divorce:

> The adults are able to work through their anger, disappointment, and loss in a timely manner and terminate their spousal relationship with each other—legally and emotionally—while at the same time retaining or rebuilding their parental alliance and commitment to their children. A "good" divorce can relieve the

children of the daily stress of overt parental conflict and associated anger and depression. Fortunately, most couples appear to be relatively successful in achieving this kind of transition.[6]

These authors then describe the "failed divorces": many years after separation, 25 to 33 percent report "high degrees of hostility and discord" surrounding the issue of their children's care:

> Probably most characteristic of this population of "failed divorces" is that these parents have difficulty focusing on their children's needs as separate from their own and cannot protect their children from their own emotional distress and anger, or from their ongoing disputes with each other.[7]

Parental Conflict

For almost all children whose parents get divorced, "the first two to three years are exceedingly difficult. Not only must they adjust to major changes in their life circumstances, they must also acquire a whole new understanding of what constitutes a 'family.'"[8] During this time the parents' conflict with each other—the level and intensity of it—is the most significant factor in a child's adjustment.[9]

Common issues triggering ongoing conflict are parenting skills (mistrust of the other parent's ability; fear that the child is endangered in the other parent's care); transition times (the child's actions and adjustment before and after visits to the other parent); time sharing (one parent wants more time, and the other parent resists); details of visits (ignoring drop-off and pick-up times; failing to communicate changes); and disparaging talk (negative remarks about the other parent made in the child's presence).[10]

Children are put in a loyalty bind predicament when parents ask them to take sides and, in effect, to form a coalition against the other parent. A loyalty bind may result from a parent's mild encouragement not to comply with the other parent's request, or the bind may be the desired effect of a serious effort to undermine all of one spouse's parental authority. All divorced parents place their children in loyalty binds from time to time, and children report feeling divided within themselves.[11]

Alienation and estrangement between a parent and child may also occur—particularly when parental conflict or domestic violence is an issue. Parents should avoid exacerbating the situation through constant disparagement of the other parent.

Parents must also remember that a child may have a strong affinity for one parent because of attachment patterns *without rejecting the other parent*. Normal developmental shifts may have occurred; a child may align with one parent for divorce-specific reasons; flawed parenting may encourage a child to take sides; and justified rejection or realistic estrangement may be the result of domestic violence, abuse, neglect, or significant parental deficiencies whereby the child develops a realistic and self-protective desire to avoid that parent.[12] After rational reasons for a child's resistance are ruled out, then other contributors should be considered – such as a parent's alienating conduct by expressing negative views of the other parent or giving guilt messages when the child expresses enjoying being with the other parent, or actively undermining the other parent's relationship with the child.[13]

Divorce is a tumultuous time for parents and children alike. Psychologist Judith Wallerstein identified six psychological tasks a child must accomplish—in no particular order—to overcome the stress of their parents' divorce:

- Acknowledging the reality of the marital rupture
- Disengaging from parental conflict and distress and resuming customary pursuits
- Resolving losses
- Resolving anger and self-blame
- Accepting the permanence of the divorce
- Achieving realistic hopes for their own relationships[14]

These significant challenges are more difficult if parents remain engaged in open combat and fail to do the appropriate parenting their child requires. Healthy boundaries when divorce is a reality "means maintaining our roles as much as possible, supporting our children in their age-appropriate activities and behaviors, and providing experiences and settings for our children to experience their lives as kids."[15]

Reduced parental conflict, appropriate respect for the other parent (Romans 13:7), and mature parenting foster a child's welfare. After all, Christians are called to "love your neighbor as yourself" (Matthew 22:39) by living the Golden Rule: "whatever you wish that others would do to you, do also to them" (7:12). Christians are also called to love one another sacrificially the way God has sacrificially loved us (1 John 4:7–12) and to "strive for peace" (Hebrews 12:14). We are to live peaceably with everyone "so far as it depends on [us]" (Romans 12:18; *see also* James 3:17–18; 1 Peter 3:11).

Consider the familiar words of 1 Corinthians 13:4–7 as a how-to for relating to your ex:

Love is patient and kind; love does not envy or boast; it is not arrogant or rude. It does not insist on its own way; it is not irritable or resentful; it does not rejoice at wrongdoing but rejoices with the truth. Love bears all things, believes all things, hopes all things, endures all things.

Although the romantic love may have ended, both parties must do the critical work of cultivating a post-separation parental commitment to love and respect one another's status as God's image-bearer and as a co-parent of the children who are a blessing and a gift from Him.

Authoritative Parenting
Whether living in an intact family or in two separate households, children benefit from a meaningful relationship with two functioning parents who are able to do things like this:

- Consistently place a child's needs above their own desires
- Don't abdicate their parental role
- Maintain clear boundaries for their child
- Provide necessary guidance and discipline
- Unconditionally love and cherish their child.

This approach to being a mom or dad has been termed *authoritative* parenting.

Parental love and guidance contribute to "self-confident, independent, and well behaved" children.[16] In fact, studies show that "the most important predictor of children's successful coping with divorce is having *one* authoritative parent."[17] Authoritative parenting unites parental love with "clear, firm, fair, and well-reasoned" discipline.[18]

God's discipline of his children is a model for a parent's discipline of a child: discipline proceeds from love and is intended to bring forth "the peaceful fruit of righteousness to those who have been trained by it."[19] Discipline is a parental responsibility exercised for a child's own good and mature development (Proverbs 22:15; 23:13–14; 29:17; Hebrews 12:11). Scripture also admonishes parents to "not provoke your children to anger but bring them up in the discipline and instruction of the Lord" (Ephesians 6:4). Parents are also to teach and instruct their children to reverence God, treasure wisdom, exercise prudence, and pursue righteousness, justice, and equity.

Authoritative parenting differs from *authoritarian parenting* that is characterized by strict or harsh discipline and lacking to some degree in parental love.[20] Children may be outwardly compliant, but they may experience diminished self-esteem and confidence, feel unhappy, and choose to rebel later.[21] Authoritative parenting "supports a child's growth through healthy guidance, despite the child's preference for the path of least resistance."[22]

Also according to research, "children seek firm and loving support from a parent who demonstrates the authoritative parenting style."[23] If this kind of parenting cannot be provided in both households, consider providing your child with greater stability by placing him/her in the better home environment as much as possible. Straddling two radically different situations will be neither easy nor helpful.[24]

Services to Protect Children from Harm

Courts have increasingly moved away from viewing child custody as simply a legal dispute and are now taking a more therapeutic approach. Resolving parenting issues involves multiple approaches and services, both court-sponsored and community-based. Many of the services offered focus on reducing the conflict that children are exposed to, particularly domestic violence. For better or worse, as this shift expands the customary role of courts, it increasingly encroaches on traditional parental roles and responsibilities.

Driving this trend is the rapid rise in the number of court cases where one or both parties represent themselves throughout the divorce process. In response, some programs now provide both lower income and unrepresented parties with *meaningful* access to courts as well as to services that are available to people who have attorneys and greater financial means.

In a sense, it not only takes a village to raise a child, but a village is also required to protect a child from becoming tragic collateral damage in the parents' divorce. Courts have sought to manage cases and match services to the particular needs of the families impacted by the litigation.

Enhanced Access to Justice

Many parents choose to pursue child custody litigation without legal representation; others lack the financial resources to retain an attorney. The prevalence of parties representing themselves in family law matters not only stretches judicial resources, but it also presents challenge like making the court process more understandable and affiliated services more accessible to unrepresented litigants.

Some courts provide uniform family law forms for parties to complete and file in dissolution or divorce proceedings.[25] In other states, courts provide forms primarily for individuals who are not represented by an attorney and need to file papers in divorce, custody, visitation, child support, alimony, or contempt actions.[26] These forms help provide litigants who are unfamiliar with the judicial process access to courts. Many courts and bar associations support self-help clinics at a courthouse or other community location. Often on an income-eligibility basis, these clinics provide legal advice to self-represented litigants as well as help completing the court forms.

Many local bar associations run clinics that provide income-eligible parents free legal advice and lawyer referral services for either *pro bono* or reduced-fee legal representation. Some nonprofit legal aid offices and family justice centers provide free representation or referral to counsel, particularly in domestic violence cases. Because *pro bono* programs depend on volunteer attorneys, interested parties may encounter a waiting period, and there is no assurance that counsel will be available.

Progress has been made throughout the United States: more and more individuals are obtaining free or reduced-fee legal counsel. But available services still lag behind the increased demand. As a result—and very unfortunately—many parents who cannot afford legal counsel remain compelled to represent themselves in child custody litigation, sometimes to the detriment of their children.

One approach that makes a greater access to justice more affordable is *unbundled legal services*, also known as limited scope representation or discrete task representation. Ordinarily, an attorney in a court case is responsible for full representation of the party in all related court proceedings until new counsel takes over the case or the court permits the attorney to withdraw from representation. But many clients cannot afford a full-service attorney. The ABA Model Rules of Professional Conduct—Rule 1.2(c)—states, however, that "a lawyer may limit the scope of representation if the limitation is reasonable under the circumstances and the client gives informed consent."

This rule has been adopted by most states, often with modifications. Court rules and professional ethics rules have become more receptive to permitting limited scope representation. This makes legal counsel more financially accessible to a parent needing help with some of the critical aspects of child custody or other family law cases.

Court-Affiliated Parent Education Programs[27]

Most states have court-affiliated parent education programs to promote enhanced parenting skills, improved working relationships between parents, and reduced parental conflict for their children's benefit.[28] Most states either require attendance by statute or give courts discretion to mandate attendance.

The six-hour PEACE (Parent Education And Custody Effectiveness) program is representative of parent education programs.[29] The class leaders are usually mental health professionals, and typically the newly divorced parents attend separate classes. Scheduled as two three-hour sessions or three two-hour sessions, the class provides parents with information about the emotional, financial, and educational difficulties their children may experience as a result of the separation and divorce. Parents also learn about the adverse impact that their conflict with one another can have on their children. In addition, the parents receive information about the legal process, court determinations in custody matters, the effects of separation and divorce on divorcing parents and their children, and how they can help their children adjust to a restructured family. The program encourages the separated or divorced couples to develop an effective co-parenting relationship that places their children's needs first.

Parents are generally satisfied with parent education classes like PEACE, and some evidence suggests that the classes result in changed behavior and reduced parental conflict.[30] Some states or local courts also provide programs for children of divorcing parents.[31] Furthermore, completion of a parent education class prior to mediation can provide a good foundation for discussing and developing parenting plans.

Custody Mediation[32]

Most courts order mediation of child custody and visitation disputes when such intervention is appropriate, it is likely to benefit the parties and/or the child, and a properly qualified mediator is available. Mediation programs screen for a history of family violence, and courts will not order mediation when past incidents of domestic violence make mediation inappropriate.[33]

Court orders requiring attendance at mediation usually limit the number of hours that the parties must attend: the order may read "a single three-hour session subject to extension." Parents are not required to reach agreement; they are only required to make a good-faith effort. Through mediation parents have an opportunity to develop an agreed-upon parenting plan that addresses their particular situation and their child's needs, all without an adversarial court trial. Mediation resulting in a settlement maximizes self-determination and reduces the financial costs of litigation.

In some court-based programs, where the mediation occurs at the courthouse, the parties may have the opportunity to put their agreement on the record before a magistrate or judge at the end of the mediation session instead of waiting for a formal written agreement to be prepared. This is an efficient conclusion to the matter, and the judge may ask the parents questions to make sure they understand the terms and have agreed voluntarily.

Custody Evaluations

In order to make more informed decisions that are in the best interest of the child, courts often order a custody or visitation evaluation. The evaluation considers the parties' respective strengths and deficiencies as well as the best fit for the child. The focus is on "skills, deficits, values, and tendencies relevant to parenting attributes and a child's psychological needs."[34]

In this kind of evaluation, qualified mental health professionals act as impartial examiners and report their findings and recommendations to the court, the parties, and the parties' counsel. Some courts have an evaluator's office that appoints an investigator—a social worker, psychiatrist, psychologist, or trained investigator—to do the evaluation and then submit a report with or without recommendations to the court. Sometimes an independent private evaluation is ordered. The typical evaluation protocol includes the following:

- Conduct at least one in-person interview with each parent.[35] Compile a psychosocial—social, educational, medical, mental health, criminal, and marital/relationship—history.
- If doing so does not put the child at risk, observe the interaction between each parent and child. Note the parenting skills that are in place as well as the parent's ability to respond to the child's needs.
- Conduct a home visit that provides a brief opportunity to meet the child. Look for how comfortable the child is in the home environment and pay attention to the interaction between the parent and child. (The evaluator may interview the child later without the parents being present.)
- Interview significant collateral witnesses—extended family members, friends, neighbors, teachers, pediatricians, coaches, and others—who can provide relevant information about the child. The parent usually cooperates and provides the evaluator with contact information for the most significant persons.
- Review the child's school, medical, and mental health records.
- Review the parents' mental health records.
- Primarily when assigned from outside the court, the evaluator uses appropriate formal assessment instruments and runs psychological tests.
- Present the evaluator's oral or written report, including the bases for the opinions shared and specific reasons for the recommendations made. The evaluator's report should be "accurate, objective, fair, and independent,."[36] Ordinarily the report is used only in the pending proceeding, and disclosure to third parties is restricted or prohibited.

Parenting Coordinators

Parenting coordination is an alternative dispute resolution process primarily used in cases involving high conflict between the parents. This field is still developing and is authorized by statutes or rules in a minority of states. The interdisciplinary Association of Family and Conciliation Courts approved *Guidelines for Parenting Coordination* for jurisdictions wanting to develop and implement parenting coordination programs.[37] These parenting coordinators may be granted limited authority to decide certain matters or to make recommendations, but courts generally don't delegate judicial decision-making authority to a third party.

A parenting coordinator is an impartial professional—usually a licensed mental health or legal professional—who has mediation experience and parent coordination training. This professional may (1) help parents implement and comply with court orders or their parenting plan; (2) resolve parenting disputes and make timely decisions that promote the child's best interests; (3) reduce conflict between the parents that could harm the child; and (4) foster cooperation between the parents.

Because parenting coordination does not fall under standard privilege or confidentiality statutes, these coordinators must clearly communicate the nature and extent of any confidentiality—and be sure that the parents understand. The coordinators should address these items at least:

- The parenting coordinator's access to court records
- Whether a parent is required to release any confidential or privileged information
- The extent to which the parenting coordinator may testify in court regarding communications with a parent
- Whether the parenting coordinator may disclose to one parent confidential or privileged information—received by consent—regarding the other parent

Best Interest Attorneys (or Guardians Ad Litem)

Statutes in forty-four states and the District of Columbia authorize courts to appoint an attorney or guardian *ad litem* to represent the child in custody cases.[38] The counsel for a child could be a *best interest attorney* (BIA and in many states also called a guardian *ad litem*), a child's privilege attorney, or a child advocate.[39]

If you believe that counsel for a child should be appointed, make sure the court's order clearly defines what the *role* of the appointed counsel will be—BIA, privilege attorney, or child advocate. One attorney may be appointed to represent some or all of the parents' children when there is no conflict between what is best for each of the children.

In some states the BIA is not required to be an attorney; he or she is sometimes a trained layperson or mental health professional. The BIA's assignment is to make an independent evaluation of the relevant facts and then advocate for the child's best interests even if that goal is not what the child desires. Many states do not permit the child's BIA to testify at the trial or file a written report with the court, as their role is that of an attorney rather than a witness.[40] Although the BIA should ensure that the child's preference is disclosed to the court, they promote the child's best interest, not the child's wishes.

A *child's privilege attorney* decides whether to waive the patient-psychiatrist/psychologist privilege—or any other statutory privilege—for the child.[41] The primary reason a waiver may be declined is to maintain the trust and confidentiality of the child's therapeutic relationship. The benefit to the child of an ongoing therapeutic relationship may outweigh the benefit of the court receiving information from the therapist.

Court-appointed to provide independent legal counsel for a child, a *child advocate attorney* "owes the same duties of undivided loyalty, confidentiality, and competent representation as are due an adult client."[42] If this attorney determines that the child has considered judgment, then they advocate for the child's wishes; if the child doesn't have considered judgment, this attorney asks the court to change their role to that of a BIA—or to appoint a separate BIA.

Judicial Interviews of Children

The child's wishes regarding custody must be considered in virtually every jurisdiction.[43] According to the Uniform Marriage and Divorce Act (UMDA), the court "may interview the child in chambers to ascertain the child's wishes as to his custodian and as to visitation. The court may permit counsel to be present at the interview. The court shall cause a record of the interview to be made and to be part of the record in the case."[44]

Professor Schepard notes some significant concerns about relying on child interviews:

- Many experts recommend child interviews be conducted only if required by statute because a brief interview provides a judge "very little information of value" to the custody determination.

- Clinicians report that a judicial interview is "a very stressful experience in which a child experiences loyalty conflicts, guilt, and fear of retribution."

- Judges generally lack necessary training "in the child-interviewing skills that might reduce the problems children experience in these interviews."

- The interview may "expose the judge to unreliable evidence that may influence the decision in the case, evidence that the parents will not have the opportunity to confront."[45]

Larry Wright emphasizes that "the judge should have a general background in the area of child development in order for the questioning to be effective. The judge must know what questions to ask; how to ask them; and how to interpret the child's answers."[46] Often, judges resist interviewing children, and they may even form an unfavorable view of a parent who insists on such an interview.

Restrictions on Custody and Visitation

Visitation is an important natural and legal right, and courts generally hold that access to both parents benefits children, yet the child's welfare must take priority over visitation rights. The complete denial of visitation with a parent is rare, though sometimes it is necessary for courts to set certain restrictions and limitations to assure the child's safety.

The court restrictions address issues like these:

- Spouse abuse
- Child abuse
- Alcohol and substance abuse that impairs functioning
- Harmful exposure to the other parent's significant other
- Smoking affecting a child's asthma
- Mental health counseling and medication compliance
- Anger management
- Parent skills education
- Safe transfer or transition between parents
- Advance notice of intended relocation
- Proper use of an infant or child car seat
- Interfering with visitation
- Appropriate make-up visitation[47]

Sometimes courts order supervised visitation, and in some jurisdictions a supervised visitation program may be available. Any referral to the court's supervised visitation program must come through the court's protocol and procedures, and that referral is subject to space availability.

When no supervised visitation program is available, the visitation order should designate an appropriate third-party supervisor—a neutral and mature individual who is able to supervise the parent, protect the child, report on the visit, and be available for the entire visit. [48]

A copy of the order and the supervisor's responsibilities should be distributed to the visiting parent and the supervisor, who should also be informed of the reason supervision is necessary. The order should set forth the visitation schedule, including appropriate restrictive provisions concerning alcohol and controlled substances, any provisions pertinent to batterer's prevention programs, and provision for the visiting parent to post bond if concern regarding child abduction arises.

Family members should *not* be selected as supervisors when the supervision is required due to domestic violence. Community members—from churches, community groups, childcare facilities, schools, child protective services, and mental health professionals—may provide more neutral supervision than family members and friends could.

Child Abduction Preventive Measures

When a credible risk of child abduction (i.e., wrongful removal or retention) exists, courts may take preventive measures.[49] Travel restrictions, for instance, offer the child protection. The parent traveling with the child must provide an itinerary; contact information (i.e., a physical address and telephone numbers so the child can be reached during specified windows of time); and copies of all travel documents (e.g., airline tickets, hotel reservations). Courts may also outline prohibitions against removing the child from the state, country, or other area without the court's permission and/or the other parent's consent; and prohibitions against removing the child from school or a childcare center or against approaching the child at any location other than a designated supervised visitation site.

Other preventive measures might address the child's passport. The court could: require the surrender of the child's passport to the court; prohibit a parent from applying for a child's new or replacement passport; have mirror orders entered in a relevant foreign country containing terms identical to the child custody determination issued in the United States; require a parent to post a bond or provide other security that would pose as a financial deterrent and, if necessary, be used to pay reasonable attorney's fees and other costs involved in recovering the child.[50]

What Does *Custody* Mean?

Custody—or *custodial responsibility*—refers to both legal custody (the decision-making responsibility) and physical or residential custody (also known as parenting time). In the past, courts addressed the traditional topics of *custody awards* and *visitation rights*. The clear trend today, however, is to direct parents to focus on their child's needs by developing parenting plans that cover *parenting time* and *decision-making responsibility.*[51]

Here's a representative description of legal custody terms:

Legal custody carries with it the right and obligation to make long-range decisions involving education, religious training, discipline, medical care, and other matters of major significance concerning the child's life and welfare.[52]

The core of legal custody is parental decision-making authority over significant matters that arise during childhood. The routine day-to-day decisions regarding a child's welfare are ordinarily left to whichever parent the child is physically with whether as a matter of physical custody, visitation/access, or a parenting time award. This authority includes matters of discipline and the right to consent to emergency medical care when there is insufficient time to contact the parent who has legal custody.[53]

The American Law Institute (ALI) publication *Principles* advocates that courts "presume that an allocation of decision-making responsibility jointly to each . . . parent . . . who has been exercising a reasonable share of parenting functions is in the child's best interests." This presumption would be overridden if shared decision-making proves not to be in the child's best interests or if there is a history of domestic violence or child abuse.[54]

Parents are frequently designated joint legal custodians. In other words, the two parents share the decision-making authority: "Joint legal custody means that both parents have an equal voice in making those decisions, and neither parent's rights are superior to the other parent's rights."[55] This definition reflects the natural state of parents as joint guardians, charged with the responsibility for their child's support, care, nurture, welfare, and education. They have the same powers and duties; neither is presumed to have any superior right to custody.[56]

California's statute provides important parameters: "In making an order of joint legal custody, the court shall specify the circumstances under which the consent of both parents is required to be obtained to exercise legal control of the child and the consequences of the failure to obtain mutual consent." In all other circumstances, either parent acting alone may exercise legal control of the child.

Most states permit the court to include a provision in its joint legal custody award for one parent to have tie-breaking (or final decision-making) authority. Tie-breaking authority is appropriate in many jurisdictions "precisely because of the parties' inability to make decisions for their children" and in other jurisdictions as "pragmatic solutions to the problem of parents failing to make decisions in a timely manner for their children's benefit."[57] When the parents reach an impasse regarding an important decision involving their child's welfare, the parent with this tie-breaking authority may make the final decision.

The ALI *Principles* supports allocating joint decision-making authority to parents and notes that "decision-making responsibility may be allocated as a whole, *or by separate areas*" (emphasis added).[58] For example, one parent may have ultimate authority on educational issues, and the other, on medical or mental health treatment decisions.

Parents are obligated to communicate in good faith and attempt to reach joint decisions before one parent exercises tie-breaking authority: "Because this arrangement requires a genuine effort by both parties to communicate, it ensures each has a voice in the decision-making process."[59] This good faith effort should be made in any joint legal decision-making situation.

Although joint custody is authorized in every state, less than one-third of the states apply some sort of presumption that an award of joint custody to the parents is in the child's best interest, and several of these states only presume it's in the child's best interests if both parents request joint custody.[60] Presumptions and preferences remain subject to the best interests of the child.

Physical or residential custody is now commonly called parenting time, and it is defined like this:

> The right and obligation to provide a home for the child and to make the day-to-day decisions required during the time the child is actually with the parent having such custody. Joint physical custody is in reality "shared" or "divided" custody. Shared physical custody may, but need not, be on a 50/50 basis, and in fact most commonly will involve custody by one parent during the school year and by the other parent during summer vacation months.[61]

The term *split custody* describes "the situation in which one parent is given sole custody of some of the children of the parties, with sole custody of the remaining children going to the other parent, and cross rights of visitation."[62] Sometimes split custody is also called divided custody, but *divided custody* is also used to describe an arrangement where the custody is divided or alternated between parents.

Thus, the focus of *legal* custody is the allocation of decision-making authority; the focus of *physical* custody is the allocation of the child's time with each parent. The adoption of the more neutral language of parenting plans—custodial responsibility, decision-making responsibility, and parenting time—will undoubtedly become even more widespread.

Strategic Parenting Plans

Parenting plans are another significant way courts encourage conflict reduction and the resolution of disputes. Submitting written custody agreements to courts for approval is nothing new, and about 90 percent of these cases settle prior to a contested court trial. Parents who reach agreements through negotiation or mediation often place their agreement on the court record in open court at a pretrial settlement conference or even on the day of a scheduled trial. What's relatively new is the court's trend toward requiring parties to submit proposed parenting plans that identify specific child custody–related matters that have been agreed to. If some child custody matters have not been agreed to, each parent will present their proposed resolution.

A parenting plan is a written agreement between the two parties, detailing their roles and responsibilities as parents. The plan, for instance, addresses arrangements concerning the children's living situation, and contact schedules with the parents, allocation of the decision-making responsibilities between the parents, and mechanisms for resolving future parenting disputes.[63]

Along these same lines, the ALI *Principles* recommends that parents be required to file with the court a proposed parenting plan containing provisions for the child's living arrangements and for each parent's custodial responsibility, including "a custodial schedule that designates in which parent's home each minor child will reside on given days of the year"; "an allocation of decision making responsibility as to significant matters reasonably likely to arise with respect to the child"; and a dispute resolution provision and remedies for violation of the plan.[64]

Some states require certain details: holidays and school vacations noted on the parenting time schedule; various procedures for the exchanges of the child, including the meeting point(s) and who is responsible for transportation; for the parents' periodic review of the plan's provisions; and for the means and the frequency of parental communication about the child.[65] The plan may include other matters and address other issues the parents agree to about the child. The plan outlines how the parents are going to work together to best meet their children's needs. Parents have the opportunity to develop plans uniquely suited to their family situation and their child's needs.

Many states require parents to submit parenting plans for their post-divorce arrangements. If the parents can't agree on all the terms, the court would consider the two proposed plans and create a parenting plan based on those.[66] Several states also require parents to file a proposed temporary parenting plan when the parent is seeking a temporary or interim order relating to parenting.[67]

Consider this Washington statute, a sample of those described parenting plan objectives:

> (a) Provide for the child's physical care; (b) Maintain the child's emotional stability; (c) Provide for the child's changing needs as the child grows and matures, in a way that minimizes the need for future modifications to the permanent parenting plan; (d) Set forth the authority and responsibilities of each parent with respect to the child . . . ; (e) Minimize the child's exposure to harmful parental conflict; (f) Encourage the parents, where appropriate . . . , to meet the responsibilities to their minor children through agreements in the permanent parenting plan rather than relying on judicial intervention; and (g) To otherwise protect the best interests of the child.[68]

Clearly, parenting plans are more than visitation schedules and guidelines for decision-making. Parenting plans provide an opportunity for both parents to contribute to their child's development; to promote some consistency and stability across two homes; to—consistent with safety—be involved in a meaningful way in their children's lives; and to design a plan that would address the particular needs of their child while allowing for some future flexibility as the children's needs change. Greater structure and detail may be necessary for clarity, to limit the need for parental communication or contact, and to prevent future disputes between parents where the level of parental conflict is higher.

States that require parents to submit a parenting plan also provide checklist forms and instructions to complete them. These parenting plan forms provide options for parents to select and allow them to write in a choice that is not listed. The American Academy of Matrimonial Lawyers (AAML) has an extensive 32-page Model for a Parenting Plan that contains many detailed options that might not be on your state's parenting plan form. My clients—and the mediating parties in cases I have taken on—have found this AAML parenting plan model helpful. Sample parenting plans are useful no matter what your state requires. In fact, you might not have considered some of the choices presented but, upon seeing them, would now like to include in your custody agreement.

Summary

Children are not combatants in the divorce proceedings. Neither are they to be spoils of war. Yet many parents consciously and/or irresponsibly place their child in the crossfire of their divorce war and custody battle. Sometimes a parent simply doesn't consider the consequences; other times parents march on, recklessly disregarding both the short-term and long-range impact on their child's welfare.

Parents have the duty to limit potential harm to their child by reducing parental conflict and exercising authoritative parenting during the separation/divorce process and its aftermath. Maintaining a meaningful relationship with two well-functioning parents promotes a child's welfare.

Today, courts and communities are combining their efforts to provide services and resources that can strengthen co-parenting relationships, keep children out of the conflict and mitigate harm to them. Some of those resources are parent education, parenting coordinators, mediation, best interest attorneys, and custody evaluations. When necessary, courts can also protect children by setting appropriate restrictions and conditions on a parent's access to a child.

In discussions about the desired allocation of both time with the child and decision-making authority, identifying each parent's real objectives and underlying interests is essential. A parent, for instance, may be litigating over a particular title when the real concern is an acceptable access schedule or meaningful participation in certain decisions. Emery says that parents should focus on children's needs and happiness rather than on "getting their share."[69] After all, children don't count overnights; they *experience parenting,* which means quality time really does count.[70]

Requiring parents to submit proposed parenting plans to each other and to the court may speed up the resolution process. This assignment compels parents (and their attorneys, if any) to focus on reasonable and realistic proposals that will define areas of agreement and disagreement. Parenting plans also provide a template that helps self-represented parents make more informed proposals for how to resolve custody issues. Without the forms and the instructions to guide them, many self-represented parents are in the difficult spot of not knowing what to include.

Parents won't always agree on what terms are best for their children, but their proposed parenting plans can help start the dialogue as well as reduce misunderstandings about decision-making responsibilities and parenting time. If parents cannot agree, courts will make the determination.

CHAPTER 12

Child Custody:
How Courts Decide What's in the
Children's Best Interests

WHEN PARENTS come together to establish a parenting plan and custody arrangement, they present this agreement to a court for entry of an order approving their agreement. When parents cannot agree and are unable to resolve their dispute, a court may ultimately be called upon to decide.

This kind of situation is hardly new. A well-known Old Testament narrative concerns two women who lived in the same house and gave birth to sons a few days apart. One child died, and both women claimed to be the mother of the living baby. They brought the matter to wise King Solomon.[1]

And Solomon ordered the living baby to be cut in two, and each claimant would receive one-half of the infant. The baby's true mother, revealing her genuine maternal love, relinquished her claim in order to spare her baby's life. The other woman's malice became evident when she urged Solomon to divide the baby so that neither woman would have the living child. With total confidence, Solomon gave the child to the true parent: "She is his mother" (1 Kings 3:27).

Clearly, Solomon in his wisdom understood God's character as well as the heart of human beings created in God's image, and Solomon did justice. Similarly, today's judges often face two parents who claim they deserve custody of their children, and these judges have the daunting task of evaluating the situation and determining what custodial arrangement will best serve the interests of a minor child.

Fundamental and Constitutional Parental Rights

Although the parents' constitutional rights are not an issue in most custody cases, they do provide an important context. Parents have a constitutionally protected, fundamental liberty to make decisions concerning the care of their minor children and to direct their children's upbringing as they deem appropriate.[2]

The parents' own constitutionally protected freedom of religion includes the right to guide the religious upbringing of their children.[3] Parents also have a constitutional right to travel[4]: they are free to travel from one state to another, to "migrate, resettle, find a new job, and start a new life."[5] However, nothing in U.S. jurisprudence even suggests that the constitutional right to travel takes precedence over a state's responsibility to preserve a child's best interest.[6] Indeed, parental rights are not absolute. The government may intervene in the parent-child relationship in order to protect children and ensure their welfare.[7]

Generally, in custody disputes between fit parents who both have fundamental constitutional rights to parent, the legal standard of the best interests of the child will be the deciding factor.[8] And regarding "pure third-party" custody disputes, the majority view is that there "must first be a finding of parental unfitness or extraordinary circumstances before custody can be transferred to a third party based on a 'best interest' analysis."[9]

Some states have adopted the concept of a *de facto* parent (i.e., "parent in fact"). The term generally describes an individual who claims custody or visitation rights based upon that person's parent-like relationship, in fact, with a child who is not that claimant's biological or adopted child.[10] *De facto* parents have standing to contest custody or visitation without having to show parental unfitness or exceptional circumstances before a trial court may apply a best interests of the child analysis to decide custody rights.[11]

Common Legal Standard: "Best Interests of the Child"

The prevalent legal standard applied by courts in child custody determinations is the "best interests of the child" test. The child's best interest "is not considered as one of many factors, but as the objective to which virtually all other factors speak."[12]

This standard gives the court broad discretion in making the custody decision, and a judge's decision in one case gives little reliable guidance to parties in another case.[13] Determining a child's future best interest "requires an element of prediction. . . . The aim is necessarily to structure custody and visitation to accommodate the *future* best interest of the child."[14] The desired outcome of this best-interests standard is "a parenting arrangement and parenting plan or other court-ordered arrangement which provides for a child's safety, emotional growth, health, stability, and physical care and regular and continuous school attendance and progress for school-age children."[15]

Factors Courts Consider

More than forty states and the District of Columbia have enacted statutes that specify numerous factors to be considered by a court required to determine a child's best interest, and case law in other states reveals their requisite factors.[16] Here are some of the most significant considerations.

Fitness to Care for the Child

Courts must consider the psychological and physical capabilities of both parents.[17] The court is to look for any conduct and/or characteristic of a parent that may impact their ability to care for a child or have an adverse impact on the child's welfare. The court will take into account the character and reputation of both parents.[18]

The court's focus is whether a parent's conduct has adversely impacted the child. In most states a child's exposure to a parent's significant other is not deemed detrimental *per se*. In this regard an adulterous parent is no longer presumed unfit to be custodian. Like all other pertinent factors, the adultery is evaluated only to determine whether it affects the child's welfare.[19]

Courts, however, may restrict a parent's right to visit with a child if sufficient evidence shows that such access is detrimental or not in the child's best interest. To limit visitation, the court must see a link between harm to the child and contact with the parent's significant other. Parents must always be careful about whom they permit to interact with their children, including housemates, significant others, and so on.

Although parents often dispute the fitness of the other parent, usually both are found to be fit custodians, so the court is determining which fit parent's custody of the child will be in the child's best interests.

Mental and Physical Health

All states permit consideration of the parents' and the children's mental and physical health. This also includes any "chemical health" issue.[20] It may also be appropriate to consider the health of third parties, such as significant others or family members who may be in regular contact with the child. The court is particularly interested in whether the child's intellectual, physical, or emotional welfare is negatively affected by the mental or physical health of any person residing in the custodial household.

When one parent's mental health is a disputed issue, the other parent often focuses only on the diagnosis—such as depression or bipolar—as if that's all that matters. But the court is interested in parental functioning and the steps a parent is taking—like seeing a counselor regularly and/or following the prescribed medication regimen—to address a condition. It is important that parents seek treatment and follow the reasonable recommendations of mental health professionals. A parent's untreated, deteriorating mental health may be particularly troublesome to a court especially when that deterioration is accompanied by erratic behavior, an apparent lack of control, insensitivity to how such behavior impacts the child and family, and a minimizing of personal responsibility.[21]

In a judicial proceeding a psychiatrist-patient or psychologist-patient privilege may grant a patient the "privilege to refuse to disclose, and to prevent a witness from disclosing: (1) communications relating to diagnosis or treatment of the patient; or (2) any information that by its nature would show the existence of a medical record of the diagnosis or treatment."[22]

Jurisdictions differ as to whether a party seeking a custody award places his or her mental health in controversy so as to require disclosure of privileged mental health records.[23] Courts do have the discretion to order current mental and physical health evaluations of the parents and the children.

Also, a parent's disability is relevant only to the extent that the court finds, based on evidence already in the record, that the disability affects the best interest of the child.

Additionally, a parent's commitment to a disabled child should not imply that such commitment is detrimental to that parent's other children unless evidence of such adverse impact is available.[24]

The Role of "Friendly Parent"

When Missouri adopted the Uniform Marriage and Divorce Act (UMDA), it added a "friendly parent" (or "cooperative parent") custody factor, namely, "Which parent is more likely to allow the child frequent and meaningful contact with the other parent?"[25] This question has become increasingly significant in custody determinations: thirty-eight jurisdictions apply this factor.[26]

After all, encouraging the child's ongoing relationship with the other parent and demonstrating this through providing parent-child contact is a positive for the child; placing obstacles in the way of both parent-child contact and the natural development of their relationship is not.

Generally, a child will fare better when parents respect the importance of their child's relationship with both of them and foster it.

Parents should be aware of the negative impact on their child when they undermine the other parent's role in the child's life. Courts view a parent's conduct negatively when it marginalizes or devalues the other parent's role in their child's life. Of course, as many statutes show, courts are sensitive to the reluctance or resistance of a victim of domestic violence to encourage visitation with the abuser.

The Child's Preference

The child's preference should be considered when the child is of sufficient age, discretion, and intelligence to form a rational judgment, but the child's preference is not determinative. The court must be sensitive to some possible influences on the choice: one parent is the Disneyland dad or the Magic Mountain mom; the child may express a preference for joint custody in hopes of reuniting the parents; and a parent's conduct may be alienating the child from the other parent.

Courts have various ways to obtain information about the child's desires—the "voice of the child"—through an attorney appointed to represent the child's best interests, a therapist's testimony if the child's privilege is waived, a custody evaluator, a judicial interview of the child, or evidence submitted by the parents. The court seeks to balance the right of the parents to present evidence as to what they deem to be in the child's best interest against the possible psychological impact of the child testifying.

The Parents' Preference

The desires of the parents and agreements between the parties—including "any prior agreement or course of conduct between the parents relating to caretaking functions with respect to the child"[27]—should be considered. Generally, a court may modify any provision of an agreement between parents regarding the care, custody, education, or support of their minor child if the modification would be in the best interest of the child.[28] The willingness to share custody and the sincerity of the parent's request are also important. Generally, an expression of unwillingness to share custody does not give that parent veto power over the possibility of joint custody.[29]

The Ability to Reach Shared Decisions

The parents' capacity to communicate with each other and to reach shared decisions regarding the child's welfare "is clearly the most important factor in the determination of whether an award of joint legal custody is appropriate, and is relevant as well to a consideration of shared physical custody."[30] Joint custody is rarely warranted when the parents have shown the inability to effectively communicate on matters involving the child and when there is no indication or even potential for effective communication to happen in the future.[31]

In some particular circumstances, however, joint custody may be the only option that will keep the parents from totally cutting each other out of the child's life. When the court awards joint custody to parents who lack mature communication skills, the court must articulate clearly the justification for its award.

When allocating decision-making responsibility, the court should consider whether the parents' past involvement with the child "reflects a system of values, time commitment, and mutual support that would indicate an ability as mutual decision makers to provide a positive and nourishing relationship with the child."[32]

A History of Alcohol or Substance Abuse

This factor includes (1) a party's history of drug or alcohol abuse, abuse of prescription medication, or illegal use of controlled substances; (2) a history of drug or alcohol abuse by a member of a party's household; and (3) each party's demonstrated ability to maintain a substance abuse–free environment for the children.

According to the National Institute on Drug Abuse, the "misuse of and addiction to opioids—including prescription pain relievers, heroin, and synthetic opioids such as fentanyl—is a serious national crisis that affects public health as well as social and economic welfare."[33]

Alcohol and drug abuse—including opioids—can have a devastating effect on a parent's ability to function as a caretaker.

Incidents of Domestic Violence or Child Abuse

In child custody and visitation proceedings, all jurisdictions in the United States consider the issues of child abuse and domestic violence committed by one parent against the other.[34] In some states, when evidence of abuse exists, the court must specifically find no likelihood that the parent may abuse or neglect a child whose custody/visitation is within the court's jurisdiction: "The focus is not on a particular child but on the party guilty of the previous abuse or neglect."[35] Neglect or abuse refers to the neglect or abuse of *any* child in the past, not only the child whose custody is being decided in the current proceeding. A substantial minority of states imposes a rebuttable presumption against awarding custody to the abusive parent.

The flip side of this domestic violence consideration is whether either parent has been convicted of falsely reporting child abuse or neglect or has intentionally misused protection from domestic violence proceedings to gain a tactical advantage in a custody proceeding.[36]

Of course a distinction is made between reasonable corporal punishment and abuse.[37] The line is not always clear, and parents must be circumspect about their overall approach to disciplining the children in their care. In 1979 Sweden banned corporal punishment, and many other countries have also banned it.[38] But proverbs that advocate the rod of discipline "should never be used to legitimize any form of child abuse."[39] Parental differences concerning appropriate child discipline—whether corporal punishment, time-outs, reasoning with a child, or other approaches—may be a source of conflict in marriages as well as in custody disputes. Courts should zealously promote a child's welfare and do all they can to protect children from abuse.

The Child's Key Relationships

This factor encompasses not only a child's past and current interaction and relationship with each parent, but also relationships with siblings and others who may significantly affect the child's best interests. Courts also consider the length of the child's separation from the natural parents[40] and the child's ability "to maintain a relationship with any sibling."[41]

States tend to dislike separating siblings from one another, and ordinarily the children of the same parents are best served by keeping them together to grow up as siblings under the same roof.[42] The American Law Institute (ALI) Principles recommend as an objective "to keep siblings together where the court finds that doing so is necessary to their welfare."[43] Another aspect of this factor is "the availability of extended family."[44]

The Ability to Meet the Child's Needs

It's important that parents be attuned to their child's needs—physical, emotional, mental, educational, cultural, and spiritual. They also must demonstrate their ability to address those needs in ways that benefit the child. Parents should show themselves informed about their child's "friends, teachers, medical care providers, daily activities, and favorite things"[45] as well as demonstrate their ability to be actively involved in the life of the child.

A parent's capacity and disposition "to give the child love, affection, and spiritual guidance and to continue the education and rearing of the child"[46] and "to continue the education and raising of the child in his or her religion or creed, if any,"[47] are important. Also significant is providing "a consistent routine for the child, such as discipline, and daily schedules for homework, meals, and bedtime."[48]

Also impacting the parents' ability to meet the child's needs are the demands of their place of employment, their work schedules, and the "ability to make appropriate child-care arrangements."[49] A parent must also attend to the child's medical needs, providing necessary medications and altering their own lifestyle as reasonably necessary. In light of the health risks that exposure to secondhand smoke pose to children, the court will consider parental smoking particularly when a child has asthma or some other health or respiratory condition.

Age and Gender

Although the maternal preference doctrine—the presumption that a younger child is better off with the mother—has been abolished in all states, some consideration of age and gender may still be appropriate where these factors bear upon the parents' respective "ability to provide the care needed by the child at that time."[50] For example, whether a child of less than one year old is being breastfed may significantly impact custody decisions.[51] In one case I heard as a family magistrate, I fashioned a temporary access schedule that provided the father with regular, brief, and frequent access to the parties' infant that did not disrupt the mother's regular nursing schedule.

Stability and Continuity for the Child

The need to maintain and promote continuity and stability in a child's life is a significant factor. Courts assess potential disruption of a child's social life and school life.[52] This assessment includes adjustment to and the stability of the child's home, school, and community environments.

The Geographic Proximity of the Parents' Homes

The physical proximity of the parties' respective homes may have a practical impact on the amount of parenting time each is awarded.[53] Consider these points:

Parental homes within the same school district offer certain advantages in a joint custody situation. The child may enjoy joint physical custody without changing schools or being required to constantly change a circle of friends, and the parents may find proximity a benefit in discussing the decisions to be made concerning the child. However, distance is not a bar, and when the distance between homes is great, a joint custody arrangement may offer the only practical way to preserve for the child a meaningful relationship with each parent.[54]

Often when parties separate, one parent moves—or desires to move—away for a fresh start, a job transfer, or a new opportunity; to go back to school; or to be closer to family and the emotional and financial support they can offer. A move or an intended move raises many additional considerations for the court that will be discussed later in this chapter.

Primary Care Provider of the Child

Which parent has been the child's primary caregiver? The court will consider the parties' respective parenting tasks and their prior division of responsibilities, "including the extent to which parenting responsibilities were undertaken by third parties."[55] The court might also consider "any necessary changes to the parents' custodial roles and any reasonable life-style changes that a parent proposes to make to be able to spend time with the child in the future."[56]

The ALI *Principles* advocates an "approximation" presumption—or "past caretaking" standard—whereby "the court should allocate custodial responsibility so that the proportion of custodial time the child spends with each parent approximates the proportion of time each parent spent performing caretaking functions for the child prior to the parents' separation."[57]

This is not merely a factor; it's a criterion advocated to replace the "best interest of the child" standard. Basing custody guidelines on past caretaking is a way to preserve stability and attachments in the child's life and to, at the same time, align reasonably well with the parents' expectations: "The way parents chose to divide responsibility when the family lived together anchors the negotiations in their own lived experience rather than in unrealistic or emotion-based aspirations about the future."[58]

Consider Andrew Schepard's favorable description of the approximation/past caretaking guideline:

> The approximation principle preserves after divorce the relationship between caregiving and custody before it. If the parents shared care-giving responsibilities equally before divorce, they share it after divorce. If one parent provided most of the child's

care before divorce, he or she receives the right to provide most of the care after divorce. The approximation principle thus reduces the risk to the child of being placed with a less experienced caregiver.[59]

Schepard also notes these objections: (1) This arrangement "runs the risk of confusing the quantity of time spent with the quality of the interaction between parent and child"; (2) there is "no reason to assume that a child's current primary caretaker is also his or her most important emotional attachment" because the comparative time spent with a parent may not adequately reflect the relative strength of the attachments; (3) it "does not take into account the probability of post-divorce change in parenting roles"; and (4) "the importance of both parents in the post-divorce life of the child" should be heeded.[60]

The approximation standard does allow for certain exceptions that are intended to protect a child from a parent's abuse or neglect, domestic violence, or substance abuse that interferes with caretaking functions. Always "the court should impose limits that are reasonably calculated to protect the child, child's parent, or other member of the household from harm."[61]

Although the approximation standard may have little impact on your state's child custody law, a parent's respective past parental involvement, that parent's ongoing role in the child's life, and the quality of the parent-child emotional attachment are significant factors in custody determinations. Courts notice, too, the significance of the parent who has had greater responsibility for the child being especially attuned to the child's needs and who has a solid record of competently meeting those needs.

Religion

Parents' constitutionally protected freedom of religion includes the right to oversee the religious upbringing of their children. Several statutes mention the child's spiritual needs and each party's capacity "to give the child . . . spiritual guidance and to continue the education and rearing of the child."[62]

Other states emphasize that a parent's religion and the child's religious upbringing is a factor to the extent it impacts the child's physical or emotional welfare. The court may not weigh the merits of different religions or nonreligious upbringing. That said, "Disapproval of mere *belief or nonbelief* cannot be a consideration in a custody determination, . . . Yet consideration of religiously motivated *behavior* with an impact on a child's welfare cannot be ignored."[63]

Before the court will interfere, however, one parent has to clearly show that the other parent's religious practices have been or are likely to be harmful to the child. This requirement necessitates more than a statement that the child is confused or upset by conflicting religious practices. A causal relationship between the practices and the actual or probable harm is required.[64]

Protecting the Child from Parental Conflict

This factor includes the "capacity and disposition of each parent to protect the child from the ongoing litigation as demonstrated by not discussing the litigation with the child, not sharing documents or electronic media related to the litigation with the child, and refraining from disparaging comments about the other parent to the child."[65] Any manipulation by or coercive behavior of either or both parents in an effort to involve the child in their adult dispute is also relevant.

Military Deployment

The Uniform Deployed Parents Custody and Visitation Act (2012) addresses child custody and visitation issues that arise due to military deployment, including expedited court resolutions of custody and temporary custody arrangements.[66] The act seeks to promote a just balance of both the service member's and the other parent's rights as well as the children's best interests. When deployment is not imminent, a court may not use a parent's past deployment or possible future deployment as an adverse factor in determining a child's best interest.

The Maryland statute states that any order based on deployment shall require the following:

1. The other parent reasonably accommodate the leave schedule of the parent who is subject to the deployment;

2. the other parent facilitate opportunities for telephone and electronic mail contact between the parent who is subject to the deployment and the child during the period of deployment; and

3. the parent who is subject to the deployment provide timely information regarding the parent's leave schedule to the other parent.[67]

These reasonable provisions help a deployed service member maintain his or her parental role.

Relocation-Specific Considerations

The American Academy of Matrimonial Lawyers (AAML) Proposed Model Relocation Act (§ 405) lists factors that overlap with the standard of the child's best interest, but many of these points are specific to a relocation case:

1. The nature, quality, extent of involvement, and duration of the child's relationship with the person proposing to relocate and with the nonrelocating person, siblings, and other significant persons in the child's life;

2. The age, developmental stage, needs of the child, and the likely impact the relocation will have on the child's physical, educational, and emotional development, taking into consideration any special needs of the child;

3. The feasibility of preserving the relationship between the nonrelocating person and the child through suitable [visi-

tation] arrangements, considering the logistics and financial circumstances of the parties;

4. The child's preference, taking into consideration the age and maturity of the child;

5. Whether there is an established pattern of conduct of the person seeking the relocation, either to promote or thwart the relationship of the child and the nonrelocating person;

6. Whether the relocation of the child will enhance the general quality of life for both the custodial party seeking the relocation and the child, including but not limited to, financial or emotional benefit or educational opportunity;

7. The reasons of each person for seeking or opposing the relocation;

8. Any other factor affecting the best interests of the child.

The ALI *Principles* states that "the court should allow a parent who has been exercising the clear majority of custodial responsibility to relocate with the child if that parent shows that the relocation is for a valid purpose, in good faith, and to a location that is reasonable in light of the purpose."[68] The following purposes should be considered valid:

1. To be close to significant family or other sources of support

2. To address significant health problems

3. To protect the safety of the child or another member of the child's household from a significant risk of harm

4. To pursue a significant employment or educational opportunity

5. To be with one's spouse or domestic partner who lives in, or is pursuing a significant employment or educational opportunity in, the new location

6. To significantly improve the family's quality of life

The court should find that a move for a valid purpose is reasonable unless its purpose is shown to be achievable without moving—or by moving to a location less disruptive to the other parent's relationship with the child.

Even if neither the AAML Proposed Model Relocation Act nor the ALI *Principles* has been adopted in your state, they still present factors to consider in a case involving parental relocation.

Which Courts Have Jurisdiction When Parents Live in Different States?

Sometimes separated parents live in different states or countries, and the appropriate court must make the initial child custody determination. Forty-nine states and the District of Columbia have enacted a form of the Uniform Child Custody Jurisdiction and Enforcement Act (UCCJEA).[69] Under this act a court may make an initial child custody determination only if it qualifies for jurisdiction.

The UCCJEA has four grounds for jurisdiction: home state, significant connection, more appropriate forum, and vacuum or default jurisdiction. Courts may also issue orders for temporary relief on emergency grounds.[70]

Primacy of Home State Jurisdiction

The UCCJEA gives priority to a child's home state to make an initial determination that addresses, among other things, custody and visitation orders.[71] A state is the home state if the child has lived there for six consecutive months on the date the case is filed.[72]

A state with a significant connection (i.e., with the child and the child's parents, or with the child and at least one parent or the person acting as a parent)—and when substantial evidence of the child's care, protection, training, and personal relationships is available—may assume jurisdiction only if no state has home state jurisdiction or the home state declines to exercise jurisdiction.[73]

Sometimes all states with home state or significant connection jurisdiction decline to exercise jurisdiction, permitting another more appropriate forum to decide the case.[74] For example, it would be more efficient to have one court decide custody of two siblings who reside in different states that each has jurisdiction over one of them. Provisions also govern whether jurisdiction should be declined due to someone's unjustifiable conduct, such as a parent's abducting/removing the child to another state.[75] The UCCJEA authorizes courts to communicate about any proceeding, and communication is required in certain instances.[76] The best interests of the child, however, are not part of the jurisdictional inquiry.

Continuing Exclusive Jurisdiction

The UCCJEA provides for continuing exclusive jurisdiction: the original decree state retains jurisdiction as long as a significant connection remains with the child or the child and one parent—and as long as substantial evidence relating to the child is still available in that state. This jurisdiction is lost if the child and both parents have moved away, a change that is significant in child custody modification proceedings.

Enforcement of Custody and Visitation Orders

States are required to enforce a custody or visitation order from another state when the order conforms to the UCCJEA.[77] A child custody determination must be registered in the appropriate court of the foreign state in order to be recognized by that court.[78] The enforcing court's inquiry is limited to whether the court issuing the order had jurisdiction and whether it complied with due process. Due process requires reasonable notice and a meaningful opportunity to be heard.[79]

The UCCJEA also has international application. A foreign country shall be treated as if it were a state of the United States in applying the act. To be specific, a foreign country's child custody determination made "under factual circumstances in substantial conformity with the jurisdictional standards of [the UCCJEA] must be recognized and enforced under [Article] 3."[80] Additionally, courts "enforce an order for the return of the child made under the Hague Convention (Hague Convention on the Civil Aspects of International Child Abduction (October 25, 1980)) as if it were a child-custody determination."[81]

Summary

When parents can't agree on a parenting plan, the court will decide where the child will reside and allocate the decision-making responsibilities it deems to be in the child's best interest. In most cases the court is deciding between two parents who are both fit to have custody and parenting responsibilities. The "child's best interest" legal standard gives judges wide discretion in their determinations, and a court's custody decision is difficult to overturn on appeal.

Yet child custody determinations are not permanent. They are subject to modification by courts when a material change in circumstances affecting the child's welfare occurs and a modification would be in the child's best interest.[82]

The UCCJEA addresses jurisdictional issues and the appropriate court that should make the initial custody determination. The relocating parent should be prepared to inform the court what the child's life will be like in the new location. Stability is important for children, and in some cases the stability comes from continuing in a familiar environment. For other children, the stability may come primarily from the continuing close relationship with a particular parent.

Compelling interests exist on both sides in a custody and visitation case, and the decision is quite difficult. The greater the extent to which each parent is able to consider the situation from the other parent's perspective, the greater the chance that a resolution can be reached that allows the child to maintain a meaningful relationship with each parent.

CHAPTER 13

Child Support: Protecting Children From Financial Harm

A PARENT'S OBLIGATION to support her or his minor child is a natural and moral duty as well as a legal obligation required by public policy and statutes.[1] To establish a child support order requires personal jurisdiction over the obligor (the person bound by a legal obligation) and the obligee (the person to whom another is obligated). If the obligor is a nonresident, jurisdiction may be obtained under the Uniform Interstate Family Support Act (UIFSA), a version of which has been adopted by all jurisdictions in the United States.[2]

Jurisdiction Over Obligor

UIFSA gives states broad, "long arm" jurisdiction over a child support obligor, even when the obligor is a nonresident. There can be only one controlling order, and the state that issues the controlling order retains continuing, exclusive jurisdiction to modify the order as long as either parent or child remains in the issuing state.

A state can lose its continuing, exclusive jurisdiction if neither parent and none of the children live in the state or if an agreement was made to transfer jurisdiction to another state. When a state loses jurisdiction, it can no longer modify the order it issued or enforce it once it has been modified by another state.[3] A support order may be sent to another state for registration and enforcement. Each state is required to give full faith and credit to another state's child support order.[4]

Age of Majority and Duration of Support

The age of majority in most states is eighteen, and these states typically extend the child support obligation to age nineteen or even up to twenty-one if the child remains enrolled in high school. Child support may terminate prior to the child attaining majority when the obligor parent dies or the child marries, becomes emancipated, or dies.

Parents may agree to continue supporting a child past a state's age of majority. For example, child support may be awarded to an adult child who is destitute and, due to a mental or physical disability, cannot be self-supporting.[5]

Child Support Guidelines

The Family Support Act of 1988 requires states to enact child support guidelines that provide a rebuttable presumption that the amount calculated under the guidelines is correct. When a child support decision deviates from these guidelines, written findings must state the amount of support required under the guidelines, why that amount is unjust or inappropriate, and, consequently, why the order varies from the guidelines.[6]

Guidelines make awards more consistent, predictable, and equitable; increase the amount of awards; promote voluntary settlement; and provide more efficient court hearings. The three models are the Income Shares Model (used in most states) and the less common Percentage of Income and Melson Formula Models.

The premise of the Income Shares Model is "that the children should receive the same proportion of parental income that he or she would have received if the parents lived together."[7] Child support is based on the parents' income—rather than the child's expenses—and the number of children owed support.[8] It is then apportioned between the parents based on each one's percentage of the combined income.

Example: Family with two children living in Maryland

Financial Information

Custodial parent's gross monthly income:	$2,000
Noncustodial parent's gross monthly income:	$3,500
Work-related childcare expense:	$250
Children's health insurance premium:	$200
Extraordinary medical expenses:	$50

Income Shares Model Guidelines Applied

Parents' combined income:	$5,500
Custodial parent's share of income:	36.4%($2,000 ÷ $5,500)
Noncustodial parent's share of income:	63.6% ($3,500 ÷ $5,500)
Child support obligation:	$1,319[9]
Plus childcare, health insurance, medical expenses:	$500
Total child support obligation:	$1,819
Noncustodial parent's pro rata obligation (63.6%):	$1,157
Custodial parent's pro rata obligation (36.4%):	$662

The Percentage of Income Model calculates child support as a percentage of the noncustodial parent's income. I'm using the same information from the above example:

Noncustodial parent's income:	$3,500
Percentage to apply:	25%
Basic child support obligation:	$875 (25% x $3,500)

Adjustments are then made for the add-ons and deductions before the final presumptive obligation is determined. The Percentage of Income model doesn't necessarily result in a fair and consistent award. Neither does it adequately account for the wide range of a custodial parent's income and financial circumstances: a low-income custodian receives the same amount of child support as a high-income custodian.

The Melson Formula Model—used in Delaware, Hawaii, and Montana—is "a more complicated version of the Income Shares Model," and it factors in each parent's minimal self-support need to determine a Standard of Living Allowance.[10]

Income

Income covers "all income . . . from any source,"[11] and typically includes:

- Salaries and wages, including overtime,[12] commissions, tips, and bonuses[13]
- Income from second jobs[14]
- Investments, interest, and dividends
- Pension[15]
- Trust and estate income, annuities
- Stock options/incentives[16]
- Social Security benefits, worker's compensation,[17] unemployment insurance benefits, disability insurance benefits, disability pensions, military disability benefits, military fringe benefits[18]
- Alimony or maintenance[19]
- Severance pay
- Capital gains (recurring)
- Gifts[20]
- Prizes, lottery and gambling winnings
- Education grants (not education loans)
- Expense reimbursements or in-kind payments received by a parent in the course of employment, self-employment, or operation of business (to the extent the reimbursements or payments reduce the parent's personal living expenses)[21]
- Income from self-employment, rent, royalties, proprietorship of a business, or joint ownership of a partnership or closely held corporation[22]
- Benefits from means-tested public assistance programs (TANF, SSI, food stamps, etc.) are excluded.[23]

States typically recognize when a party is underemployed or has "voluntarily impoverished" himself or herself,[24] and that person's potential income or earning capacity will be attributed for determining their obligation to pay—or entitlement to receive—child support.[25] Potential income is income attributable to the parent factoring in employment potential and probable earnings level based on, but not limited to, recent work history, occupational qualifications, the job market, and earnings in the community.

Parties must complete and file standardized forms disclosing income and other required information.[26] Most states require parents to provide verification of income, which typically includes pay stubs, receipts, expenses if self-employed, W-2s, 1099s, and copies of each parent's three most recent tax returns. The court may also require a current financial statement under oath.

Health Insurance and Extraordinary Medical Expenses

Child support must "provide for the child(ren)'s health care needs, through health insurance coverage or other means."[27] States generally address health insurance costs either by deducting the cost from the paying parent's income or treating the cost as an add-on that may be further apportioned or divided between the parents.[28] All states consider uninsured and extraordinary medical expenses in their determinations. Most states handle it as a mandatory or permissive add-on to the support award; the other states treat it as a deviation factor.[29] Generally, the add-on amount is then apportioned between the parents in the same manner as the basic child support obligation is allocated. In states where these expenses are a deviation factor, the court must give reasons supporting its decision that these expenses require deviation.

Ordinary medical expenses are deemed built into the basic support award computation.[30] The definition of *extraordinary medical expenses* varies. Many states distinguish between ordinary and extraordinary medical expenses by a threshold dollar amount. Some states have a threshold amount for a single illness or condition; others use an annual amount; and a few use a percentage of the child support award as the dividing line.

For example, in Maryland the actual cost of health insurance—including medical insurance, dental insurance, prescription drug coverage, and vision insurance—for the child and extraordinary medical expenses (namely, uninsured costs for medical treatment in excess of $250.00 in any calendar year) are treated as add-on expenses and apportioned between the parents.[31] These medical expenses could be reasonable and necessary costs for orthodontia, dental treatment, vision care, asthma treatment, physical therapy, treatment for any chronic health problem, and professional counseling or psychiatric therapy for diagnosed mental disorders.[32]

Childcare Expenses

Every state considers childcare expenses in its child support awards. States generally handle childcare costs by treating the coverage cost as an add-on that may be further apportioned or divided between the parents (thirty-four states); deducting the cost from the paying parent's income (three states and DC); or as a deviation factor (thirteen states).[33]

Childcare costs are generally limited to work-related childcare. Some states also include childcare costs incurred for a parent's "vocational, career, or occupational training; and educational training that will lead to better employment opportunities or greater income."[34] Summer camp expenses may, in some instances, be included especially when camp serves as a substitute for childcare.

Generally, the childcare expense must be reasonable. That amount may be determined by the family's actual experience unless the court finds the experience not in the child's best interests. If the family does not have any actual childcare experience or if the court finds that the family's experience is not in the child's best interest, then the amount included is "the level required to provide quality child care from a licensed source" or the lower actual cost of unlicensed quality care.[35]

Education Expenses

Expenses for a child attending a special or private school to meet particular educational needs may be apportioned between the parents in proportion to their incomes and added to the basic child support obligation, or this cost can be added as a deviation factor.

A child does not have to suffer from a disability for a court to find the child's particular education needs sufficient to order the payment of private school costs. Factors considered include (1) the child's educational history; (2) the child's performance in the private school; (3) the family history of private school; (4) whether the parents had made the choice to send the child to the school prior to their divorce; (5) any particular factor that might impact the child's best interest; and (6) the parents' ability to pay.[36]

Determining Whether to Adjust the Calculated Amount

To determine whether the use of the guidelines is unjust or inappropriate, the court may consider the terms of any agreement made between the parties—or a court order—that addresses the payment of mortgages, marital debts, or college education expenses; the use and possession order or the right to occupy the family home; or any direct payments made for the benefit of the children.[37]

It may be appropriate to deviate from the guidelines if either parent has other children in his or her household to whom he or she owes a duty of support and to whose expenses the parent directly contributes.[38] The court may also deviate if the child's income would make the application of the guidelines unjust or inappropriate. Also, most states credit the obligor parent for certain third-party payments such as Social Security disability dependency benefits received by a child on account of the obligor parent's disability.[39]

The court should assure that any child support agreements between the parents are consistent with the child support guidelines—and should provide reasons for approving any agreement that deviates from the guidelines.[40]

Impact of Shared Parenting Time

All states provide for some type of offset or adjustment—by formula or deviation—for shared parenting time. The threshold that activates the offset differs in various states.[41] For example, in Maryland when a child spends more than 35 percent of overnights per year with each parent, and both parents contribute to the children's expenses in addition to the payment of child support, child support is calculated under a formula relating to shared physical custody.[42]

The important point is, when states apply shared parenting time formulas, it results in a lesser child support obligation. Referring back to our previous Income Shares example, the noncustodial parent's $1,157 monthly obligation would be reduced to $883 when their overnights meet the 128 minimum; $730 at 156 overnights; and $590 when the parents have had the same number of overnights.

The presumption of these shared parenting time offsets is that at a certain point, the increased parenting time with a noncustodial parent results in greater expenses incurred by the noncustodial parent and reduced expenses for the primary custodial parent. An unfortunate consequence of this precipitous approach, however, is that conflict can arise during negotiations about a parenting time schedule. Parents may contend over the number of overnights rather than focusing on what may be in the child's best interest.

Split Custody

Although parenting plans usually keep siblings together, sometimes one parent may have sole custody of one or more minor children while the other parent has custody of their other minor children. This is called *split custody*. In this situation many states determine child support separately for the number of children in each parent's custody, and the lesser amount of child support is offset against the greater amount.[43] The parent with the greater obligation pays the difference in support. A minority of states treat a split custody situation as a deviation factor.

Income Exceeding the Guidelines Schedule

Child support guidelines schedules usually have a maximum income, such as $10,000 or $15,000 monthly. When the parents' income exceeds the highest amount on the chart, states have three primary ways to address the situation: (1) provide a formula that applies to the high income; (2) use the guidelines' highest amount; or (3) essentially disregard the guidelines, consider the child's needs and the parents' ability to provide support, and have the court exercise its discretion.[44] One approach is to view the maximum support award under the schedule as the presumptive minimum that should be awarded.[45] The court is required to fully explain its reasoning when child support awarded in an above-the-guidelines case is an amount lower than the maximum support award.

Retroactive Obligation to Pay Child Support

The court is required to award child support for the period of time from the filing of an initial pleading requesting child support *pendente lite* unless the court finds that this would produce an inequitable result. In a modification proceeding or a proceeding other than an initial request for *pendente lite* support, the court has the discretionary authority to award child support from the date of the filing of the proceeding.[46] A parent, however, must receive credit for payments made during the case.

Modification of Child Support

Courts may modify a child support award upon a showing of a material and substantial change in circumstances. This change may be in either income or the child's needs.[47] No change in circumstances is necessary when a court modifies child support contained in an agreement that has not become part of a court order.

When a parent requests modification of child support set by the agreement of both parties, the court must determine that the current provision does not serve the best interest of the child and that the proposed modification does. The court may not retroactively modify an award prior to the date of the filing of the motion for modification.[48] Upon the motion of either party, the court is required to review a child support award upon the expiration of a use and possession order or the expiration of the right to use a family home under an agreement.[49]

Enforcement of Child Support

The primary child support enforcement tool is income withholding through an Earnings Withholding Order (EWO). All support orders constitute an immediate and continuing withholding on all earnings of the obligor although EWOs are not effective when the obligor is self-employed or an independent contractor. Income subject to earnings withholding is not limited to wages and salaries – it also includes any form of periodic payments to an individual such as an annuity, a pension, Social Security payments, workers' compensation payments, unemployment insurance benefits, as well as commissions or fees paid in connection with the obligor's employment. Withholding can be established for both current support obligations and any accumulated overdue payments.If the recipient is being paid directly by the obligor, the order can be enforced by an EWO if the obligor accumulates arrears amounting to more than thirty days of support.[50] When an obligor does not comply with the court-ordered obligation, contempt proceedings can be another important enforcement mechanism to compel payment.

Various administrative enforcement measures also exist: income tax intercept; revocation or suspension of driver's license or occupational license;[51] and notifying a consumer credit reporting agency.[52] These additional enforcement tools are a benefit that comes with using the services of an Office of Child Support Enforcement. These offices also provide assistance with establishing paternity, establishing support obligations, locating absent parents, collecting support obligations, enforcing support obligations, and cooperating with other states in interstate child support cases.

Summary

Whether or not they live in the home and whether or not they have custody of the children, parents have an obligation to support their minor children. Child support guidelines can be an effective tool that compels parents to pay reasonable child support. A broad definition of income is also significant to determining a reasonable support obligation. While child support awards vary from state-to-state for families in similar situations, guidelines generally result in greater consistency and perceived fairness.

CHAPTER 14

The Way of Wisdom
Divorce That is Just, Fair, and Right

SEPARATION AND DIVORCE can disorient the strongest and steadiest of us. The often heart-wrenching experience challenges our beliefs, life principles, identity, relationships, emotions, and ability to function. Divorce impacts the people around us, especially the children who are caught in the middle. The tearing asunder what God has joined together causes us to reexamine the meaning of love and reevaluate where we find peace, contentment, and security. And our life plans have been radically altered.

Even when the *path* of divorce seems clear, the *way* the divorce plays out may be full of unexpected twists and turns, and you may struggle to cope with the destructive tactics of a formerly close ally. The *fog of war* is an oft-used phrase describing the complexity and uncertainty soldiers experience in the midst of war. Similarly, the *fog of divorce* is very real.

It's my hope that the principles you've read in this book will help you answer the hard questions and make the tough decisions you are facing. May what you've read also encourage you to walk before God in humility, showing justice and mercy to others (yes, even to your spouse). Finally, the principles set forth in this book will also make a difference as you pursue what's best for your child.

The *Just Divorce* considerations may provide you with a broadened perspective on divorce, one that look beyond marital misconduct alone. The legal insight is meant to help you pursue a resolution that is just, fair, and right. This legal information along with biblical wisdom will not always provide specific answers, but they will point you in the right direction. With your prayerful application of Scripture, your understanding of the legal process, and the wise counsel of others, you can pursue an outcome pleasing to God.

It is important that the Christian community, individually and collectively, exhibit compassion and extend love to individuals and families who are struggling through the painful reality of a ruptured marriage and the turmoil of divorce. We must "develop a balanced, biblical attitude toward divorce—on the one hand, hating all those things that God hates about divorce, while recognizing that in this sinful world there are those situations in which (as God Himself demonstrated) it may be necessary to obtain a divorce."[1] Ultimately we who are in a position to make a difference must seek to ensure a Just Divorce, one where both parties are treated with righteousness, justice, and equity.

Bibliography

AAML. *Bounds of Advocacy: Goals for Family Lawyers*. AAML National. Accessed July 16, 2020. https://cdn.ymaws.com/aaml.org/resource/resmgr/bookstore/bounds_of_advocacy.pdf.

————. "Child Custody Evaluation Standards." *Journal of the American Academy of Matrimonial Lawyers* 25 (2013): 251–94. Accessed July 16, 2020. https://cdn.ymaws.com/aaml.org/resource/collection/65D445D0-6C82-4D5C-8F70-D4BBC6DFA12D/MAT201_3.pdf.

Adams, Jay E. *From Forgiven to Forgiving: Learning to Forgive One Another God's Way*. Amityville, NY: Calvary Press, 1994.

————. *Marriage, Divorce, and Remarriage in the Bible: A Fresh Look at What Scripture Teaches*. Grand Rapids: Zondervan, 1980.

ALI. *Principles of the Law: Family Dissolution; Analysis and Recommendations*. Philadelphia: ALI, 2000.

————. *Restatement of the Law Second: Conflict of Laws*. American Law Institute, 1971.

Allender, Dan B., and Tremper Longman III. *Intimate Allies: Rediscovering God's Design for Marriage and Becoming Soul Mates for Life*. Carol Stream, IL: Tyndale, 1995.

Alsdurf, James, and Phyllis Alsdurf. *Battered Into Submission: The Tragedy of Wife Abuse in the Christian Home*. Downers Grove, IL: InterVarsity Press, 1989.

American Medical Association. "Diagnostic and Treatment Guidelines on Domestic Violence," *Archives of Family Medicine* 1 (September 1992). Accessed July 16, 2020. https://www.nlm.nih.gov/exhibition/confrontingviolence/materials/OB11102.pdf.

American Psychological Association. "Guidelines for Child Custody Evaluations in Family Law Proceedings." Accessed July 16, 2020. https://www.apa.org/practice/guidelines/child-custody

————. "Guidelines for the Practice of Parenting Coordination." *American Psychologist* 67, no. 1 (January 2012): 63–71. Accessed July 16, 2020. http://www.apa.org/pubs/journals/features/parenting-coordination.pdf.

BIBLIOGRAPHY

Aquinas, St. Thomas. *Summa Theologiae: A Concise Translation*. Edited by Timothy McDermott. Notre Dame: Ave Maria, 1989.

Atkinson, David. *To Have and to Hold: The Marriage Covenant and the Discipline of Divorce*. Grand Rapids: Eerdmans, 1979.

Augustine. *Concerning the City of God Against the Pagans*. Translated by Henry Bettenson. London: Penguin, 2003.

———. Letter 189 to Boniface. In *The Confessions and Letters of St. Augustine*. Vol. 1 of *NPNF¹*, edited by Philip Schaff. Peabody, MA: Hendrickson, 1994.

———. "On Marriage and Concupiscence." In *St. Augustine: Anti-Pelagian Writings*. Vol. 5 of *NPNF¹*, edited by Philip Schaff. Peabody, MA: Hendrickson, 1994.

———. "On the Good of Marriage." In *St. Augustine: On the Holy Trinity, Doctrinal Treatises, Moral Treatises*. Vol. 3 of *NPNF¹*, edited by Philip Schaff. Peabody, MA: Hendrickson, 1994.

———. "Reply to Faustus the Manichaean 22." In *St. Augustine: The Writings Against the Manichaeans, and Against the Donatists*. Vol. 4 of *NPNF¹*, edited by Philip Schaff. Peabody, MA: Hendrickson, 1994.

Avery, Bruce E., Kristina Badalian, and Maureen Glackin. "CLE: Military Retirement Benefits, Disability Pay, and Related Issues," panel discussion on September 26, 2017, Bar Association of Montgomery County, Rockville, MD.

Babb, Barbara, Gloria Danziger, Judith D. Moran, and Itta Englander. *Parent Education Programs: Review of the Literature and Annotated Bibliography*. Maryland Judiciary Research Consortium, 2009. Accessed July 16, 2020. https://law.ubalt.edu/downloads/law_downloads/June2009_ParentEdPrograms_FINAL.pdf.

Barrett, C. K. *The First Epistle to the Corinthians*. Baker's New Testament Commentary, Peabody, MA: Hendrickson, 2006.

Bazerman, Max H., and Margaret A. Neale. *Negotiating Rationally*. New York: Free Press, 1992.

Beale, G. K., and D. A. Carson, eds. *Commentary on the New Testament Use of the Old Testament*. Grand Rapids: Baker Academic, 2007.

Beeke, Joel R., and Sinclair B. Ferguson, eds. *Reformed Confessions Harmonized.* Grand Rapids: Baker Books, 1999.

Bell, Daniel M., Jr. *Just War as Christian Discipleship: Recentering the Tradition in the Church rather than the State.* Grand Rapids: Brazos Press, 2009.

Blocher, Henri. *In the Beginning: The Opening Chapters of Genesis.* Downers Grove, IL: InterVarsity Press, 1984.

Blomberg, Craig L. *1 Corinthians.* NIV Application Commentary. Grand Rapids: Zondervan, 1994.

———. "Marriage, Divorce, Remarriage, and Celibacy: An Exegesis of Matthew 19:3–12." *Trinity Journal* 11 (1990): 161–96.

———. *Matthew.* Vol. 22 of The New American Commentary. Nashville: Broadman & Holman, 1992.

Bock, Darrell L. *Luke: 9:51–24:53.* Vol. 3B of Baker Exegetical Commentary on the New Testament. Grand Rapids: Baker Academic, 1996.

Bowermaster, Janet M. "Sympathizing with Solomon: Choosing Between Parents in a Mobile Society." *University of Louisville Journal of Family Law* 31 (1992): 791, 884.

Brauns, Chris. *Unpacking Forgiveness: Biblical Answers for Complex Questions and Deep Wounds.* Wheaton, IL: Crossway, 2008.

Burns, Bob. *Through the Whirlwind: A Proven Path to Recovery from the Devastation of Divorce.* Nashville: Oliver-Nelson, 1989.

Calvin, John. *Institutes of the Christian Religion.* Vol. 31 of *Library of Christian Classics,* edited by John T. McNeill and translated by Ford Lewis Battles. Philadelphia: Westminster, 1960.

Camp, Jim. *No: The Only Negotiating System You Need for Work and Home.* New York: Crown, 2007.

———. *Start with No: The Negotiating Tools That the Pros Don't Want You to Know.* New York: Crown, 2002.

Carson, D. A. *Matthew: Chapters 13–28.* The Expositor's Bible Commentary. Grand Rapids: Zondervan, 1995.

Chapman, Gary. *One More Try: What to Do When Your Marriage Is Falling Apart.* Chicago: Moody, 2014.

Chirban, John T. *Collateral Damage: Guiding and Protecting Your Child Through the Minefield of Divorce.* Nashville: W Publishing, 2017.

CLS. "About Us." Accessed July 16, 2020. www.christianlegalsociety.org/about.

Collins, Raymond F. *First Corinthians.* Vol. 7 of *Sacra Pagina*, edited by Daniel J. Harrington. Collegeville, MN: Liturgical Press, 1999.

Corman, Marjorie. *Negotiating Outcomes: Expert Solutions to Everyday Challenges.* Pocket Mentor Series. Boston: Harvard Business Publishing, 2007.

Craver, Charles. *The Intelligent Negotiator: What to Say, What to Do, and How to Get What You Want—Every Time.* Roseville, CA: Prima, 2002.

Davis, John Jefferson. *Evangelical Ethics: Issues Facing the Church Today.* 3rd ed. Phillipsburg, NJ: P&R Publishing, 2004.

Demby, Steven. "Commentary on Entrenched Postseparation Parenting Disputes: The Role of Interparental Hatred." *Family Court Review* 55, no. 3 (July 2017): 417–23.

Douglas, Emily M. *Mending Broken Families: Social Policies for Divorced Families: How Effective Are They?* Lanham, MD: Rowman & Littlefield, 2006.

Elrod, Linda D., and Robert G. Spector. "A Review of the Year in Family Law 2014–2015: Family Law Continues to Evolve as Marriage Equality is Attained," *Family Law Quarterly* 49, no. 4 (Winter 2016): 589–614.

———, "A Review of the Year in Family Law 2015–2016: Domestic Dockets Stay Busy," *Family Law Quarterly* 50, no. 4 (Winter 2017): 565–603.

--------, "A Review of the Year in Family Law 2017-2018: Courts Tackle Immigration, Jurisdiction, and the Usual Family Law Disputes," *Family Law Quarterly* 52, no. 4 (Winter 2019): 519-625.

Ellis, Elizabeth M. *Divorce Wars: Interventions with Families in Conflict.* Washington, DC: American Psychological Association, 2000.

Emery, Robert E. *Two Homes, One Childhood: A Parenting Plan to Last a Lifetime.* New York: Avery, 2016.

Fahnert, Marie, and Melyse Mpiranya. *Child-Custody Jurisdiction.* Chicago: ABA Section of Family Law, 2015.

Fee, Gordon. *The First Epistle to the Corinthians.* New International Commentary on the New Testament. Grand Rapids: Eerdmans, 1987.

Feldhahn, Shaunti. *The Good News About Marriage: Debunking Discouraging Myths About Marriage and Divorce.* Colorado Springs: Multnomah, 2014.

Ferguson, Everett. *Backgrounds of Early Christianity*, 3rd ed. Grand Rapids: Eerdmans, 2003, 74.

Ferguson, Sinclair B. *Kingdom Life in a Fallen World: Living Out the Sermon on the Mount.* Colorado Springs: NavPress, 1987.

———. *Let's Study Mark.* Carlisle, PA: Banner of Truth, 1999.

Fisher, Roger, William Ury, and Bruce Patton. *Getting to Yes: Negotiating Agreement Without Giving In.* 2nd ed. New York: Penguin, 1991.

Frame, John M. *The Doctrine of the Christian Life.* Phillipsburg, NJ: P&R Publishers, 2008.

——— *The Doctrine of the Knowledge of God.* Phillipsburg, NJ: P&R, 1987.

———. "Spousal Abuse: Grounds for Divorce?" *IIIM Magazine Online* 4, no. 22 (June 3–9, 2002). Accessed July 16, 2020. http://thirdmill.org/newfiles/joh_frame/PT.Frame.divorce.abuse.html.

Gardner, Richard. "Recent Trends in Divorce and Custody Litigation," *Academy Forum* 29, no. 2 (1985): 3–7.

Garland, David E. *1 Corinthians.* The Baker Exegetical Commentary on the New Testament. Grand Rapids: Baker Academic, 2003.

Garner, Bryan A., ed. *Black's Law Dictionary*, 10th ed. St. Paul, MN: Thomson Reuters, 2014.

Garrity, Carla B., and Mitchell A. Baris. *Caught in the Middle: Protecting the Children of High-Conflict Divorce.* San Francisco: Jossy-Bass, 1994.

Gay, Craig M. *The Way of the (Modern) World: Or, Why It's Tempting to Live as if God Doesn't Exist*. Grand Rapids: Eerdmans, 1998.

Gershoff, Elizabeth T., and Susan H. Bitensky. "The Case Against Corporal Punishment of Children." *Psychology, Public Policy, and Law* 13, no. 4 (2007): 231–72.

Gillum, Tameka L., and Shondrah Tarrezz Nash. "Faith-Based Programs and Interventions." Chap. 16 in *Sourcebook on Violence Against Women*, edited by Claire M. Tenzetti, Jeffrey L. Edleson, and Raquel Kennedy Bergen. 2nd ed. Los Angeles: Sage, 2011.

Green, Joel B. *The Gospel of Luke*. New International Commentary on the New Testament. Grand Rapids: Eerdmans, 1997.

Hoff, Patricia M. "UCAPA: Understanding and Using UCAPA to Prevent Child Abduction." *Family Law Quarterly* 41, no. 1 (Spring 2007): 1–21.

Holcomb, Justin S., and Lindsey A. Holcomb. *Is It My Fault?: Hope and Healing for Those Suffering Domestic Violence*. Chicago: Moody, 2014.

Holmes, Arthur F. "The Just War," in *War: Four Christian Views*, edited by Robert G. Clouse, 115–35. Downers Grove, IL: InterVarsity Press, 1981.

———, ed. *War and Christian Ethics*. 2nd ed. Grand Rapids: Baker Academic, 2005.

Horowitz, Robert, Kathi Grasso, and Diane Boyd Rauber. *A Judge's Guide: Making Child-Centered Decisions in Custody Cases*. ABA Center on Children and the Law, 2001.

Hugenberger, Gordon P. *Marriage as a Covenant: Biblical Law and Ethics as Developed from Malachi*. Grand Rapids: Baker Books, 1998.

Instone-Brewer, David. *Divorce and Remarriage in the Bible: The Social and Literary Context*. Grand Rapids: Eerdmans, 2002.

———. *Divorce and Remarriage in the Church: Biblical Solutions for Pastoral Realities*. Downers Grove, IL: InterVarsity Press, 2003.

Johnston, Janet R. "Commentary on Entrenched Postseparation Parenting Disputes: The Role of Interparental Hatred," *Family Court Review* 55, no. 3 (July 2017): 424–29.

Johnston, Janet R., Vivienne Roseby, and Kathryn Kuehnle. *In the Name of the Child: A Developmental Approach to Understanding and Helping Children of Conflicted and Violent Divorce.* 2nd ed. New York: Springer, 2009.

Johnston, Janet R., and Kinda K. Girdner, "Early Identification of Parents at Risk for Custody Violations and Prevention of Child Abductions." *Family and Conciliation Courts Review* 36, no. 3 (1998): 392–409.

Johnston, Janet R., Inger Sagatun-Edwards, Martha-Elin Blomquist, and Linda K. Girdner. "Early Identification of Risk Factors for Parental Abduction." *OJJDP Juvenile Justice Bulletin* (March 2001). Accessed January 22, 2017, https://www.ncjrs.gov/pdffiles1/ojjdp/185026.pdf.

Jones, David Clyde. *Biblical Christian Ethics.* Grand Rapids: Baker Books, 1994.

———. "The Westminster Confession on Divorce and Remarriage." *Presbyterian* 16 (1990): 17–40.

Josephus, Flavius. *The Works of Josephus: Complete and Unabridged.* Translated by William Whiston. Peabody, MA: Hendrickson, 1987.

Kaiser, Walter C., Jr. *Malachi: God's Unchanging Love.* Grand Rapids: Baker Books, 1984.

———. "True Marital Love in Proverbs 5:15–23 and the Interpretation of Song of Songs." In *the Way of Wisdom: Essays in Honor of Bruce K. Waltke,* edited by J. I. Packer and S. K. Soderlund, 106–16. Grand Rapids: Zondervan, 2000.

Keener, Craig S. *A Commentary on the Gospel of Matthew.* Grand Rapids: Eerdmans, 1999.

Keller, Timothy. *The Meaning of Marriage: Facing the Complexities of Commitment with the Wisdom of God.* New York: Penguin Group, 2011.

Kelly, Joan B., and Janet R. Johnston. "The Alienated Child: A Reformulation of Parental Alienation Syndrome," *Family Court Review* 39 (2001): 249–66.

Kendrick, Alex, and Stephen Kendrick. *The Love Dare.* Nashville: B&H, 2008.

Kidner, Derek. *Proverbs: An Introduction & Commentary.* Tyndale Old Testament Commentaries. Downers Grove, IL: InterVarsity Press, 1964.

Kisthardt, Mary Kay. "Rethinking Alimony: The AAML's Considerations for Calculating Alimony, Spousal Support, or Maintenance." *Journal of the American Academy of Matrimonial Lawyers* 21 (2008): 61–85.

Köstenberger, Andreas J. "The Mystery of Christ and the Church: Head and Body, 'One Flesh.'" *Trinity Journal* 12, no. 1 (Spring 1991): 79–94.

Köstenberger, Andreas J., with David W. Jones. *God, Marriage, and Family: Rebuilding the Biblical Foundation.* Wheaton, IL: Crossway Books, 2004.

Kovach, Kimberlee K. *Mediation: Principles and Practice.* 2nd ed. St. Paul, MN: West Group, 2000.

Kroeger, Catherine Clark, and Nancy Nason-Clark. *No Place for Abuse: Biblical and Practical Resources to Counteract Domestic Violence.* Downers Grove, IL: InterVarsity Press, 2001.

Kübler-Ross, Elisabeth. *On Death and Dying: What the Dying Have to Teach Doctors, Nurses, Clergy, and Their Own Families.* New York: Macmillan, 1969.

Laney, J. Carl. *The Divorce Myth: A Biblical Examination of Divorce and Remarriage.* Minneapolis: Bethany House, 1981.

Lewis, C. S. *Mere Christianity.* New York: HarperCollins, 2001.

Lind, Goran. *Common Law Marriage: A Legal Institution for Cohabitation.* New York: Oxford University Press, 2008.

Lohse, Eduard. *The New Testament Environment.* Translated by John E. Steely. Nashville: Abingdon, 1976.

Longman, Tremper, III. *Genesis.* The Story of God Bible Commentary. Grand Rapids: Zondervan, 2006.

———. "God's Law and Mosaic Punishments Today." In *Theonomy: A Reformed Critique*, edited by William S. Barker and Robert W. Godfrey, 41–54. Grand Rapids: Zondervan, 1990.

———. *Proverbs.* Baker Commentary on the Old Testament Wisdom and Psalms. Grand Rapids: Baker Academic, 2006.

Luther, Martin. *The Estate of Marriage (1522).* In *Martin Luther's Basic Theological Writings*, 2nd ed. Edited by Timothy F. Lull. Minneapolis: Fortress Press, 2005.

Malhotra, Deepak, and Max H. Bazerman. *Negotiation Genius: How to Overcome Obstacles and Achieve Brilliant Results at the Bargaining Table and Beyond.* New York: Bantam, 2007.

Marshall, I. Howard. *The Gospel of Luke: A Commentary on the Greek Text.* The New International Greek Testament Commentary. Grand Rapids: Eerdmans, 1978.

Marz, Stacy. "Early Resolution for Family Law Cases in Alaska's Courts." *Alaska Justice Forum* 31, nos. 1–2 (Spring–Summer 2014): 13–17. Accessed July 16, 2020. https://www.uaa.alaska.edu/academics/college-of-health/departments/justice-center/alaska-justice-forum/31/1-2spring-summer2014/d_erp.cshtml.

Mayo Clinic Staff. "Anger Management." Mayo Clinic. Accessed July 16, 2020. http://www.mayoclinic.org/tests-procedures/anger-management/basics/results/prc-20014603.

McKane, William. *Proverbs: A New Approach.* The Old Testament Library Series. Philadelphia: Westminster Press, 1970.

Merriam-Webster's Collegiate Dictionary. 11th ed. Springfield, MS: Merriam-Webster, 2003.

Miles, Al. *Violence in Families: What Every Christian Needs to Know.* Minneapolis: Augsburg, 2002.

MNADV. *It Shouldn't Hurt to Go Home: The Domestic Violence Victim's Handbook.* Lanham, MD: MNADV, 2011. Accessed July 16, 2020. http://mnadv.org/_mnadvWeb/wp-content/uploads/2011/07/shouldnthurt2013.pdf.

_____. *A Vision for the Future: Recommendations for a More Coordinated Community Response to Domestic Violence in Maryland.* Lanham, MD: MNADV, 2006.

Mnookin, Robert H., and D. Kelly Weisberg. *Child, Family, and State: Problems and Materials on Children and the Law.* 6th ed. New York: Aspen, 2009.

Morgan, Laura W. *Child Support Guidelines: Interpretation and Application.* 2nd ed. New York: Wolters Kluwer, 2016 Sup.

Morris, Leon. *The Gospel According to St. Luke.* Tyndale New Testament Commentaries. Grand Rapids: Eerdmans, 1974.

Murphy, Roland E. *Proverbs.* Vol. 22 of Word Biblical Commentary. Nashville: Thomas Nelson, 1998.

Murray, John. *Divorce.* Philadelphia: Presbyterian and Reformed, 1961.

———. *Principles of Conduct: Aspects of Biblical Ethics.* Grand Rapids: Eerdmans, 1957.

Nason-Clark, Nancy, and Barbara Fisher-Townsend. *Men Who Batter.* New York: Oxford University Press, 2015.

Neusner, Jacob. *The Mishnah: A New Translation.* New Haven: Yale University Press, 1988.

Newheiser, Jim. *Marriage, Divorce, and Remarriage.* Phillipsburg: P&R, 2017.

———, *Opening Up Proverbs.* Leominster, England: DayOne, 2008.

Ortlund, Raymond C., Jr. *God's Unfaithful Wife: A Biblical Theology of Spiritual Adultery.* Downers Grove, IL: InterVarsity Press, 2002.

———. "Marriage." In *New Dictionary of Biblical Theology*, edited by T. Desmond Alexander, Brian S. Rosner, D. A. Carson, and Graeme Goldsworthy, 654–57. Downers Grove, IL: InterVarsity Press, 2000.

———. *Marriage and the Mystery of the Gospel.* Wheaton, IL: Crossway, 2016.

PCA. "Report of the Ad Interim Committee on Divorce and Remarriage: To the Twentieth General Assembly." *PCA Digest: Position Papers* (1992): 182–295. Accessed July 16, 2020. https://pcahistory.org/pca/digest/studies/divorce-remarriage.pdf.

———. "Appendix B: A Second Marriage Service." In *The Book of Church Order of the Presbyterian Church in America.* 6th ed. Lawrenceville, GA: Office of the Stated Clerk of the General Assembly of the Presbyterian Church in America, 2016.

Phillips, Roderick. *Untying the Knot: A Short History of Divorce.* Cambridge: Cambridge University Press, 1991.

Piper, John. *This Momentary Marriage: A Parable of Permanence*. Wheaton, IL: Crossway, 2009.

———. *What Jesus Demands from the World*. Wheaton, IL: Crossway, 2006.

Plumb, with Susanna Foth Aughtmon. *Need You Now: A Story of Hope*. Nashville: Shoe Publishing, 2014.

Popenoe, David. "The Future of Marriage in America." In *the State of Our Unions 2007: The Social Health of Marriage in America*, 5–12. Piscataway, NJ: National Marriage Project, 2007. Accessed June 13, 2017. http://www.stateofourunions.org/past_issues.php.

Poythress, Vern S. *The Shadow of Christ in the Law of Moses*. Phillipsburg, NJ: Presbyterian and Reformed, 1991.

Pratt, Richard L., Jr. *Designed for Dignity: What God Has Made It Possible for You to Be*. 2nd ed. Phillipsburg, NJ: P&R Publishers, 2000.

Raiffa, Howard. *Negotiation Analysis: The Science and Art of Collaborative Decision Making*. Cambridge, MS: Harvard University Press, 2007.

Regan, Richard J. *Just War: Principles and Cases*. 2nd ed. Washington, DC: Catholic University of America Press, 2013.

Roberts, Barbara. *Not Under Bondage: Biblical Divorce for Abuse, Adultery, and Desertion*. Ballarat, AU: Maschil Press, 2008.

Rosner, Brian S. *Paul, Scripture & Ethics: A Study of 1 Corinthians 5–7*. Vol. 22 of the *Biblical Studies Library*. Grand Rapids: Baker Books, 1999.

Rushdoony, R. J. *The Institutes of Biblical Law*. Nutley, NJ: Presbyterian and Reformed, 1973.

Sande, Ken. *Peacemaking for Families: A Biblical Guide to Managing Conflict in Your Home*. Carol Stream, IL: Tyndale, 2002.

———. *The Peace Maker: A Biblical Guide to Resolving Personal Conflict*. 3rd ed. Grand Rapids: Baker Books, 2004.

Schepard, Andrew I. *Children, Courts, and Custody: Interdisciplinary Models for Divorcing Families*. Cambridge: Cambridge University Press, 2004.

Sells, Benjamin L. *The Soul of the Law*. Rockport, MS: Element, 1994.

Shapiro, Ronald M., and Mark A. Jankowski. *The Power of Nice: How to Negotiate So Everyone Wins—Especially You!* Rev. ed. New York: Wiley, 2001.

Smyth, Bruce M., and Lawrence J. Moloney. "Entrenched Postseparation Parenting Disputes: The Role of Interparental Hatred?" *Family Court Review* 55, no. 3 (July 2017): 404–16.

Society for Human Resource Management. *Harvard Business Essentials: Negotiation.* Boston: Harvard Business Publishing, 2003.

Starnes, Cynthia Lee. *The Marriage Buyout: The Troubled Trajectory of U.S. Alimony Law.* New York: New York University Press, 2014.

Stott, John R. W. *Christian Counterculture: The Message of the Sermon on the Mount.* Bible Speaks Today. Downer's Grove, IL: InterVarsity Press, 1978.

———. *Issues Facing Christians Today.* 4th ed. Grand Rapids: Zondervan, 2006.

———. *Human Rights and Human Wrongs: Major Issues for a New Century.* Grand Rapids: Baker Books, 1999.

———. "Marriage and Divorce." In *Our Social & Sexual Revolution: Major Issues for a New Century,* 133–155. 3rd ed. Grand Rapids: Baker Books, 1999.

Tesler, Pauline H., and Peggy Thompson. *Collaborative Divorce: The Revolutionary New Way to Restructure Your Family, Resolve Legal Issues, and Move On with Your Life.* New York: HarperCollins, 2006.

Tetlow, Elisabeth Meier. *Women, Crime, and Punishment in Ancient Law and Society.* Vol. 1 of *The Ancient Near East.* New York: Continuum, 2004.

Thiselton, Anthony C. *First Corinthians: A Shorter Exegetical and Pastoral Commentary.* Grand Rapids: Eerdmans, 2006.

———. *The First Epistle to the Corinthians: A Commentary on the Greek Text.* The New International Greek Testament Commentary. Grand Rapids: Eerdmans, 2000.

Thompson, Leigh L. *The Mind and Heart of the Negotiator.* 3rd ed. Upper Saddle River, NJ: Pearson Prentice Hall, 2005.

———. *The Truth About Negotiations.* Upper Saddle River, NJ: FT Press, 2007.

Tifft, Larry L. *Battering of Women: The Failure of Intervention and the Case for Prevention.* Boulder, CO: Westview Press, 1993.

Tolman, Richard M., and Jeffrey L. Edleson. "Intervening with Men for Violence Prevention," Chap. 18 in *Sourcebook on Violence Against Women,* ed. Claire M. Tenzetti, Jeffrey L. Edleson, and Raquel Kennedy Bergen. 2nd ed. Los Angeles: Sage, 2011.

Tomson, Peter J. *Paul and the Jewish Law: Halakha in the Letters of the Apostle to the Gentiles.* Minneapolis: Fortress Press, 1990.

Truax, Louise T., and Jeffrey P. Wittmann. "Alienation: Identification Is Not Enough." Session 1 presented at the "AFCC-AAML 2015 Conference on Advanced Issues in Child Custody: Evaluation, Litigation and Settlement." Washington, DC, October 1, 2015.

Turner, Brett R. *Equitable Distribution of Property.* 3 vols. 3rd ed. Thomson-West, 2005, 2017–18 Sup.

Ury, William. *Getting Past No: Negotiating in Difficult Situations.* New York: Bantam, 1991.

———. *Getting to Yes with Yourself (and Other Worthy Opponents).* New York: HarperOne, 2015.

———. *The Power of a Positive No: How to Say No and Still Get to Yes.* New York: Bantam, 2007.

Via, Dan O., and Robert A. J. Gagnon. *Homosexuality and the Bible: Two Views.* Minneapolis: Fortress Press, 2003.

Walker, Lenore E. *The Battered Woman.* New York: Harper, 1979.

———. *The Battered Woman Syndrome.* 3rd ed. New York: Springer, 2009.

Wall, John, Don Browning, William J. Doherty, and Stephen Post, eds. *Marriage, Health, and the Professions: If Marriage Is Good for You, What Does This Mean for Law, Medicine, Ministry, Therapy, and Business?* Grand Rapids: Eerdmans, 2002.

Wallerstein, Judith. "Children of Divorce: The Psychological Tasks of the Child." *American Journal of Orthopsychiatry* 53 (1983): 263–79.

Waltke, Bruce K. *Genesis: A Commentary.* Grand Rapids: Zondervan, 2001.

———. *An Old Testament Theology: An Exegetical, Canonical, and Thematic Approach.* Grand Rapids: Zondervan, 2007.

Webb, Stuart G., and Ron D. Ousky. *The Collaborative Way to Divorce: The Revolutionary Method That Results in Less Stress, Lower Costs, and Happier Kids—Without Going to Court.* New York: Hudson Street Press, 2006.

Wenham, Gordon. *The Book of Leviticus.* New International Commentary on the Old Testament. Grand Rapids: Eerdmans, 1979.

Westminster Confession of Faith. Reprint. Glasgow: Free Presbyterian Publications, 1983.

Witte, John, Jr. *From Sacrament to Contract: Marriage, Religion, and Law in the Western Tradition.* Louisville: Westminster John Knox, 1997.

Wood, Robert G., Brian Goesling, and Sarah Avellar. "The Effects of Marriage on Health: A Synthesis of Recent Research Evidence." Office of the Assistant Secretary for Planning and Evaluation, U.S. Department of Health and Human Services. Mathematica Policy Research, 2007. Accessed July 16, 2020. http://aspe.hhs.gov/hsp/07/marriageonhealth/index.htm.

Wright, Christopher. *Deuteronomy.* New International Biblical Commentary on the Old Testament. Peabody, MA: Hendrickson, 1996.

———. *Old Testament Ethics for the People of God.* Downers Grove, IL: InterVarsity Press, 2004.

Wright, Larry. "Interviewing Children in Child Custody Cases." *Journal of the American Academy of Matrimonial Lawyers* 18 (2002): 295–309.

Yoder, John Howard. *Christian Attitudes to War, Peace, and Revolution.* Edited by Theodore J. Koontz and Andy Alexis-Baker. Grand Rapids: Brazos Press, 2009.

———. *When War Is Unjust: Being Honest in Just-War Thinking.* Eugene, OR: Wipf & Stock, 2001.

Endnotes

PREFACE

1. John M. Frame, *The Doctrine of the Knowledge of God* (Phillipsburg, NJ: P&R, 1987), 76.
2. John M. Frame, *The Doctrine of the Christian Life* (Phillipsburg, NJ: P&R, 2008), 33.
3. See Arthur F. Holmes, "The Just War," in *War: Four Christian Views*, ed. Robert G. Clouse (Downers Grove, IL: InterVarsity Press, 1981), 120–35.

CHAPTER 1

1. WCF 1.1; 1.6: "The whole counsel of God concerning all things necessary for His own glory, man's salvation, faith and life, is either expressly set down in Scripture, or by good and necessary consequence may be deduced from Scripture."
2. John Howard Yoder, *Christian Attitudes to War, Peace, and Revolution*, ed. Theodore J. Koontz and Andy Alexis-Baker (Grand Rapids: Brazos Press, 2009), 97–98; John Howard Yoder, *When War Is Unjust: Being Honest in Just-War Thinking* (Eugene, OR: Wipf & Stock, 2001), 150–51.
3. Yoder, *Christian Attitudes to War*, 98.
4. In practice, the requirement of at least two witnesses to establish a charge (Deut. 19:15) and the severe penalty for bearing false witness (vv. 16–21) would make any prosecution and punishment difficult.
5. David Instone-Brewer, *Divorce and Remarriage in the Bible: The Social and Literary Context* (Grand Rapids: Eerdmans, 2002), 94; David Instone-Brewer, *Divorce and Remarriage in the Church: Biblical Solutions for Pastoral Realities* (Downers Grove, IL: InterVarsity Press, 2003), 56. The man and woman would become betrothed through a legal agreement, customarily a written document (*ketubah*), with the bride's father that contained the husband's obligations to his wife and a sum of money as the marriage obligation to which she was entitled in case of divorce or his death.
6. Num. 5:11–31 indicates that death is not always the legal penalty for adultery.
7. G. K. Beale and D. A. Carson, eds., *Commentary on the New Testament Use of the Old Testament* (Grand Rapids: Baker, 2007), 705–6, 709–10. The goal of church discipline is redemptive rather than punitive, restorative rather than vindictive (cf. Prov. 3:11–12; Matt. 18:15–20; 2 Cor. 2:5–11; 1 Tim. 5:20; Heb. 12:5-11).
8. See John M. Frame, *The Doctrine of the Christian Life* (Phillipsburg, NJ: P&R Publishers, 2008), 774–75n8, regarding divorce as a substitute for death. John Murray affirms that adultery retains "its heinousness as a violation of God's law," but "our Lord instituted divorce as the proper recourse for the innocent spouse who had been wronged by adultery on the part of the other. By implication our Lord abrogated the death penalty for adultery." *Principles of Conduct: Aspects of Biblical Ethics* (Grand Rapids: Eerdmans, 1957), 54–55.
9. See Rom. 1:18–32; 1 Cor. 5:9–11; 6:9–10; Gal. 5:19–21; Eph. 5:3, 5, 7–17; Rev. 21:8; 22:15.
10. See Linda D. Elrod and Robert G. Spector, "A Review of the Year in Family Law 2017–2018: Courts Tackle Immigration, Jurisdiction, and the Usual Family Law Disputes," *FLQ* 52, no. 4 (Winter 2019): 519, 600-608, chart 4.
11. Mal. 2:13–16. Scripture sometimes symbolically depicts entering into a marriage covenant as a man covering a woman with his garment (Ruth 3:9; Ezek. 16:8). In stark contrast, God says "the man who hates and divorces . . . covers his garment with violence" (Mal. 2:16 ESV).
12. Similarly, Prov. 2:17 describes an adulteress who seeks to seduce others as one "who forsakes the companion of her youth and forgets the covenant of her God."
13. Gordon D. Hugenberger, *Marriage as a Covenant: Biblical Law and Ethics as Developed from Malachi* (Grand Rapids: Baker Books, 1998), 51, 67–76, 83.
14. Hugenberger, *Marriage as a Covenant*, 76.
15. See *m. Git.* 9:3: "The text of the writ of divorce [is as follows]: 'Lo, you are permitted to any man.' R. Judah says, '[In Aramaic]: Let this be from me your writ of divorce, letter of dismissal, and deed of liberation, that you may marry anyone you want.'" Jacob Neusner, *The Mishnah: A New Translation* (New Haven: Yale University Press, 1988), 485.
16. Beale and Carson, *Commentary on the New Testament Use*, 23.

17. See *m. Git.* 9:10, Neusner, *Mishnah*, 487.

18. Josephus reports that a Palestinian Jew who desires to divorce his wife "for any cause whatsoever (and many such causes happen among men), let him in writing give assurance that he will never use her as his wife anymore; for by this means she may be at liberty to marry another husband, although before this bill of divorce be given, she is not permitted so to do." *Antiq.* 4.8.23 (4.253), in *The Works of Josephus: Complete and Unabridged*, trans. William Whiston (Peabody, MA: Hendrickson, 1987), 120.

19. See Instone-Brewer, *Divorce and Remarriage in the Church*, 58–59, 145–46. Instone-Brewer notes that any first-century reader of Mark's account (10:2) would have mentally added "for 'Any Cause'" to complete the recorded question "Is it lawful for a man to divorce his wife?" (59).

20. Blomberg, "Marriage, Divorce, Remarriage," 171; Blomberg, *Matthew*, 291. Darrel L. Bock comments that Jesus is "in effect saying that if you make a vow to marry and be faithful to your spouse before God, then breaking that vow and entering into another marital union can be called adultery because the original vow was not kept." *Luke: 9:51–24:53*, vol. 3B of Baker Exegetical Commentary on the New Testament (Grand Rapids: Baker Academic, 1996), 1356.

21. See Instone-Brewer, *Divorce and Remarriage in the Church*, 59–60.

22. Instone-Brewer, *Divorce and Remarriage in the Church*, 61. Instone-Brewer notes that Christian interpreters make the mistake of not giving appropriate weight to the context of the phrase. "Nothing except 'sexual immorality' was a question about the meaning of Deuteronomy 24:1. Jesus used exactly the same words as the Shammaites in exactly the same context (a debate about Deut. 24:1) with exactly the same people (the Pharisees) in the same time and place (first-century Palestine), so we have to conclude that Jesus and the Shammaites meant the same thing—there is only one valid type of divorce in Deuteronomy 24:1. Neither he nor the Shammaites implied by this that there is only one valid type of divorce *in the whole of Scripture*" (98, emphasis original).

23. See Craig S. Keener, *A Commentary on the Gospel of Matthew* (Grand Rapids: Eerdmans, 1999), 466–67; see *m. Yebam.* 2:8; *m. Sotah* 5:1, Neusner, *Mishnah*, 341, 454.

24. Matt. 5:32; Mark 10:11–12; Luke 16:18. Blomberg, *Matthew*, 289; I. Howard Marshall, *The Gospel of Luke: A Commentary on the Greek Text*, New International Greek Testament Commentary (Grand Rapids: Eerdmans, 1978), 631; Joel B. Green, *The Gospel of Luke*, New International Commentary on the New Testament (Grand Rapids: Eerdmans, 1997), 603.

25. Blomberg, "Marriage, Divorce, Remarriage," 177; Blomberg, *Matthew*, 292. See also D. A. Carson, *Matthew: Chapters 13–28*, Expositor's Bible Commentary (Grand Rapids: Zondervan, 1995), 413; John R. W. Stott, *Christian Counter-Culture: The Message of the Sermon on the Mount*, Bible Speaks Today (Downers Grove, IL: InterVarsity Press, 1978), 96–97; Frame, *Christian Life*, 764, 774–76; Bock, *Luke: 9:51–24:53*, 1358; Instone-Brewer, *Divorce and Remarriage in the Church*, 60.

26. Frame, *Christian Life*, 775–76. In a report on divorce and remarriage, the PCA asserts that when such conduct becomes a substitute for fulfilling a spouse's marital conjugal rights, the conduct may not only harm the marriage relationship but may also be understood to break the one-flesh union as an "equivalent of *porneia*." PCA, "Report of the Ad Interim Committee on Divorce and Remarriage: To the Twentieth General Assembly, *PCA Digest: Position Papers* (1992), 182–295. Additionally, note the tenth commandment's demand that "you shall not covet your neighbor's wife" (Ex. 20:17).

27. Blomberg, *Matthew*, 110–11; Frame, *Christian Life*, 775, 776.

28. Leon Morris asserts that, "Jesus is not here suggesting a law for society at large. He is saying that this is how God's people regard marriage." *The Gospel According to St. Luke*, Tyndale New Testament Commentaries (Grand Rapids: Eerdmans, 1974), 251. In discussing Matt. 5:32 Blomberg argues that (1) "divorce itself, except when it is for sexual sin, is metaphorical adultery–faithlessness to the person to whom one promised permanent loyalty," (2) "the adultery (faithlessness) occurred at the time of divorce," and (3) "even if one divorces for unbiblical reasons and remarries, such a person does not enter into an ongoing adulterous relationship. The commission of adultery is a one-time act." "Marriage, Divorce, Remarriage," 174–75. "There is no indication here that a second marriage, even following an illegitimate divorce, is seen as permanently adulterous. Divorced Christians who have remarried should not commit the sin of a second divorce to try to resume relations with a previous spouse (see again Deut. 24:1–4) but should begin afresh to observe God's standards by remaining faithful to their current partners." Blomberg, *Matthew*, 111. In his discussion of Matt. 19:9, John

Jefferson Davis notes that the grammatical sense of "commits adultery" "would imply that while divorce and remarriage apart from unchastity constitute an *act* of adultery, they do not necessarily constitute a continuing *state* of adultery. This conclusion should encourage churches in their efforts to restore to full fellowship those couples whose divorces and subsequent remarriages were in violation of the divine standards." *Evangelical Ethics: Issues Facing the Church Today*, 3rd ed. (Phillipsburg, NJ: P&R, 2004), 106.

29. Apart from the exception clause, a significant difference between Matt. 5:32 and Luke 16:18 is that Matthew asserts that the one who divorces his wife makes or causes her to commit adultery, while Luke states the man himself is guilty of adultery if he marries another woman. Marshall, *Luke*, 630–31. The underlying assumption of Matt. 5:32 and Luke 16:18 "is that divorce will lead inevitably to remarriage." Bock, *Luke: 9:51–24:53*, 1357.

30. Stott, *Our Social & Sexual Revolution*, 144. "We may assume, then, that Mark 10:2–12 and Luke 16:18 omit this exception because they take it for granted." See also Blomberg, "Marriage, Divorce, Remarriage," 163. Davis notes that "It is likely that Jesus, like most preachers and teachers, repeated the same material in slightly different forms on various occasions. The differences would reflect not a fundamental change in content, but an adaptation of the message to different contexts and audiences." Davis, *Evangelical Ethics*, 105.

31. Carson, *Matthew: Chapters 13–28*, 412.

32. Blomberg, *Matthew*, 111.

33. Keener, 192.

34. Bock, *Luke: 9:51–24:53*, 1358 n27.

35. Blomberg, 164–65.

36. Ancient Jews, Greeks, and Romans "almost universally agreed that lawful divorce granted a person the right to remarry," and "Jesus' words would almost certainly have been taken as permission for remarriage when divorce was permitted, i.e., after marital unfaithfulness. In other cases divorce causes adultery." Blomberg, *Matthew*, 111; Keener asserts that "a valid divorce by definition included the right to remarry, as is attested by ancient divorce contracts . . . and the very meaning of the term." *Matthew*, 469. Indeed, both parties may remarry after divorce on the ground of sexual immorality. Frame writes that following divorce for sexual immorality, "with John Murray, I agree that remarriage is permitted to both parties, both the innocent party and the guilty party. While it may be best in many cases for the two to be reconciled and remarried to one another, they are not obligated to do this. It is not wrong for them to seek other partners, for divorce has annulled the original marriage bonds. In this case (which, I reiterate, is an exception to the general rule), a second marriage is not adulterous." *Christian Life*, 777.

37. Blomberg, "Marriage, Divorce, Remarriage," 192.

CHAPTER 2

1. Craig L. Blomberg, *1 Corinthians*, NIV Application Commentary (Grand Rapids: Zondervan, 1994), 134·

2. Gordon Fee writes that "Divorce in Greco-Roman culture could be 'legalized' by means of documents; but more often it simply happened. In this culture divorce was divorce, whether established by a document or not." *First Epistle to the Corinthians*, 293–94.

3. Adams, *Marriage, Divorce, and Remarriage*, 41. Adams also notes that the "modern view of separation is an anti-biblical substitution for the biblical requirement of reconciliation or (in some cases) divorce. These two options alone are given by God. Modern separation settles nothing" (33n3). "This wicked substitute for the biblical solution (peace by reconciliation or by divorce) fights against true peace. All is held in limbo. It deceives by its temporary sense of relief, (often mistaken for peace). But nothing is settled (made truly peaceful) by it" (49).

4. Adams, 40n1.

5. C. K. Barrett, *The First Epistle to the Corinthians*, Black's New Testament Commentaries (Peabody, MA: Hendrickson, 2006), 164–65; Collins, *First Corinthians*, 266; Fee, *First Epistle to the Corinthians*, 299–302.

6. See WCF 14.1; 14.2; 25.2; 38.6; 2 Tim. 3:14–15; cf. Rom. 9:1–13.

7. See Garland, *1 Corinthians*, 291–93; Barrett, *First Epistle to the Corinthians*, 166.

8. The passage we are discussing relates to mixed (believer/unbeliever) marriages. However, John Frame writes, "Through the discipline of the church, a person recognized as a believer at one time can, through excommunication, be later regarded as an unbeliever. So a marriage between two believers can, by the action of the church, become a marriage between a believer and an unbeliever. Then verse 15 can enter the picture." *Christian Life*, 780.

9. Blomberg, *1 Corinthians*, 140; Davis, *Evangelical Ethics*, 109; Instone-Brewer, *Divorce and Remarriage in the Church*, 112–13. See also Adams, *Marriage, Divorce, and Remarriage*, 48; cf. Fee, *First Epistle to the Corinthians*, 302–3.

10. Blomberg, "Marriage, Divorce, Remarriage," 188; Instone-Brewer, *Divorce and Remarriage in the Bible*, 288–89.

11. Adams, *Marriage, Divorce, and Remarriage*, 48.

12. WCF 24:6 states that "Although the corruption of man be such as is apt to study arguments, unduly to put asunder those whom God hath joined together in marriage; yet nothing but adultery, or *such willful desertion as can no way be remedied by the church or civil magistrate*, is cause sufficient of dissolving the bond of marriage: wherein a public and orderly course of proceeding is to be observed, and the persons concerned in it not left to their own wills and discretion in their own case" (emphasis added). This section is not limited to desertion by an unbelieving spouse; where one spouse—whether an unbeliever or believer—irremediably abandons the other, the abandoned Christian spouse would be justified in pursuing a divorce. This will be discussed further in chapter five.

13. Adams, *Marriage, Divorce, and Remarriage*, 47. Adams goes on to say: "So then, the general principle seems clear enough: where there is no consent (agreement) by the unbeliever to continue the marriage (vv. 12, 13) but (on the contrary) there is a desire to dissolve it, the Christian must not stand in the way of the separation. Paul uses a permissive imperative: 'let him separate.' This is a command; it is the one instance in which divorce is *required*" (48, emphasis original).

14. John Frame says, "What is needed is a focus on the question of whether the unbeliever makes a credible claim to be upholding his marital vows. When that claim is no longer credible, because of physical or verbal abuse, emotional entanglements with people other than the spouse, failure to provide, literal desertion, and so on, the church may declare the original marriage null and void and the partners free to remarry. But, as the WCF says, these forms of 'desertion' must be such as 'can no way be remedied by the church, or civil magistrate.' The church should recognize divorces in these cases only when all available remedies have failed." *Christian Life*, 781. See also Davis, *Evangelical Ethics*, 110.

15. Keener, *Matthew*, 191.

16. Blomberg, *Matthew*, 293.

17. Keener, *Matthew*, 192. David Atkinson writes that "any action which constitutes unfaithfulness to the marriage covenant so persistent and unrepentant that reconciliation becomes impossible may be sufficient to break the bond of marriage and so may release the other partner from their covenant promise." *To Have and To Hold*, 154.

18. R. J. Rushdoony, *The Institutes of Biblical Law* (Nutley, NJ: Presbyterian and Reformed, 1973), 403.

CHAPTER 3

1. MNADV, *A Vision for the Future*, 1; see also Barbara Roberts, *Not Under Bondage: Biblical Divorce for Abuse, Adultery, and Desertion* (Balarat, AU: Maschil Press, 2008), 18–24; Justin S. Holcomb and Lindsey A. Holcomb, *Is It My Fault: Hope and Healing for Those Suffering Domestic Violence* (Chicago: Moody, 2014), 55–59.

2. Westminster Larger Catechism 136; see also Heidelberg Catechism 106, which states, "In forbidding murder, God teaches us that He abhors the cause thereof, such as envy, hatred, anger, and desire of revenge; and that He accounts all these as murder." Joel R. Beeke and Sinclair B. Ferguson, eds., *Reformed Confessions Harmonized* (Grand Rapids: Baker Books, 1999), 156.

3. Prov. 12:18; 15:1,18; 27:3–4; 29:20, 22; cf. 1 Sam. 25:9–42; Prov. 16:32; 17:27; 19:11.

4. Westminster Larger Catechism 135; see also Heidelberg Catechism 105 teaching that in the sixth commandment God requires "that neither in thoughts, nor words, nor gestures, much less in deeds, I dishonor, hate, wound, or kill my neighbor, by myself or by another; but that I lay aside all desire of revenge; also, that I hurt not myself, nor willfully expose myself to any danger. Wherefore also

the magistrate is armed with the sword to prevent murder." Beeke and Sinclair, *Reformed Confessions Harmonized*, 156.

5. James Alsdurf and Phyllis Alsdurf, *Battered into Submission: The Tragedy of Wife Abuse in the Christian Home* (Downers Grove, IL: InterVarsity Press, 1989), 128–29.

6. See Kroeger and Nason-Clark, *No Place for Abuse*, esp. 13–37.

7. Two publications provided general background and statistical information cited in this section: *It Shouldn't Hurt to Go Home: The Domestic Violence Victim's Handbook* (Lanham, MD: MNADV, 2001), accessed October 27, 2017, http://mnadv.org/_mnadvWeb/wp-content/uploads/2011/07/shouldnthurt2013.pdf, and *A Vision for the Future: Recommendations for a More Coordinated Community Response to Domestic Violence in Maryland* (Lanham, MD: MNADV, 20.

8. *It Shouldn't Hurt to Go Home*, MNADV, 2; Kroeger and Nason-Clark, *No Place for Abuse*, 82.

9. Kroeger and Nason-Clark, *No Place for Abuse*, 119, esp. 13–37.

10. Alsdurf and Alsdurf, *Battered Into Submission*, 108; Kroeger and Nason-Clark, *No Place for Abuse*, 33, 37, 83.

11. The "Battered Spouse Syndrome" is sometimes used as a defense in certain criminal actions. The Syndrome may help the court understand why a victim may not have reported abuse previously, why a victim may have remained with or reconciled with her abuser in the past, and why seemingly minor threats or incidents may raise fear in the abuse victim.

12. Alsdurf and Alsdurf, *Battered Into Submission*, 29–30.

13. Miles, *Violence in Families: What Every Christian Needs to Know* (Minneapolis: Augsburg, 2002), 32.

14. See MNADV, *It Shouldn't Hurt to Go Home*, 12.

15. See MNADV, 13.

16. Concerning spiritual abuse, see Miles, *Violence in Families*, 35–36.

17. Miles, 34.

18. Miles, 34.

19. MNADV, *A Vision for the Future*, 6.

20. MNADV, *It Shouldn't Hurt to Go Home*, 7. For helpful guidance in developing a personalized safety plan, see Holcomb, *Is It My Fault?*, 187–97.

21. Kroeger and Nason-Clark, *No Place for Abuse*, 35–36.

22. Kroeger and Nason-Clark, 36.

23. Miles, *Violence in Families*, 57–68.

24. Miles, 62, 68.

25. Alsdurf and Alsdurf, *Battered into Submission*, 34–37.

26. See Miles, *Violence in Families*, 29–32.

27. Lenore Walker, *The Battered Woman* (New York: Harper, 1979), 42–54.

28. See, e.g., Roberts, *Not Under Bondage*, 84: "Some authors have suggested that *porneia* could also cover domestic violence, but this is not really sustainable. *Porneia* is only used figuratively for spiritual infidelity (human worshiping a false god). When it refers to human relationships it always refers to sexual sin, not some non-sexual variety of covenantal violation. It is important to recognize that Jesus did not use the word *moicheia* ('adultery') but the broader word *porneia* and therefore all forms of illicit sex (including sodomy, incest, enforced prostitution, bestiality, marital rape) qualify as exceptions as well as adultery. This is quite relevant to abusive marriages, as such practices sometimes occur in marital abuse scenarios."

29. Davis, *Evangelical Ethics*, 110.

30. *Painter v. Painter*, 113 Md. App. 504, 522, 688 A.2d 479 (1997).

31. Holcomb, *Is It My Fault?*, 136–37.

32. Jones, 204.

33. Instone-Brewer, *Divorce and Remarriage in the Bible*, 99–110. If a man took a Hebrew slave or bonded woman as a wife, he was not permitted to "diminish her food, her clothing, or her marital rights" if he took another wife; "if he does not do these three things for her, she shall go out for nothing, without payment of money" (Ex. 21:10–11; cf. Deut. 21:10–14). Presenting an "argument from major to minor," Instone-Brewer argues that the rights of the slave wife were the rights of both partners in a marriage: "If a slave wife has these rights, then surely a free wife would also have equivalent rights.

And: If a wife has these rights, then surely a husband would also have equivalent rights" (100–101); see also Instone-Brewer, *Divorce and Remarriage in the Church*, 35–37.

34. Instone-Brewer, *Divorce and Remarriage in the Bible*, 106–10.

35. Rushdoony, *Institutes of Biblical Law*, 403. Rushdoony notes Paul's reference to this law in 1 Cor 7:3–5, where Paul wrote that the failure to give each other conjugal rights defrauded the marital partner, and Rushdoony said it could also constitute a form of desertion. See also Instone-Brewer, *Divorce and Remarriage in the Bible*, 99–110, 192–97; Köstenberger, *God, Marriage, and Family*, 41, 355n25.

36. Instone-Brewer, *Divorce and Remarriage in the Bible*, 184; see also 166, 181–82, 184–88; Instone-Brewer, *Divorce and Remarriage in the Church*, 95–96, 99. Similarly, it has been asserted that "The fact that Jesus says nothing about non-'no-fault' divorces is probably best understood as an acceptance of those grounds as outlined in Exod. 21:10–11 (hence Matt. 19:9's exception and Paul's instructions in 1 Cor. 7:10–16)." Beale and Carson, *Commentary on the New Testament*, 199.

37. Instone-Brewer, *Divorce and Remarriage in the Bible*, 192–97, 212; see also Rosner, *Paul, Scripture & Ethics*, 159; Tomson, *Paul and the Jewish Law*, 107.

38. Köstenberger, *God, Marriage, and Family*, 355n25.

39. WCF 24.6.

40. Robert Nisbet, *The Present Age: Progress and Anarchy in Modern America* (New York: Harper & Row, 1988), 84, quoted in Craig M. Gay, *The Way of the (Modern) World: Or, Why It's Tempting to Live as if God Doesn't Exist* (Grand Rapids: Eerdmans, 1998), 193.

41. The Barna Group study found that "born again Christians who are not evangelical were indistinguishable from the national average on the matter of divorce: 33% have been married and divorced"; that Catholics (28%) and evangelical Christians (26%) were among those with the "lowest likelihood of having been divorced"; and that "when evangelicals and non-evangelical born again Christians are combined into an aggregate class of born again adults, their divorce figure is statistically identical to that of non-born again adults: 32% versus 33%, respectively." "New Marriage and Divorce Statistics Released," *Barna Update*, March 31, 2008, https://www.barna.com/research/new-marriage-and-divorce-statistics-released. Shaunti Feldhahn discusses the Barna data and several other studies that show a marked reduction in the divorce rate among Catholics and evangelical Christians who attend church. *The Good News About Marriage: Debunking Discouraging Myths About Marriage and Divorce* (Colorado Springs: Multnomah, 2014), 66–91. The active practice of faith, shown by church attendance and other activities rather than reported beliefs alone, makes a significant difference in divorce rate.

42. Adams, *Marriage, Divorce, and Remarriage*, 23. See Jer. 3:6–8.

CHAPTER 4

1. The names of clients and their spouses have been changed.

2. *Merriam-Webster's Collegiate Dictionary*, 11th ed. (Springfield, MA: Merriam-Webster, 2003).

3. Yoder, *When War Is Unjust*, 152–53; Yoder, *Christian Attitudes to War*, 90.

4. Yoder, *Christian Attitudes to War*, 99.

5. Yoder, *When War Is Unjust*, 152. Augustine similarly notes "The real evils in war are love of violence, revengeful cruelty, fierce and implacable enmity, wild resistance, and the lust of power, and such like;" *Reply to Faustus the Manichean 22*, in *St. Augustine: The Writings Against the Manichaeans, and Against the Donatists*, vol. 4 of *NPNF1*, ed. Philip Schaff (Peabody, MA: Hendrickson, 1994), 301.

6. Stott, *Issues Facing Christians Today*, 107.

7. See also Lev. 19:17–19; Ps. 7:4–5; Prov. 20:22; 24:17–18; 27:5; Matt. 5:43–48; 18:15; Gal. 6:1.

8. Murray, *Principles of Conduct*, 179.

9. Murray, 179.

10. Murray, 179.

11. Murray, 179.

12. See also Prov. 10:12: "Hatred stirs up dissension, but love covers a multitude of sins"; Matt. 6:12, 14–15; 18:21–35 (the parable of the unforgiving servant); Col. 3:12–14.

13. Regan, *Just War*, 86.

14. Yoder, *Christian Attitudes to War*, 90–91; Yoder, *When War Is Unjust*, 152–53.
15. Deut. 6:5–6; Matt. 22:37–40; Mark 12:29–31; Luke 10:26–28; Rom. 13:9; Gal. 5:14; James 2:8.
16. A contrite King David acknowledged that the sacrifices of God that he will not despise are "a broken spirit; a broken and contrite heart" (Ps. 51:16–19).
17. WCF 16.7.
18. 1 Chron. 28:9; Ps. 139:23–24; 2 Tim. 3:16–17.
19. Yoder, *Christian Attitudes to War*, 99; cf. Yoder, *When War Is Unjust*, 152–53).
20. This sentence was influenced in part by lyrics to the song "Even Though," written by Christa Wells (More Than Rubies, 2013).

CHAPTER 5

1. Davis, *Evangelical Ethics*, 111.
2. "A bruised reed he will not break, and a faintly burning wick he will not quench; he will faithfully bring forth justice" (Isa. 42:3). God's faithful servant is called to minister to—and plead justice for—the weak, needy, and those whose hope is wavering. The "bruised reed" image also aptly serves as the logo of Prison Fellowship.
3. Regan, *Just War*, 65.
4. Adams, *Marriage, Divorce, and Remarriage*, 57–59. The WCF states that "Church censures are necessary for the reclaiming and gaining of offending brethren; for deterring of others from the like offences; for purging out of that leaven which might infect the whole lump; for vindicating the honor of Christ, and the holy profession of the gospel; and for preventing the wrath of God, which might justly fall upon the church, if they should suffer his covenant, and the seals thereof, to be profaned by notorious and obstinate offenders" (WCF 30.3).
5. In order to attain appropriate church censures or discipline, the church officers may use admonition, suspension of the offender from partaking in the Lord's Supper, and excommunication as the circumstances warrant (WCF 30.4).
6. See also Davis, *Evangelical Ethics*, 111–12, regarding someone divorced on nonbiblical grounds who seeks to remarry: "In such cases the improperly divorced believer is obligated to repent of the divorce and the sinful behavior that contributed to it, and to seek reconciliation with the spouse (1 Cor. 7:11), assuming the spouse has remained unmarried. The process of reconciliation would include making restoration for personal and financial obligations that may have been abandoned and seeking the offended spouse's forgiveness. If the spouse persistently refuses all attempts at reconciliation, he has *de facto* placed himself in the position of an unbelieving, deserting spouse, and the partner who has been seeking reconciliation is free to remarry another. If either of the spouses remarries without seeking reconciliation and forgiveness—in violation of 1 Corinthians 7:11—he or she commits adultery against the former partner (Matt. 19:9; Mark 10:11). The spouse remaining single may then be free to remarry, after having sought forgiveness for any wrongs committed in the prior marriage."
7. Blomberg, "Marriage, Divorce, Remarriage," 193–94.
8. See Lenore E. A. Walker, *The Battered Woman Syndrome*, 3rd ed. (New York: Springer, 2009); and Larry L. Tifft, *Battering of Women: The Failure of Intervention and the Case for Prevention* (Boulder, CO: Westview Press, 1993).
9. Holcomb, *Is It My Fault?*, 89.
10. Alsdurf, *Battered Into Submission*, 100–101.
11. Kroeger and Nason-Clark, *No Place for Abuse*, 115. See also Miles, *Violence in Families*, 76: "Forgiveness is the decision on the part of a person who has been abused, betrayed, or wronged to let go of, or put aside, the justifiable anger, bitterness, and hurt that arises from being victimized."
12. Alsdurf, *Battered Into Submission*, 107–8.
13. Newheiser, *Marriage, Divorce, and Remarriage*, 261.
14. Holcomb, *Is It My Fault?*, 202–3.
15. Newheiser, *Marriage, Divorce, and Remarriage*, 251–52.
16. Adams, *Marriage, Divorce, and Remarriage*, 57.
17. Frame, *Christian Life*, 770.

18. Instone-Brewer, *Divorce and Remarriage in the Church*, 105.

CHAPTER 6

1. See Md. Code Ann., Fam. Law § 1-201(b) (2019 Repl. Vol.). The state's residence requirement must be satisfied; typically, one of the spouses must have resided in the state for a specified period of time or the cause of action must have occurred in the state.

2. Personal jurisdiction is necessary to satisfy Constitutional due process requirements and is a matter of fairness in assuring that the party from whom relief such as alimony or a monetary award is due has at least "minimum contacts" with the state making the award. Generally, personal jurisdiction may be exercised by a state "as to any cause of action over a person domiciled in, served with process in . . . or who maintains his principal place of business in this state." Md. Code Ann., Cts. & Jud. Proc. § 6-102 (2016). A court lacking personal jurisdiction may still award alimony to the extent of property owned in the state by the nonresident defendant. It is important to be familiar with a state's requirements concerning subject matter and personal jurisdiction.

3. Md. Code Ann., Fam. Law, § 11-106(a)(2) (2019 Repl. Vol.); *Connecticut*: Conn. Gen. Stat. § 46b-83(a) (2017); *D.C.*: D.C. Code § 16-913(c) and §16-911(a)(1) (2016).

4. In addition to a temporary maintenance award, "the court may award such sum as may be necessary to enable a spouse to pay the expenses of job training and education." Tenn. Code Ann. § 36-5-121(b) (2017).

5. *Karmand v. Karmand*, 145 Md. App. 317, 327, 802 A.2d 1106 (2002). The UMDA (1973) would limit alimony awards to only situations where the court finds that the spouse seeking alimony both "(1) lacks sufficient property to provide for himself; and (2) is unable to support himself through appropriate employment or is the custodian of a child whose condition or circumstances make it appropriate that the custodian not be required to seek employment outside the home." UMDA (1973), §308 (a).

6. *New Jersey*: The payee's plan must show "the scope of rehabilitation, the steps to be taken, and the time frame, including a period of employment during which rehabilitation will occur." N.J. Stat. Ann. § 2A:34-23(d) (2017).

7. *Nevada's* statute is expansive in allowing the court to require payment of certain rehabilitative expenses in addition to any alimony that's awarded: "(1) Testing of the recipient's skills relating to a job, career or profession; (2) Evaluation of the recipient's abilities and goals relating to a job, career or profession; (3) Guidance for the recipient in establishing a specific plan for training or education relating to a job, career or profession; (4) Subsidization of an employer's costs incurred in training the recipient; (5) Assisting the recipient to search for a job; or (6) Payment of the costs of tuition, books and fees for: (I) The equivalent of a high school diploma; (II) College courses which are directly applicable to the recipient's goals for his or her career; or (III) Courses of training in skills desirable for employment." Nev. Rev. Stat. § 125.150(11) (2015).

8. *New Jersey*: N.J. Stat. Ann. § 2A:34-23(c) (2017).

9. *Indiana*: Ind. Code § 31-15-7-2(3) (2016).

10. In *New Mexico*, the court's award of rehabilitative spousal support "may include a specific rehabilitation plan . . . and may condition continuation of the support upon compliance with that plan." N.M. Stat. § 40-4-7(B) (2017).

11. *Massachusetts*: Mass. Gen. Laws ch. 208, § 50(b) (2017).

12. *Maine*: Me. Rev. Stat. Ann. tit. 19-A, § 951-A(2)(B) (2016).

13. *Florida*: Fla. Stat. § 61.08(5) (2017).

14. *Florida*: "Permanent alimony may be awarded following a marriage of long duration if such an award is appropriate upon consideration of the factors . . . , a marriage of moderate duration if such an award is appropriate based upon clear and convincing evidence . . . , or following a marriage of short duration if there are written findings of exceptional circumstances. In awarding permanent alimony, the court shall include a finding that no other form of alimony is fair and reasonable under the circumstances of the parties." Fla. Stat. § 61.08(8) (2017).

15. Md. Code Ann., Fam. Law §11-106 (c) (2019 Repl. Vol.).

16. *Tennessee*: Tenn. Code Ann. § 36-5-121(h)(2&3) (2017). In addition to other forms of alimony, *New Mexico* permits "(d) a single sum to be paid in one or more installments that specifies definite

amounts, subject only to the death of the receiving spouse; or (e) a single sum to be paid in one or more installments that specifies definite amounts, not subject to any contingencies, including the death of the receiving spouse. N.M. Stat. § 40-4-7(B) (2017). *South Carolina*: Lump-sum alimony terminates "only upon the death of the supported spouse, but not terminable or modifiable based upon remarriage or changed circumstances in the future." S.C. Code Ann. § 20-3-130(B)(2) (2017).

17. *Blaine v. Blaine*, 97 Md. App. 689, 701, 632 A.2d 191 (1993), *aff'd* 336 Md. 49, 646 A.2d 413 (1994); see also *Turisi v. Sanzaro*, 308 Md. 515, 521-522, 520 A.2d 1080 (1987).

18. *Maine*: Me. Rev. Stat. Ann. tit. 19-A, § 952-A(2)(D) (2016).

19. *Turrisi v. Sanzaro*, 308 Md. 515, 529-530, 520 A.2d 1080 (1987).

20. *Oregon*: Or. Rev. Stat. § 107.105(1)(d)(B) (2015). *Massachusetts*: Mass. Gen. Laws ch. 208 § 48 (2017).

21. *Freeman v. Freeman*, 318 S.C. 265, 457 S.E.2d 3 (S.C. App., 1995); The purpose of reimbursement alimony "may include, but is not limited to, circumstances where the court finds it necessary and desirable to reimburse the supported spouse from the future earnings of the payer spouse based upon circumstances or events that occurred during the marriage." *South Carolina*: S.C. Code Ann. § 20-3-130(B)(4) (2017).

22. *Utah*: Utah Code Ann. § 30-3-5(8)(g) (2017).

23. *Maine*: Me. Rev. Stat. Ann. tit. 19-A, § 952-A(2)(C) (2016).

24. ALI, *Principles of the Law: Family Dissolution; Analysis and Recommendations* (Philadelphia: ALI, 2000) §5.02, cmt a., 789.

25. A third primary compensable loss is loss of earning capacity during marriage that continues post divorce due to caregiving for a third party in fulfillment of a moral obligation.

26. ALI *Principles*, §5.02, cmt a., 788.

27. ALI *Principles*, §5.04, 804.

28. ALI *Principles*, §5.05, 833.

29. ALI *Principles*, §5.05, cmt a., 835; §5.02(3), 787; cmt f., 792.

30. ALI *Principles*, §5.02; §5.04.

31. ALI *Principles*, §5.02(2), 787.

32. ALI *Principles*, §5.04(2), 804.

33. *FLQ* 52, no. 4 (Winter 2019), 582-85.

34. Md. Code Ann., Fam. Law §11-106 (b) (2019 Repl. Vol.). Maryland's twelfth factor ("whether the award would cause a spouse who is a resident of a related institution as defined in §19-301 of the Health–General Article and from whom alimony is sought to become eligible for medical assistance earlier than would otherwise occur") does not appear to have any other state counterpart and is of limited applicability.

35. The UMDA (1973) lists some factors: "(1) the financial resources of the party seeking maintenance, including marital property apportioned to him, his ability to meet his needs independently, and the extent to which a provision for support of a child living with the party includes a sum for that party as custodian; (2) the time necessary to acquire sufficient education or training to enable the party seeking maintenance to find appropriate employment; (3) the standard of living established during the marriage; (4) the duration of the marriage; (5) the age and the physical and emotional condition of the spouse seeking maintenance; and (6) the ability of the spouse from whom maintenance is sought to meet his needs while meeting those of the spouse seeking maintenance." UMDA § 308(b).

36. *FLQ* 52, no. 4 (Winter 2019), 582-85.

37. *California*: Cal. Fam. Code § 4320(g) (2017); *Florida*: Fla. Stat. § 61.08(2)(g) (2017); *Ohio*: Ohio Rev. Code Ann. § 3105.18(C)(1)(f) (2016).

38. *FLQ* 52, no. 4 (Winter 2019), 582-85.

39. *Tennessee*: Tenn. Code Ann. § 36-5-121(C)(2) (2017). If one spouse's current income is sufficient to maintain that party's former standard of living, the standard of living makes that the measure of "necessity" in a case. *Reynolds v. Reynolds*, 216 Md. 205, 85 Al.3d 350, 362 (2014). Standard of living may exceed a party's "expressed needs." *Straus v. Straus*, 101 Md. App. 490, 512, 647 A.2d 818 (1994).

40. Md. Code Ann., Fam. Law, § 11-106 (c)(2) (2019 Repl. Vol.).

41. In *Massachusetts*, the "court may increase the length of marriage if there is evidence that the parties' economic marital partnership began during their cohabitation period prior to the marriage." Mass. Gen. Laws ch. 208 § 48 (2017).

42. *West Virginia*: W.Va. Code § 48-6-301(b)(2) (2016).

43. *Florida*: Fla. Stat. § 61.08(4) (2017).

44. *Florida*: Fla. Stat. § 61.08(2)(f) (2017). *Tennessee*'s statute recognizes that spouses have "family arrangements" concerning nurturing the family and the family's economic strength, and that "the contributions to the marriage as homemaker or parent are of equal dignity and importance as economic contributions to the marriage." Tenn. Code Ann. § 36-5-121(c) (2017).

45. *Ohio*: Ohio Rev. Code Ann. § 3105.18(C)(2) (2016).

46. *Arizona*: Ariz. Rev. Stat. Ann. § 25-319(B)(6) (2017).

47. UMDA (1973) § 307 & § 308(b); ALI, *Family Dissolution*, § 5.02(2), see Comment *e*.

48. *FLQ* 52, no. 4 (Winter 2019), 582-85, 600-608.

49. For example, *Georgia*'s statute states that: "A party shall not be entitled to alimony if . . . the separation between the parties was caused by that party's adultery or desertion. In all cases in which alimony is sought, the court shall receive evidence of the factual cause of the separation." Ga. Code Ann. § 19-6-1(b) (2017).

50. *Louisiana*: "When a spouse has not been at fault prior to the filing of a petition for divorce and the court determines that party was the victim of domestic abuse committed during the marriage by the other party, that spouse shall be awarded final periodic support or a lump sum award, at the discretion of the court, in accordance with Paragraph C of this Article." La. Civ. Code Ann. art. 112(B) (2017); *Utah*'s statute defines "fault" as certain wrongful conduct during the marriage that substantially contributed to the breakup of the marriage relationship: (i) adultery; (ii) intentionally physically harming (or attempting to harm) the other party or minor children; (iii) intentionally causing the other party or minor children to "reasonably fear life-threatening harm;" or (iv) "substantially undermining the financial stability of the other party or the minor children." Utah Code Ann. § 30-3-5(8)(c) (2017).

51. *Alaska*: Alaska Stat. § 25.24.160(a)(2)(E) (2016).

52. *Arizona*: Ariz. Rev. Stat. Ann. § 25-319(B)(11) (2017).

53. *Benkin v. Benkin*, 171 Md. App. 191, 203, 524 A.2d 789 (1987).

54. Md. Code Ann., Fam. Law, § 11-106(c)(1) (2019 Repl. Vol.). Indiana's post divorce alimony is restricted to certain situations, including, "where a spouse's physical or mental incapacity materially affects that spouse's ability to be self-supporting alimony may be awarded during the period of the incapacity." Ind. Code § 31-15-7-2(1) (2017). See also *Brashier v. Brashier*, 80 Md. App. 93, 99, 100, 560 A.2d 44 (1989) (Where a wife's psychiatric disability adversely impacted her rehabilitation efforts, modification of alimony to award indefinite alimony was appropriate).

55. *Nevada*: Nev. Rev. Stat. § 125.150(9) (2015).

56. *New Hampshire*: N.H. Rev. Stat. Ann. § 458:19(IV)(b) (2016).

57. Md. Rule 9-202(e) and 9-203(a) (2020).

58. *New York*: N.Y. Dom. Rel. Law § 236 Part B (4) (2017).

59. *Reynolds v. Reynolds*, 216 Md. App. 205, 85 A.3d 350, 359 (2014) (citations omitted); and *St. Cyr v. St. Cyr*, 228 Md. App. 163 (2016).

60. A recipient's assets do not have to be liquidated before being entitled to obtain spousal support. *Wassif v. Wassif*, 77 Md. App. 750, 756-58, 551 A.2d 935 (1989); Reuter v. Reuter, 102 Md. App. 212, 232-33, 649 A.2d 24 (1994).

61. *New Mexico*: "potential proceeds from the sale of property by either spouse shall not be considered by the court, unless required by exceptional circumstances and the need to be fair to the parties." N.M. Stat. § 40-4-7(E)(7) (2017).

62. *West Virginia*: W.Va. Code § 48-6-301(b)(14) (2016).

63. "An Employee's Guide to Health Benefits Under COBRA," accessed October 28, 2017. https://www.dol.gov/sites/default/files/ebsa/about-ebsa/our-activities/resource-center/publications/an-employees-guide-to-health-benefits-under-cobra.pdf.

64. See Md. Code Ann., Ins. §15-408 (2017 Repl. Vol.) and Md. Code Ann., Fam. Law §11-111 (2019 Repl. Vol.).

65. *Arizona*: Ariz. Rev. Stat. Ann. § 25-319(B)(12) (2017).

66. Cal. Fam. Code § 4320(j) (2016).

67. See IRS Publication 504, "Divorced or Separated Individuals."

68. See Md. Code Ann., Fam. Law § 8-101, 8-103, and 8-105 (2019 Repl. Vol).

69. *Virginia*: Va. Code Ann. § 20-107.1(E)(11) (2017).

70. See Cynthia Lee Starnes, *The Marriage Buyout: The Troubled Trajectory of U.S. Alimony Law* (New York: New York University Press, 2014), 76-88. Starnes discusses representative examples of various forms of guidelines used in certain jurisdictions. See also Mary Kay Kisthardt, "Rethinking Alimony: The AAML's Considerations for Calculating Alimony, Spousal Support, or Maintenance," *Journal of the American Academy of Matrimonial Lawyers* 21 (2008), 73–77.

71. An alimony award in *Louisiana* "shall not exceed one-third of the obligor's net income except in instances of domestic abuse." La. Civ. Code Ann. art. 112 (2017). In *Texas*: "(a) A court may not order maintenance that requires an obligor to pay monthly more than the lesser of: (1) $5,000; or (2) 20 percent of the spouse's average monthly gross income." Tex. Fam. Code Ann. § 8.055(a) (2015).

72. See *New York*: N.Y. Dom. Rel. Law § 236 Part B (2017).

73. An AAML Commission reviewed guidelines used in various jurisdictions and determined that two universal factors were applied: the parties' income and the marriage length. AAML then recommended an approach to determining both the amount and length of an alimony award, subject to application of ten specified "deviation factors." "Deviation factors: The following circumstances may require an adjustment to the recommended amount and duration: 1) A spouse is the primary caretaker of a dependent minor or a disabled adult child; 2) A spouse has pre-existing court-ordered support obligations; 3) A spouse is complying with court-ordered payment of debts or other obligations (including uninsured or unreimbursed medical expenses); 4) A spouse has unusual needs; 5) A spouse's age or health; 6) A spouse has given up a career, a career opportunity, or otherwise supported the career of the other spouse; 7) A spouse has received a disproportionate share of the marital estate; 8) There are unusual tax consequences; 9) Other circumstances that make application of these considerations inequitable; 10) The parties have agreed otherwise." Kisthardt, "Rethinking Alimony," 81. Maryland's highest court reviewed the AAML alimony guidelines and noted that a trial court may consider other factors and said, "*if* the guidelines reasonably direct the court to a fair and equitable award without supplanting or frustrating any one of the twelve enumerated statutory considerations, a court may refer to them as an aid in translating its statutorily mandated analysis into a dollar amount." *Boemio v. Boemio*, 414 Md. 118, 994 A.2d 911 (2010).

74. "'Gross Income' is defined by a state's definition of gross income under the child support guidelines, including actual and imputed income." Kisthardt, "Rethinking Alimony," 80.

75. For example, if the higher income spouse earns $80,000 and the lower income spouse earns $20,000, the alimony award would be $20,000 annually, or $1,667 monthly. Thirty percent of $80,000 equals $24,000 and 20 percent of $20,000 equals $4,000; $24,000 minus $4,000 equals $20,000. The one receiving alimony would now have $40,000 of annual income, and the payer would have $60,000. The recipient's aggregate $40,000 income does not exceed 40 percent of the parties' combined $100,000 income. The recommendations provide that this alimony calculation is made before child support is determined.

76. Kisthardt, "Rethinking Alimony," 80. Thus, if a couple is married eight years, the alimony would continue for four years (.5 x 8); if they are married sixteen years, support would last twelve years (.75 x 16); and if the marriage exceeded twenty years, the support would be permanent.

77. See Md. Code Ann., Fam. Law § 11-107(b) (2019 Repl. Vol.); *Missouri*: "The maintenance order shall state if it is modifiable or nonmodifiable. The court may order maintenance which includes a termination date. Unless the maintenance order which includes a termination date is nonmodifiable, the court may order the maintenance decreased, increased, terminated, extended, or otherwise modified based upon a substantial and continuing change of circumstances which occurred prior to the termination date of the original order." Mo. Rev. Stat. § 452.335(3) (2016).

78. UMDA (1973) § 316(a).

79. UMDA (1973) § 316(a) Comment.

80. Md. Code Ann., Fam. Law §11-107(a) (2019 Repl. Vol.): "(a) Extension of period.—Subject to the

provisions in FL § 8-103 concerning modifiability of agreements, the court may extend the period for which alimony is awarded, if (1) circumstances arise during the period that would lead to a harsh and inequitable result without an extension; and (2) the recipient petitions the court for an extension during the period." See also *New Jersey*: N.J. Stat. Ann. § 2A:34-23(d)(2017).

81. UMDA (1973) § 316(b). While states provide for alimony to terminate on the death of either party or the remarriage of the alimony recipient, some courts may require payor to purchase life insurance or provide other security for payment of amounts due to the recipient if the payor dies during the alimony term. *Connecticut*: Conn. Gen. Stat. § 46b-82(a) (2017); *Florida*: Fla. Stat. § 61.08(3) (2017). Other security for payment of alimony includes assignment of real estate or other property, including rents, profits, or income from such property. Me. Rev. Stat. Ann. tit. 19-A, § 951-A(7) (2016).

82. *Massachusetts*: Mass. Gen. Laws ch. 208 § 49(f) (2017). New Jersey has an extensive statute regarding modification or termination upon the retirement of the paying spouse who's obligated to pay alimony. *New Jersey*: N.J. Stat. Ann. § 2A:34-23 (2017). "Alimony shall terminate upon the obligor spouse or partner attaining full retirement age. 'Full retirement age' shall mean the age at which a person is eligible to receive full retirement for full retirement benefits under section 216 of the federal Social Security Act (42 U.S.C. s.416)." N.J. Stat. Ann. § 2A:34-23 (2017).

The statute also lists several factors in determining whether the rebuttable presumption has been overcome: "The ages of the parties at the time of the application for retirement; (b) The ages of the parties at the time of the marriage or civil union and their ages at the time of entry of the alimony award; (c) The degree and duration of the economic dependency of the recipient upon the payor during the marriage or civil union; (d) Whether the recipient has foregone or relinquished or otherwise sacrificed claims, rights or property in exchange for a more substantial or longer alimony award; (e) The duration or amount of alimony already paid; (f) The health of the parties at the time of the retirement application; (g) Assets of the parties at the time of the retirement application; (h) Whether the recipient has reached full retirement age as defined in this section; (i) Sources of income, both earned and unearned, of the parties; (j) The ability of the recipient to have saved adequately for retirement; and (k) Any other factors that the court may deem relevant." N.J. Stat. Ann. § 2A:34-23(j)(1) (2017).

83. "The age and health of the parties . . . The obligor's field of employment and the generally accepted age of retirement for those in that field . . . mandatory retirement dates or the dates upon which continued employment would no longer increase retirement benefits . . . motives in retiring, including any pressures to retire applied by the obligor's employer . . . expectations of the parties regarding retirement . . . ability of the obligor to maintain support payments . . . financial impact of the obligor's retirement upon the obligee." N.J. Stat. Ann. § 2A:34-23(j)(2) (2017).

CHAPTER 7

1. The *common law* system was title-based—property belonged to the spouse who had title—and courts lacked authority to transfer title. Husbands typically held legal title to property purchased during marriage, which meant divorced wives suffered an injustice only partially relieved through alimony awards. *Community property* treated the marriage like a partnership, granting both spouses rights to the property acquired during marriage.

2. *Beck v. Beck*, 112 Md. App. 197, 684 A.2d 878 (1996).

3. *New York*: N.Y. Dom. Rel. Law §236 PART B 4. (2017).

4. *Ohio*: Rev. Code Ann. § 3105.171 (E)(5) (2016).

5. *FLQ* 52, no. 4 (Winter 2019), 609-615. Married Alaska residents may elect community property regime. Alaska Stat. § 25.24.160 (2016), and Alaska Stat. § 34.77 (2016).

6. *California*: Cal. Fam. Code § 2550 (2017).

7. *Arizona*: Ariz. Rev. Stat. Ann. § 25-318.A (2017) ("equitably").

8. *Texas*: Tex Fam. Code Ann. § 3.001 (2015).

9. *New Mexico*: N.M. Stat. § 40-3-12 (2017).

10. See *Louisiana*: La. Civ. Code Ann. art. 2364, art. 2365, art. 2366, art. 2367 (2017).

11. *Arizona*: Arizona: Ariz. Rev. Stat. Ann. § 25-318 (2017).

12. See Md. Code Ann., Fam. Law § 8-205 (2019 Repl. Vol.).

13. Goodwill represents the reputation of the business and probability of future earnings. Institutional goodwill reflects the business's location, trade name reputation, long-term arrangements with customers and suppliers, and anticipated future customer base attributable to the business; individual goodwill is the reputation of the individual and is a product of the individual's skill and expertise.

14. In almost every state both vested and non-vested pension rights are subject to equitable distribution with vested rights not subject to forfeiture upon employment termination.

15. A Permanent Seat License, sometimes called a Personal Seat License, provides lifetime rights to purchase a season ticket for a particular seat in a stadium. The license is forfeited if the owner does not purchase tickets, and it may be sold to another person.

16. A nonequity country club membership that cannot be sold or transferred is not marital property, however, "those memberships that may be transferred to other parties or can be sold, exchanged, or redeemed for some monetary amount give the holder the ability to convert the membership to an asset with ascertainable value, which could be distributed equitably as marital property." *Solomon v. Solomon*, 383 Md. 176, 206-207, 857 A.2d 1109, 1126-1127 (2004).

17. Pets are generally considered personal property. Courts in a small minority of jurisdictions may award custody of a pet or service animal to a party.

18. *Maryland*: *Queen v. Queen*, 308 Md. 574, 586-587, 521 A.2d 320 (1987).

19. Medical expenses paid out of joint assets and reimbursement for lost wages during marriage are generally considered marital property; pain and suffering, loss of future earning capacity, and each spouse's loss of consortium damages are separate non-marital property. *Landwehr v. Landwehr*, 200 N.J. Super. 56, 490 A.2d 342 (App. Div., 1985).

20. The majority of decisions treat accrued leave as property where it has accrued during employment while married and it can be paid by a lump sum payment at retirement. See Turner, *Equitable Distribution of Property*, vol. 1, § 5:11, 286–89.

21. The majority rule is that a professional degree or license is not property. See *Archer v. Archer*, 303 Md. 347, 357, 493 A.2d 1074, 1079-1080 (1984).

22. Congress amended the Railroad Retirement Act and established two tiers of benefits: Tier I benefits are a Social Security substitute subject to federal preemption; Tier II benefits can be divided by the court if the marriage lasted at least ten years. See 45 U.S.C. 231a(c)(4)(I-iii) & 231m(b)(2).

23. Uniformed Services Former Spouses' Protection Act, 10 U.S.C. 1408.

24. E.g., *Vermont*: "All property owned by either or both parties, however and whenever acquired, shall be subject to the jurisdiction of the Court." Vt. Stat. Ann. tit. 15, § 751 (a) (2017). See also *FLQ 52*, no. 4 (Winter 2019), 609-615.

25. In the remainder of this chapter, marital and community property will be referred to as marital; non-marital or separate property will be referred to as separate.

26. *South Carolina*: "The court does not have jurisdiction or authority to apportion non-marital property." S.C. Code Ann. § 20-3-630(B) (2017).

27. Turner, *Equitable Distribution of Property*, vol. 1, § 2:10, 84.

28. See *Harper v. Harper*, 294 Md. 54, 448 A.2d 916 (1982).

29. *Grant v. Zich*, 300 Md. 256, 276 n 9, 477 A.2d 1163 (1984) (status changed by subsequent legislation).

30. Ky. Rev. Stat. Ann. § 403.190(2)(e) (2017); *Ohio*: Separate property includes "(iii) Passive income and appreciation acquired from separate property by one spouse during the marriage." Ohio Rev. Code Ann. § 3105.171(6)(a)(iii) (2016).

31. *Gershman v. Gershman*, 286 Conn. 341, 351, 943 A.2d 1091 (2008).

32. See *Minnesota*: Minn. Stat. § 518.58(1a) (2017): "If the court finds that a party to a marriage, without consent of the other party, has . . . transferred, encumbered, concealed, or disposed of marital assets except in the usual course of business or for the necessities of life, the court shall compensate the other party by placing both parties in the same position that they would have been in had the transfer, encumbrance, concealment, or disposal not occurred."

33. *Ohio*: Ohio Rev. Code Ann. § 3105.171(E)(4) (2016).

34. *Florida*: Fla. Stat. § 61.075 (1)(i) (2017): "(i) The intentional dissipation, waste, depletion, or destruction of marital assets after the filing of the petition or within 2 years prior to the filing of the

petition."

35. *Finan v. Finan*, 287 Conn. 491, 499, 949 A.2d 468, 473-474 (2008). The *Finan* opinion includes an extensive discussion of case law in other states and concludes that "the majority of our sister states allow trial courts to consider a spouse's dissipation of marital assets, that occurs *prior* to the spouses' physical separation, in determining the allocation of assets to each spouse."

36. *New Hampshire*: N.H. Rev. Stat. Ann. § 458:16-b (2016); *New York*: N.Y. Dom. Rel. Law §236 PART B 2.b.(2017).

37. *United States v. Cartwright*, 411 U.S. 546, 551, 93 S. Ct. 1713, 716-17, 36 L. Ed. 2d 528 (1973), quoting US Treasury regulations relating to federal estate taxes, IRS Regulation §20.2031-1.

38. *Gravenstine v. Gravenstine*, 58 Md. App 158, 175, 472 A.2d 1001 (1984).

39. See Turner, *Equitable Distribution of Property*, vol. 2, § 6:24, 143.

40. Colo Rev. Stat. § 14-10-113(6)(b)(II) (2017).

41. *District of Columbia*: D.C. Code § 16-910(c) (2016).

42. A Maryland court "may transfer ownership interest in: (1) a pension, retirement, profit sharing, or deferred compensation plan; (2) family use personal property (subject to consent of any lienholders); and (3) real property jointly owned by the parties and used as their principal residence when they lived together, by: (a) ordering transfer of ownership interest of one party in the real property to the other party if the transferee party obtains the release of the transferor party from any lien against the property; (b) authorizing one party to purchase the interest of the other party in the real property, in accordance with the terms and conditions ordered by the court; or (c) both of the above. Md. Code Ann., Fam. Law § 8-205(a)(2) (2019 Repl. Vol.).

43. Starnes, *The Marriage Buyout*, 68.

44. Md. Code Ann., Fam. Law § 8-205(b) (2019 Repl. Vol.).

45. *District of Columbia*: D.C. Code § 16-910(b)(5)(2016).

46. *Arkansas*: Ark. Code Ann. § 9-12-315(a)(1)(A)(ix) (2017).

47. *Ohio*: Ohio Rev. Code Ann. § 3105.171(F) (2016).

48. *Minnesota*: Minn. Stat. § 518.58(2) (2017). The distribution permitted in some states may be in kind—such as dividing the shares of stock between the parties—or perhaps one party will keep all the stock and one-half the value will be distributed to the other party.

49. *Florida*: Fla. Stat. § 61.075(10) (2017).

50. *Hawaii*: Haw. Rev. Stat. § 580-47(a)(4) (2017).

51. Utah Code Ann. § 15-4-6.5 (2017).

52. *In re Marriage of Coyle*, 671 N.E.2d 938 (Ind. Ct. App. 1996).

53. Turner, *Equitable Distribution of Property*, vol. 2, §6:97, 500. Some states restrict marital debt to debt that is incurred to purchase marital property.

54. See Turner, *Equitable Distribution of Property*, §6:96, 503–19.

55. Turner, *Equitable Distribution of Property*, v. 2, §6:99, 525.

56. *Kline v. Kline*, 85 Md. App. 28, 45, 581 A.2d 1300 (1990).

57. See *Deering v. Deering*, 292 Md. 115, 130-131, 437 A.2d 883 (1981).

58. Some states follow the date-of-divorce approach in determining the marital share. Here the numerator is the same—total creditable service during marriage. The denominator is different—total creditable service during marriage. The marital share would be determined by multiplying this coverture fraction by the amount of the employee's retirement benefits if he stopped working on the date of classification. Turner, *Equitable Distribution of Property*, 3d, v. 2, §6:25, 160-163.

59. For example, "*Self-only annuity* means the recurring payment to a retiree who has elected not to provide a survivor annuity to anyone." "*Gross Annuity* means the amount of a self-only annuity less only applicable survivor reduction, but before any other deduction." "*Net Annuity* means the amount of annuity payable after deducting from the gross annuity any amounts that are (1) owed by the retiree to the United States, (2) deducted for health benefits premiums . . . , (3) deducted for life insurance premiums . . . , (4) deducted for Medicare premiums, or (5) properly withheld for federal income tax purposes, if the amounts withheld are not greater than they would be if the retiree claimed all dependents to which he or she was entitled." 5 CFR 838.1003. The consequences of stating "net annuity" in an agreement, rather than "self-only" or "gross" annuity as appropriate, would mean that the former

spouse's share would be greatly reduced.

60. In *Potts v. Potts*, 142 Md. App. 448, 468, 790 A.2d 703 (2002), the Maryland Court of Special Appeals explained that a survivor benefit that is attached to a pension is property separate and apart from the pension itself. A spouse seeking to recover an interest in the survivor benefit attached to the other spouse's pension must request the survivor benefit in addition to any request for the pension benefit itself. That party bears the burden of proving that the survivor benefit is marital property (or a portion of it is marital property), and its value. If the requesting spouse meets his or her burden, the circuit court then has discretion to award the survivor benefit; the benefit is not a matter of right.

61. The USFSPA provides the state court jurisdiction to divide disposable retired pay only if the service member (1) is domiciled in the state; (2) resides in the state; or (3) consents to the state's jurisdiction. 10 U.S.C.A. § 1408(c)(4).

62. See *Howell v. Howell*, 581 U.S. ____, 137 S.Ct. 1400, 197 L.Ed. 781 (2017).

63. 10 U.S.C. §1408(d)(2).

64. 10 U.S.C. §1408(a)(2)(c). Direct payment cannot award one former spouse more than 50 percent of the service member's disposable retired pay (or more than 65 percent aggregate to all former spouses) (50/65 rule).

65. Illustration: "A Sergeant First Class (E-7) who divorces at 15 years of service and later retires at 20 years as a Master Sergeant (E-8) will have the pension divided as of 15 years of service as an E-7. Under the former Maryland law the spouse would have received 50% of the marital share, if, as, and when [the benefits are paid]. The former spouse would get one half of 15/20 or 37.5%. If the Master Sergeant's high 3 [years of pay] is $4,830, the retired pay is $2,414, so the former spouse would receive $905 per month. Under the new law the former spouse would receive one half of the retirement the Sergeant First Class would have received at 15 years. If the Sergeant First Class's high 3 at 15 years was $4,140 and had he retired with 15 years, his retired pay would have been $1,552.50, which would be divided equally so that former spouse would only get $776.25." Bruce E. Avery, Kristina Badalian, and Maureen Glackin, "CLE: Military Retirement Benefits, Disability Pay, and Related Issues," panel discussion on September 26, 2017, Bar Association of Montgomery County (Rockville, MD), 12.

66. Md. Code Ann., Fam. Law § 8-205(a)(2) (2019 Repl. Vol.).

67. Md. Code Ann., Fam. Law § 8-208 (2019 Repl. Vol.).

68. *Crawford v. Crawford*, 293 Md. 307, 309, 443 A.2d 599 (1982).

69. *Baran v. Jaskulski*, 114 Md. App. 322, 332, 689 A.2d 1283 (1997).

70. *Broseus v. Broseus*, 82 Md. App. 183, 570 A.2d 874 (1990). See also *Florida*: "In the absence of a settlement agreement involving the marital home, the court shall consider the following factors before determining the issue of credits or setoffs in its final judgment: (1) Whether exclusive use and possession of the marital home is being awarded, and the basis for the award; (2) Whether alimony is being awarded to the party in possession and whether the alimony is being awarded to cover, in part or otherwise, the mortgage and taxes and other expenses of and in connection with the marital home; (3) Whether child support is being awarded to the party in possession and whether the child support is being awarded to cover, in part or otherwise, the mortgage and taxes and other expenses of and in connection with the marital home; (4) The value to the party in possession of the use and occupancy of the marital home; (5) The value of the loss of use and occupancy of the marital home to the party out of possession; (6) Which party will be entitled to claim the mortgage interest payments, real property tax payments, and related payments in connection with the marital home as tax deductions for federal income tax purposes; (7) Whether one or both parties will experience a capital gains taxable event as a result of the sale of the marital home; and (8) Any other factor necessary to bring about   equity and justice between the parties." Fla. Stat. § 61.077 (2017).

71. *Florida*: Fla. Stat. § 61.075(5) (2017) (the court must consider the factors).

72. *North Carolina*: N.C. Gen. Stat. § 50-20(i1) (2016).

73. *Iowa*: Iowa Code § 598.21(7) (2017)

74. *Ohio*: Ohio Rev. Code Ann. § 3105.89(B) (2016).

75. *South Carolina*: S.C. Code Ann. § 20-3-620 (C) (2017).

76. *Delaware*: "The Court may also direct the continued maintenance and beneficiary designations of existing policies insuring the life of either party. The Court's power under this subsection shall extend only to policies originally purchased during the marriage and owned by or within the effective control

of either party." Del. Code Ann. tit. 13, § 1513 (e) (2017).
77. See *Hopkins v. Hopkins*, 328 Md. 263, 614 A.2d 96 (1992).
78. 11 U.S.C. § 362(a).
79. See Turner, *Equitable Distribution of Property*, vol. 1, § 3-11, 145–47.
80. See Turner, *Equitable Distribution of Property*, vol. 1, 146.
81. 11 U.S.C. § 362(b)(2)(A)(ii) & (iii).
82. See *Petrini v. Petrini*, 336 Md. 453, 467, 648 A.2d 1016 (1994); Maryland Attorneys' Rules of Professional Conduct 19-301.5(a).
83. Md. Code Ann., Fam. Law § 1-202(a)(2) (2019 Repl. Vol.).

CHAPTER 8
1. The source of the original story appears lost, and it has several versions in the retelling.
2. See Roger Fisher, William Ury, and Bruce Patton, *Getting to YES: Negotiating Agreement Without Giving In*, 2nd ed. (New York: Penguin, 1991), which contrasts typical "positional bargaining" of distributive negotiation with the integrative win-win "principled negotiation" or "negotiation on the merits" that was developed by the Harvard Negotiation Project.
3. Sande, *Peacemaker*, 92–93.
4. Leigh Thompson, *The Truth About Negotiations* (Upper Saddle River, NJ: FT Press, 2007), 21.
5. Society for Human Resource Management, *Harvard Business Essentials: Negotiation* (Boston: Harvard Business Publishing, 2003), 8, 11, 156; Marjorie Corman, *Negotiating Outcomes: Expert Solutions to Everyday Challenges*, Pocket Mentor Series (Boston: Harvard Business Publishing, 2007), 8, 93.
6. Malhotra and Bazerman *Negotiation Genius*, 111–12.
7. Fisher, Ury, and Patton, *Getting to Yes*, 4.
8. See Sande, *Peacemaking for Families*, 95–108. This provides a good pedagogical order that will be followed here.
9. Longman, *Proverbs*, 437.
10. Prov. 16:1–3, 9, 33; 19:21; 27:1; James 4:13–17.
11. Ps. 139:23–24; Matt. 6:25–33; 7:11; Rom. 8:28; 12:2; Phil. 1:9; 4:6–7; Col. 1:9–10; James 1:5.
12. Craver, *Intelligent Negotiator*, 25.
13. Ronald M. Shapiro and Mark A. Jankowski, *The Power of Nice: How to Negotiate So Everyone Wins—Especially You!*, rev. ed. (New York: Wiley, 2001), 67.
14. Shapiro and Jankowski, *The Power of Nice*, 60.
15. Danny Ertel, quoted in Harvard, *Negotiation*, 116.
16. Fisher, Ury, and Patton, *Getting to Yes*, 17–39.
17. Malhotra and Bazerman, *Negotiation Genius*, 277–79.
18. Prov. 12:18; 13:3; 15:28; 16:23, 24; James 1:19; 3:1–12.
19. Jim Newheiser, *Opening Up Proverbs* (Leominster, England: DayOne, 2008), 137.
20. Malhotra and Bazerman, 269–72.
21. Ury, *Getting Past No*, 5; Fisher, Ury, and Patton, *Getting to Yes*, 54.
22. Sande, 234.
23. Fisher, Ury, and Patton, *Getting to Yes*, 41.
24. Thompson, *Truth About Negotiations*, 91–92.
25. Ury, *Getting Past No*, 6.
26. Fisher, Ury, and Patton, *Getting to Yes*, 52.
27. Fisher, Ury, and Patton, 48.
28. Malhotra and Bazerman, *Negotiation Genius*, 108.
29. Malhotra and Bazerman, 110–11.
30. Bazerman and Neale, *Negotiating Rationally*, 23.
31. Ury, 20.
32. Malhotra and Bazerman, *Negotiation Genius*, 75.
33. Malhotra and Bazerman, 65.
34. Thompson, *Truth About Negotiations*, 110–11.
35. Malhotra and Bazerman, *Negotiation Genius*, 76.

36. Malhorta and Bazerman, 100.

CHAPTER 9

1. Kovach, *Mediation Principles*, 23.
2. Association of Family and Conciliation Courts, "Model Standards of Practice for Family and Divorce Mediation," AFCCnet, accessed October 31, 2017, http://www.afccnet.org/Portals/0/PublicDocuments/CEFCP/ModelStandardsOfPracticeForFamilyAndDivorceMediation.pdf?ver=2013-08-21-072320-000.
3. Raiffa, *Negotiation Analysis*, 87.
4. Raiffa, 319.
5. See Stuart G. Webb and Ronald D. Ousky, *The Collaborative Way to Divorce: The Revolutionary Method That Results in Less Stress, Lower Costs, and Happier Kids—Without Going to Court* (New York: Hudson Street Press, 2006).
6. For a more detailed description of the Collaborative team members' roles, see Webb and Ousky, *Collaborative Way to Divorce*, 87–96; Tesler and Thompson, *Collaborative Divorce*, 41–50.
7. Webb and Ousky, *Collaborative Way to Divorce*, 102–4.
8. See sample "Participation Agreement" in Appendix A in Webb and Ousky, *The Collaborative Way to Divorce*, 191–200.
9. "Collaborative Law Act Summary," Uniform Law Commission, accessed October 31, 2017, http://www.uniformlaws.org/ActSummary.aspx?title=Collaborative%20Law%20Act.
10. Uniform Arbitration Act (2000), § 23(a), accessed October 31, 2017, http://www.uniformlaws.org/shared/docs/arbitration/arbitration_final_00.pdf.
11. "Model Family Law Arbitration Act," AAML.org, accessed October 31, 2017, http://www.aaml.org/library/publications/21215/model-family-law-arbitration-act.
12. AAML Model Family Law Arbitration Act, § 123(a)(7).
13. "Uniform Family Law Arbitration Act," Uniform Law Commission, accessed October 31, 2017, http://www.uniformlaws.org/shared/docs/family%20law%20arbitration/2016AM_FamilyLawArbitration_Revised%20as%20approved%20act_2016aug3.pdf.
14. "Christian Conciliation Service," https://rw360.org/christian-conciliation-service/, and "Institute for Christian Conciliation," https://www.instituteforchristianconciliation.com, accessed July 3, 2020.
15. "Rules of Procedure," Christian Conciliation Service, accessed July 3, 2020, https://rw360.org/rules-procedure-christian-conciliation.

CHAPTER 10

1. Benjamin L. Sells, *The Soul of the Law* (Rockport, MA: Element, 1994), 82.
2. Kidner, *Proverbs*, 174.
3. *Maryland*: "If the grounds for divorce occurred outside of this State, a party may not apply for a divorce unless one of the parties has resided in this State for at least 6 months before the application is filed." Md. Code Ann., Fam. Law § 7-101(a) (2019).
4. *California*: "Forms & Rules," California Courts, accessed October 1, 2017, http://www.courts.ca.gov/forms.htm?filter=DI. Each form indicates whether it has been adopted for mandatory use or approved for optional use. See also *New York*: "Divorce Forms," New York State Unified Court System, accessed February 6, 2018, https://www.nycourts.gov/divorce/forms.shtml; *Washington*: "Court Forms," Washington State Courts, accessed October 31, 2017, https://www.courts.wa.gov/forms/?fa=forms.static&staticID=14.
5. *Maryland*: Department of Juvenile and Family Services, "Forms," Maryland Courts, accessed October 31, 2017, http://mdcourts.gov/family/forms.html; see also *Florida*: "Family Law Forms," Florida Courts, accessed October 31, 2017, http://www.flcourts.org/resources-and-services/family-courts/family-law-self-help-information/family-law-forms.stml.
6. See *Terry v. Terry*, 50 Md. App. 53, 435 A.2d 815 (1981); *Ledvinka v. Ledvinka*, 154 Md. App. 420, 439, 840 A.2d 173 (2003): "Pleading serves four important purposes: (1) it provides notice to the parties as to the nature of the claim or defense; (2) it states the facts upon which the claim or defense allegedly exists; (3) it defines the boundaries of litigation; and (4) it provides for the speedy resolution of frivolous claims and defenses."

7. Md. Code Ann., Cts. & Jud. Proc. § 9-109 (2013 Repl. Vol., 2019 Sup.). In Maryland the assertion of parental fitness in a child custody case does not waive psychiatrist–patient privilege. *Laznovsky v. Laznovsky*, 357 Md. 586, 745 A.2d 1054 (2000). The *Laznovsky* opinion contains an excellent legislative history analysis of this privilege statute.

8. See e.g., Md. Code Ann., Cts. & Jud. Proc. § 9-111 (2013 Repl. Vol.): "A minister of the gospel, clergyman, or priest of an established church of any denomination may not be compelled to testify on any matter in relation to any confession or communication made to him in confidence by a person seeking his spiritual advice or consolation."

9. See e.g., Md. Code Ann., Cts. & Jud. Proc. § 9-121(2013 Repl. Vol., 2019 Sup.): "A client has a privilege to refuse to disclose, and to prevent a witness from disclosing, communications made while the client was receiving counseling or any information that by its nature would show that such counseling occurred."

10. "Summary of the HIPAA Privacy Rule," US Department of Health and Human Services, accessed July 17, 2017, https://www.hhs.gov/hipaa/for-professionals/privacy/laws-regulations/index.html?language=es.

11. See e.g., Md. Code Ann., Cts. & Jud. Proc. § 9-105 (2013 Repl. Vol.).

12. *Robinson v. Robinson*, 328 Md. 507, 615 A.2d 1190 (1992), discusses the consequence of a parent asserting a Fifth Amendment privilege against compelled self-incrimination with respect to questions relating to adultery.

13. Court rules may also permit the court to order a mental or physical examination of a party under certain circumstances. Fed. R. Civ. Pro. Rule 35; Md. R. 2-423.

14. These examples are taken from Maryland Form Interrogatories, Form 5, Domestic Relations Interrogatories, with each one's number indicated in parentheses. Often subparts of an interrogatory are counted as separate against the permissible number, but form interrogatories establish that each one is treated as a single question regardless of apparent subparts. Form use also helps avoid unnecessary discovery disputes.

15. See *Pleasant v. Pleasant*, 97 Md. App. 711, 632 A.2d 202 (1993).

16. Fed. R. Civ. Proc. 30(d)(1); Md. R. 2-411.

17. Md. Rule 2-433(a) (2020).

18. "Tip: You may be able to get your tax return or return information from other sources. If you had your tax return completed by a paid preparer, they should be able to provide you a copy of the return. The IRS can provide a Tax Return Transcript for many returns free of charge. The transcript provides most of the line entries from the tax return and usually contains the information that a third party (such as a mortgage company) requires. See Form 4506-T, Request for Transcript of Tax Return, or you can call 1-800-829-1040 to order a transcript." IRS, "About Form 4506, Request for Copy of Tax Return," IRS.gov, accessed February 6, 2018, https://www.irs.gov/forms-pubs/about-form-4506.

19. E.g., for free public access to Maryland district court and circuit court judicial cases, go to www.courts.state.md.us/courtrecords.html and click on "Case Search," or go to http://casesearch.courts.state.md.us./inquiry/inquiry-index.jsp.

20. E.g., Maryland has free public access to land records at www.MDLandRec.Net.

21. WCF 24.6.

CHAPTER 11

1. AAML *Bounds of Advocacy*, § 6.1. Available through "Bounds of Advocacy," AAML.org, accessed October 14, 2017, http://aaml.org/library/publications/19/bounds-advocacy/6-children.

2. Gen. 1:27–28; Deut. 4:9, 6:1–9, 11:18–21; Prov. 1:8–10; 22:6; 2 Tim. 1:5; 3:14–15.

3. Robert E. Emery, *Two Homes, One Childhood: A Parenting Plan to Last a Lifetime* (New York: Avery, 2016), 46.

4. Emery, *Two Homes, One Childhood*, 36.

5. Andrew I. Schepard, *Children, Courts, and Custody: Interdisciplinary Models for Divorcing Families* (Cambridge: Cambridge University Press, 2004), 4.

6. Janet R. Johnston, Vivienne Roseby, and Kathryn Kuehnle, *In the Name of the Child: A Developmental Approach to Understanding and Helping Children of Conflicted and Violent Divorce*, 2nd ed. (New York: Springer, 2009), 3.

7. Johnston, Roseby, and Kuehnle, *In the Name of the Child*, 5.

8. Garrity and Baris, *Caught in the Middle*, 12.

9. See Schepard, *Children, Courts, and Custody*, 27–40; Garrity and Baris, *Caught in the Middle*, 19, 29–50; Elizabeth M. Ellis, *Divorce Wars: Interventions with Families in Conflict* (Washington, DC: American Psychological Association, 2000), 177–204.

10. Garrity and Baris, *Caught in the Middle*, 23–24.

11. Garrity and Baris, 24–25.

12. Joan B. Kelly and Janet R. Johnston, "The Alienated Child: A Reformulation of Parental Alienation Syndrome," *Family Court Review* 39 (2001): 249–66.

13. Factors that may contribute to alienation include "(1) systemic processes—triangulation into marital conflict; separation as humiliating; high conflict divorce and litigation (2) new partners, family, professionals; (3) behavior of rejected parent—passivity and withdrawal; counter-rejection of the alienated child; harsh and rigid parenting; critical/demanding style; self-centered/immature behavior; inadequate empathy for child's feelings; (4) child's developmental stage and vulnerabilities—age and cognitive capacity; feeling abandoned by rejected parent; temperament and personality vulnerabilities; other child-parent relationship factors; lack of corrective-contact; isolation with favored parent—with little support from others; (5) alienating parent's conduct—open expression of negative views; inaccurate/exaggerated opinions of dangerousness; implying the child does not need the other parent; erasure of rejected parent's presence (pictures, etc.); guilt messages when child expresses pleasure of desire for contact; insistence child can choose whether to have contact; ears get big at negative reports." Louise T. Truax and Jeffrey P. Wittmann "Alienation: Identification Is Not Enough," Sessions 1 presented at the "AF-CC-AAML 2015 Conference on Advanced Issues in Child Custody: Evaluation, Litigation, and Settlement," (Washington, DC, October 1, 2015), summarizing Kelly and Johnston's "The Alienated Child."

14. Garrity and Baris, *Caught in the Middle*, 12–13, citing Judith Wallerstein, "Children of Divorce: The Psychological Tasks of the Child," *American Journal of Orthopsychiatry* 53 (1983): 263–79.

15. Chirban, *Collateral Damage*, 41.

16. Emery, *Two Homes, One Childhood*, 29.

17. Emery, 34–35.

18. Emery, 29.

19. Ps. 94:12–13; Prov. 3:11–12; 13:24; Heb. 12:5–11; cf. Rev. 3:19.

20. Emery, *Two Homes, One Childhood*, 29.

21. See Emery, *Two Homes, One Childhood*, 29; Chirban, *Collateral Damage*, 65–66.

22. Chirban, *Collateral Damage*, 65.

23. Chirban, 66.

24. Chirban, 88.

25. See chap. 10n4.

26. See chap. 10n5.

27. See Barbara A. Babb et al., *Parent Education Programs: Review of the Literature and Annotated Bibliography*, Maryland Judiciary Research Consortium, 2009, accessed October 3, 2017, https://law.ubalt.edu/downloads/law_downloads/June2009_ParentEdPrograms_FINAL.pdf; Emily M. Douglas, *Mending Broken Families: Social Policies for Divorced Families: How Effective Are They?* (Lanham, Maryland: Rowman & Littlefield, 2006), 39–63.

28. "Rule 9-204 Educational Seminar," Maryland Code and Court Rules, accessed February 8, 2017, https://govt.westlaw.com/mdc/Document/NA3AA82B09CEB11DB9BCF9DAC28345A2A?viewType=FullText&originationContext=documenttoc&transitionType=CategoryPageItem&contextData=(sc.Default).

29. See the PEACE Handbook and Brochure, available through the Montgomery County Circuit Court, "Co-Parenting Program," accessed October 14, 2017, http://www.montgomerycountymd.gov/cct/co-parenting.html.

30. Schepard, *Children, Courts, and Custody*, 75–76.

31. See Douglas, *Mending Broken Families*, 42.

32. See the extensive discussions of negotiation (Chapter 8) and mediation (Chapter 9). See also Schepard, *Children, Courts, and Custody*, 50–67; Douglas, *Mending Broken Families*, 15–37; Ellis, *Divorce Wars*, 71–79.

33. See Domestic Violence and Mediation Workgroup, *Screening Cases for Family Violence Issues to Determine Suitability for Mediation and Other Forms of ADR: Screening Protocols and Tools for Maryland Circuit Courts* (Annapolis, MD: Maryland Judiciary, 2005), https://www.courts.state.md.us/sites/default/files/import/family/publications/screening.pdf.

34. American Psychological Association, "Guidelines for Child Custody Evaluations in Family Law Proceedings" (February 2009), §3, accessed October 11, 2017, http://www.apapracticecentral.org/news/guidelines.pdf.

35. There are ethical constraints on giving an opinion concerning a parent whom the evaluator has not interviewed.

36. AAML, "Child Custody Evaluation Standards," *Journal of the American Academy of Matrimonial Lawyers* 25 (2013): 251–94, accessed October 10, 2017, http://aaml.org/sites/default/files/MAT201_3.pdf, §10.

37. AFCC Task Force on Parenting Coordination, "Guidelines for Parenting Coordination," Association of Family and Conciliation Courts, accessed October 4, 2017, https://www.afccnet.org/Portals/0/PublicDocuments/Guidelines/AFCCGuidelinesforParentingcoordinationnew.pdf.

38. *FLQ* 52, no. 4 (Winter 2019), 586-94.

39. See Md. Code Ann., Fam. Law § 1-202 (2019 Repl. Vol.); Maryland Rule 9-205.1 (2020); Maryland Rules, Appendix 19-D, *Maryland Guidelines for Practice for Court-Appointed Attorneys Representing Children in Cases Involving Child Custody or Access* (2020).

40. Maryland Rules, *Maryland Guidelines*, Guideline 2.2–3.

41. Maryland Rules, *Maryland Guidelines*, Guideline 2.4. The parents, jointly or severally, may neither agree nor refuse to waive the privilege on a minor child's behalf. The case of *Nagle v. Hooks*, 295 Md. 127, 460 A.2d 49 (1983) holds that the court must appoint a guardian to act for a minor child to exercise the privilege of nondisclosure where the minor child is too young to personally exercise the privilege of nondisclosure.

42. Maryland Rules, *Maryland Guidelines*, Guideline 2.3.

43. *FLQ* 52, no. 4 (Winter 2019), 586-94. The child's wishes are not a criterion in Massachusetts.

44. UMDA § 404(a).

45. Schepard, *Children, Courts and Custody*, 140–41.

46. Larry Wright, "Interviewing Children in Child Custody Cases," *Journal of the American Academy of Matrimonial Lawyers* 18 (2002): 301.

47. ALI *Principles*, § 2.11(2), contains a non-exhaustive list of restrictions courts should consider imposing as may be reasonably calculated to protect the child or parent: "(a) an adjustment, including a reduction or the elimination, of the custodial responsibility of a parent; (b) supervision of the custodial time between a parent and the child; (c) exchange of the child between parents through an intermediary, or in a protected setting; (d) restraints on a parent's communication with or proximity to the other parent or the child; (e) a requirement that a parent abstain from possession or consumption of alcohol or nonprescribed drugs while exercising custodial responsibility and within a specified period immediately preceding such exercise; (f) denial of overnight custodial responsibility; (g) restrictions on the specific persons while a parent is with the child; (h) a requirement that a parent post a bond to secure return of the child following a period in which the parent is exercising custodial responsibility or to secure other performance required by the court; (i) a requirement that a parent complete a treatment program for perpetrators of domestic violence, for drug or alcohol abuse, or for other behavior addressed in this section; (j) any other constraints or conditions that the court deems necessary to provide for the safety of the child, a child's parent, or any other person whose safety immediately affects the child's welfare."

48. See ABA Center on Children and the Law, *A Judge's Guide: Making Child-Centered Decisions in Custody Cases* (ABA, 2001), 119, adapted from Robert B. Straus, "Supervised Visitation and Family Violence," *FLQ* 29 (1995), 229–52.

49. Uniform Child Abduction Prevention Act (UCAPA), Section 8(a)(1)-(5) requires certain provisions in the court's order: "(1) the basis for the court's exercise of jurisdiction; (2) the manner in which notice and opportunity to be heard were given to the persons entitled to notice of the proceedings; (3) a detailed description of each party's custody and visitation rights and residential arrangements

for the child; (4) a provision stating that a violation of the order may subject the party in violation to civil and criminal penalties; and (5) identification of the child's country of habitual residence at the time of the issuance of the order."

50. See UCAPA Section 8(c)-(f). Where there are dual-nationality children, be aware that US court orders don't prevent other countries from issuing travel documents to their citizens.

51. See the ALI *Principles* §2.03 Comment *e*.

52. *Taylor v. Taylor*, 306 Md. 290, 296, 508 A.2d 964, 967 (1986).

53. *Taylor v. Taylor*, 306 Md. 290 fn4.

54. ALI *Principles* § 2.09(2).

55. *Taylor v. Taylor*, 306 Md. 296.

56. See Md. Code Ann., Fam. Law § 5-203 (2019 Repl. Vol.).

57. *Santo v. Santo*, 448 Md. 620, 635-36, 141 A.3d 82-83 (2016).

58. ALI *Principles* § 2.09; § 2.09 Comment *a*.

59. *Santo v. Santo*, 448 Md. 633, 141 A.3d 81.

60. *FLQ* 52, no. 4 (Winter 2019), 586-94.

61. *Taylor v. Taylor*, 306 Md. 296-297.

62. *Taylor v. Taylor*, 306 Md. 297 fn5.

63. The ALI *Principles* define a parenting plan as "a set of provisions for allocation of custodial responsibility and decision[-]making responsibility on behalf of a child and for resolution of future disputes between the parents." ALI *Principles* § 2.03(2).

64. ALI *Principles* § 2.05(1), (5).

65. *Arizona*: Ariz. Rev. Stat. Ann. § 25-403.02.C. (2016).

66. Arizona: Ariz. Rev. Stat. Ann. § 25-403.02 (2016).

67. *South Carolina*: S.C. Code Ann. § 63-15-220 (2017).

68. *Washington*: Wash. Rev. Code § 26.09.184(1) (2017). In 1987 Washington was the first state to implement detailed temporary and permanent parenting plan requirements.

69. Emery, *Two Homes, One Childhood*, 69.

70. Emery, 70.

CHAPTER 12

1. First Kings 3:16–28. Solomon was king of a united Israel following the end of his father David's reign ca. 970 BCE. According to the Biblical narrative, Solomon asked God for wisdom—"discernment in administering justice"—and God blessed him with a "wise and discerning heart" (vv. 7–12). Solomon was known throughout the ancient world for his wisdom (4:31), and he displayed his wisdom in his judicial rulings (see 3:16–28).

2. See *Meyer v. Nebraska*, 262 U.S. 390, 399, 401 (1923); *Pierce v. Society of the Sisters of the Holy Names of Jesus and Mary*, 268 U.S. 510, 535 (1925); *Stanley v. Illinois*, 405 U.S. 645 (1972); *Troxel v. Granville*, 530 U.S. 57, 66 (2000).

3. *Wisconsin v. Yoder*, 406 U.S. 205 (1972).

4. See *Saenz v. Roe*, 526 U.s. 489, 498 (1999)

5. *Shapiro v. Thompson*, 394 U.S. 618, 629 (1969), overruled on other grounds by *Edelman v. Jordan*, 415 U.S. 651, 671 (1974).

6. See *Braun v. Headley*, 131 Md. App. 588, 750 A.2d 624 (2000).

7. For example, parental refusal to permit necessary blood transfusions or required vaccinations for their children on religious grounds has been overridden. See *Levitsky v. Levitsky*, 231 Md. 388 (Md. 1963) (blood transfusion); and *Brown v. Stone*, 378 So.2d 218 (Miss. 1979) (vaccinations).

8. *McDermott v. Dougherty*, 385 Md. 320, 869 A.2d 751, 770, 808 (2005).

9. *McDermott v. Dougherty*, 385 Md. 320, 374-75, 869 A.2d 751 (2005). "The analysis in third party custody and visitation disputes is the same, i.e., parents are presumed to act in the best interests of their children, and a court may not apply the best interests standard absent a threshold showing of parental unfitness or exceptional circumstances." *Aumiller v. Aumiller*, 183 Md. App. 71, 80, 959 A.2d 849, 854 (2008); See also *Burak v. Burak*, 455 Md. 564 (Md. Court of Appeals, 2017).

10. ALI *Principles* define *de facto* parent as: "An individual other than a legal parent or a parent by estoppel

who, for a significant period of time not less than two years, (i) lived with the child and, (ii) for reasons primarily other than financial compensation, and with the agreement of a legal parent to form a parent-child relationship, or as a result of a complete failure or inability of any legal parent to perform caretaking functions, (A) regularly performed a majority of the caretaking functions for the child, or (B) regularly performed a share of caretaking functions at least as great as that of the parent with whom the child primarily lived." ALI *Principles* § 2.03(1)(c), 107-08. Under the Wisconsin four-factor test, which has been followed by other states, a third-party seeking to establish *de facto* parent status has the burden of proving (1) that the biological or adoptive parent consented to, and fostered, the petitioner's formation and establishment of a parent-like relationship with the child; (2) that the petitioner and the child lived together in the same household; (3) that the petitioner assumed obligations of parenthood by taking significant responsibility for the child's care, education, and development, including contributing towards the child's support without expectation of financial compensation; and (4) that the petitioner has been in a parental role for a length of time sufficient to have established with the child a bonded, dependent relationship parental in nature. *Conover v. Conover,* 450 Md. 51, 73-74, 146 A.3d 433, 446-47 (quoting *H.S.H.–K.,* 533 N.W.2d 419 (Wisc. 1995)).

11. See *Conover v. Conover,* 450 Md. 51, 146 A.3d 433 (2016). *Idaho's* statute states: "In any case where the child is actually residing with a grandparent in a stable relationship, the court may recognize the grandparent as having the same standing as a parent for evaluating what custody arrangements are in the best interests of the child." Idaho Code Ann. § 32-717 (2017).

12. *Taylor v. Taylor,* 306 Md. 290, 303, 508 A.2d 964, 970 (1986).

13. "Because most decisions are not subjected to appellate review, and because appellate review is properly limited in scope . . . the burden of making an appropriate decision necessarily rests heavily upon the shoulders of the trial judge." *Taylor,* 306 Md. at 311, 508 A.2d at 974 (citations omitted).

14. *Domingues v. Johnson,* 323 Md. 486, 499 (1990) (emphasis added).

15. Neb. Rev. Stat. § 43-2923(1) (2017).

16. *FLQ* 52, no. 4 (Winter 2019), 586-94. UMDA §402 lists some factors to be considered: the desires of the parents and child; the child's relationship with parents, siblings and third persons who may be significantly involved; the child's stability in the present situation; the physical and mental health of the parties and the child; and the reminder that certain conduct of one seeking custody is important only insofar as it impacts the child.

17. *Taylor v. Taylor,* 306 Md. 290, 508 A.2d 964 (1986). The assertion of parental fitness in a child custody case does not waive psychiatrist-patient privilege. *Laznovsky v. Laznovsky,* 357 Md. 586, 745 A.2d 1054 (2000). The *Laznovsky* opinion contains an excellent legislative history analysis of the privilege statute.

18. *Montgomery County Department of Social Services v. Sanders,* 38 Md. App. 406, 381 A.2d 1154 (1977).

19. See *Davis v. Davis,* 280 Md. 119, 372 A.2d 231 (1977); Swain v. Swain, 43 Md. App. 645, 406 A.2d 680 (1979).

20. *Minnesota*: Minn. Stat. § 518.17 (2016).

21. See *Gillespie v. Gillespie,* 206 Md. App. 146, 47 A.3d 1018 (2012).

22. Md. Code Ann., Cts. & Jud. Proc. § 9-109 (2013 Repl. Vol., 2019 Sup.). In Maryland the assertion of parental fitness in a child custody case does not waive psychiatrist-patient privilege. *Laznovsky v. Laznovsky,* 357 Md. 586, 745 A.2d 1054 (2000). The *Laznovsky* opinion contains an excellent legislative history analysis of this privilege statute.

23. *Indiana:* simply filing a custody action places a parent's mental health in dispute and constitutes a waiver of the privilege for the custody proceeding. Owen v. Owen, 563 N.E.2d 605, 608 (Ind. 1990). *Alabama's* rules of evidence provide that there is no psychotherapist-patient privilege "for relevant communications offered in a child custody case in which the mental state of a party is clearly an issue and a proper resolution of the custody question requires disclosure." Ala. R. Evid. 503(d)(5). *Maryland:* "a person seeking an award of child custody that claims to be a fit parent, does not, without more, waive the confidential psychiatrist/psychologist-patient privilege in respect to her or his past mental health 'diagnosis and treatment' communications and records." *Laznovsky v. Laznovsky,* 357 Md. 586, 620-21, 745 A.2d 1054, 1072-73 (2000). The court noted that in some cases, "the party exercising the privilege may be at a disadvantage because the portion of the party's own treatment records that is favorable to him or her may not be available to the trial court."

24. *Hadick v. Hadick*, 90 Md. App. 740, 603 A.2d 915 (1992).

25. *Missouri*: Mo. Rev. Stat. § 452.375(2)(4) (2016).

26. *FLQ* 52, no. 4 (Winter 2019), 586-94.

27. *Illinois*: 750 Ill. Comp. Stat. 5/602.7(b)(4) (2017).

28. See Md. Code Ann., Fam. Law § 8103(a) (2019 Repl. Vol.).

29. *Taylor v. Taylor*, 306 Md. 290, 308, 508 A.2d 964, 972-973 (1986).

30. *Taylor v. Taylor*, 306 Md. 290, 304, 508 A.2d 964, 971 (1986). See also *Florida*: Fla. Stat § 61.13(3) (l) (2017); *Michigan*: Mich. Comp. Laws § 722.26a (b) (2017).

31. See also *McCarty v. McCarty*, 147 Md. App. 268, 807 A.2d 1211 (2002). Moreover, "if the evidence discloses the parents do not share parenting values and each insists on adhering to irreconcilable theories of child-rearing, joint legal custody is not appropriate." *Taylor*, 306 Md. at 305, 508 A.2d at 972.

32. *Colorado*: Colo. Rev. Stat. § 14-10-124(1.5)(b) (2016).

33. National Institute on Drug Abuse, "Opioid Overdose Crisis," NIDA, accessed August 24. 2017, https://www.drugabuse.gov/drugs-abuse/opioids/opioid-crisis. Statistically, about 21–29 percent of patients prescribed opioids for chronic pain misuse them; 8–12 percent develop an opioid disorder; 4–6 percent who misuse prescription opioids transition to heroin; and about 80 percent of heroin users first misused prescription opioids.

34. *FLQ* 52, no. 4 (Winter 2019), 586-94.

35. *In Re: Adoption No. 12612*, 353 Md. 209, 725 A.2d 1037 (1999).

36. *Arizona*: Ariz. Rev. Stat. Ann. § 25-403(11) (2016).

37. Mnookin and Weisberg, *Child, Family, and State*, 235, citing Elizabeth T. Gershoff and Susan H. Bitensky, "The Case Against Corporal Punishment of Children," *Psychology, Public Policy, and Law* 13, no. 4 (2007), 231, 247. For example, Maryland's Domestic Violence statute's definition of "abuse" states that "nothing in this subtitle shall be construed to prohibit reasonable punishment, including reasonable corporal punishment, in light of the age and condition of the child, from being performed by a parent or stepparent of the child." Md. Code Ann., Fam. Law § 4-501(b)(2) (2012 Repl. Vol., 2016 Sup.).

38. See Mnookin and Weisberg, *Child, Family, and State*, 228–38. Twenty-two additional countries later banned corporal punishment in all settings, including the home (United Nations, "Convention on the Rights of the Child," (1989), articles 19, 37); an international committee that interprets the Convention emphasizes corporal punishment as "incompatible with the Convention" and recommended its prohibition; several international organizations (e.g., the U.N. Committee on the Rights of the Child, the Council of Europe's Parliamentary Assembly, and the Council of Europe's Commissioner for Human Rights) now provide that corporal punishment of children is a violation of international human rights law.

39. Longman, *Proverbs*, 564–65: "Prov. 3:11–12; 10:13; 13:24. . . . And again it must be borne in mind that the application of any proverb depends on the people involved as well as the situation. These proverbs do not imply that parents must apply physical punishment when they judge that a simple verbal reprimand will do. Discipline is never to be done out of anger or hate or a desire to harm, but out of love and a desire that the person improve. In this way, the parent follows the model of God, who disciplines his children (3:11–12)."

40. *Montgomery County Department of Social Services v. Sanders*, 38 Md. App. 406, 381 A.2d 1154 (1977).

41. *Nevada*: Nevada Rev. Stat. § 125C.0035 (4)(1) (2015).

42. See *Hadick v. Hadick*, 90 Md. App. 740, 603 A.2d 915 (1992), and cases discussed therein.

43. ALI *Principles* § 2.08(c) (2002).

44. *Pennsylvania*: 23 Pa. Cons. Stat. § 5328(a)(5) (2017).

45. *Florida*: Fla. Stat § 61.13(3)(j) (2017).

46. *Louisiana*: La. Civ. Code Ann. art. 134 (2) (2016).

47. *Michigan*: Mich. Comp. Laws § 722.23 (2017).

48. Fla. Stat § 61.13(3)(k) (2017).

49. *Pennsylvania*: 23 Pa. Cons. Stat. § 5328(a)(14) (2017).

50. *McAndrew v. McAndrew*, 39 Md. App. 1, 382 A.2d 1081 (1978).

51. *Maine*: Me. Rev. Stat. Ann. tit.19-A, §1653(3)(P) (2016).

52. *Taylor v. Taylor*, 306 Md. 290, 309-309, 508 A.2d 964, 973 (1986).

53. *Kansas*: Factors include the location of the parties' residences and places of employment and the location of the child's school. Kan. Stat. Ann. § 23-3205(a)(13) & (14) (2016).

54. *Taylor*, 306 Md. at 309, 508 A.2d at 973.

55. The *Illinois* statute focuses on "the amount of time each parent spent performing caretaking functions with respect to the child in the 24 months preceding the filing of any petition for allocation of parental responsibilities or, if the child is under 2 years of age, since the child's birth." *Illinois*: 750 Ill. Comp. Stat. 5/602.7(a)(3) (2017).

56. *Wisconsin*: Wis. Stat. § 767.41(5)(am)(4) (2017).

57. ALI *Principles* § 2.08.

58. ALI *Principles* § 2.08 Comment *b*.

59. Schepard, *Children, Courts, and Custody*, 167–68.

60. Schepard, 167–70. Schepard next notes that the "presumption that the child should spend 50% of his or her time with each parent is the principal competitor to the approximation presumption advocated by the ALI." He says, "Whereas the approximation presumption emphasizes the parents' pre-divorce allocation of child-rearing responsibilities too much, a presumption of equal physical custody does not emphasize it enough. A fifty-fifty post divorce residence presumption departs radically from the child-care arrangements that exist in most families prior to divorce. . . . There is little evidence that most non-primary-caretaking parents actually want 50% of the child's residence time after divorce and are willing to make the changes in their lifestyles to accommodate equal physical custody" (170–71).

61. ALI *Principles* § 2.11(1–2).

62. *Louisiana*: La. Civ. Code Ann. art. 134 (2) (2016).

63. *Harrison v. Tauheed*, 256 P.3d 851, 864 (Kan. 2011).

64. See *Kirchner v. Caughey*, 326 Md. 567, 606 A.2d 257 (1992); *Bienenfeld v. BennetWhite*, 91 Md. App. 488, 507, 605 A.2d 172, cert. denied, 327 Md. 625, 612 A.2d 256 (1992).

65. *Florida*: Fla. Stat § 61.13(3)(r) (2017).*

66. Uniform Law Commission, "Delayed Parents Custody and Visitation Act," UniformLaws.org, accessed October 26, 2017, http://www.uniformlaws.org/Act.aspx?title=Deployed%20Parents%20 Custody%20and%20Visitation%20Act.

67. Md. Code Ann., Fam. Law § 9-108(d) (2019 Repl. Vol.).

68. ALI *Principles* § 2.17(4)(a).

69. National Conference of Commissioners on Uniform State Laws, "Uniform Child Custody Jurisdiction and Enforcement Act," UniformLaws.org, accessed September 2, 2017, http://www.uniformlaws.org/shared/docs/child_custody_jurisdiction/uccjea_final_97.pdf. Massachusetts follows the Uniform Child Custody Jurisdiction Act, UCCJEA's predecessor statute, but there are legislative efforts to adopt a form of UCCJEA.

70. The UCCJEA permits *temporary emergency jurisdiction* to secure the threatened person's safety until the proceeding is transferred to the home state (or if there's no home state, then to a state with another jurisdiction basis). The child's abandonment, mistreatment, or abuse, as well as threats to siblings or a parent, are bases for a court to exercise emergency jurisdiction. This may lead to continuing jurisdiction only if no other state with grounds for continuing jurisdiction can be found or, if found, declines to take jurisdiction.

71. Section 201(1) specifies that a state qualifies as a home state if the child lived in the "home state within six months before the commencement of the proceeding." Courts follow the more expansive jurisdictional description of § 201(1).

72. The requirement of "at least six consecutive months" does not have to continue right up to the filing date, but it must have continued to some point within six months of filing. Home state jurisdiction continues for six months after a child has been removed if a parent or person acting as a parent remains in the home state.

73. UCCJEA § 201(a)(2); UCCJEA § 207. The factors to be considered by the court include: "(1) whether domestic violence has occurred and is likely to continue in the future and which State could best protect the parties and the child; (2) the length of time the child has resided outside this State; (3) the

distance between the court in this State and the court in the State that would assume jurisdiction; (4) the relative financial circumstances of the parties; (5) any agreement of the parties as to which State should assume jurisdiction; (6) the nature and location of the evidence required to resolve the pending litigation, including testimony of the child; (7) the ability of the court of each State to decide the issue expeditiously and the procedures necessary to present the evidence; and (8) the familiarity of the court of each State with the facts and issues in the pending litigation." UCCJEA § 207(b).

74. UCCJEA § 201(a)(3).

75. UCCJEA § 208. The Comment to this section provides examples: "removing, secreting, retaining, or restraining the child," and "abducting parents will not receive an advantage for their unjustifiable conduct."

76. This communication is required under Sections 204 (Temporary Emergency Jurisdiction) and 206 (Simultaneous Proceedings) and is suggested in applying Section 207 (Inconvenient Forum).

77. UCCJEA § 313. A provision of the 1980 Parental Kidnapping Prevention Act is an addendum that extends full faith and credit to child custody determinations for uniformity of interstate recognition. 28 U.S.C.A. § 1738A.

78. UCCJEA § 305.

79. UCCJEA § 205.

80. UCCJEA § 105. There's an exception to recognition and enforcement of a foreign country's determination "if the child custody laws of a foreign country violates fundamental principles of human rights." UCCJEA § 105(c).

81. UCCJEA § 305. See also International Child Abduction Remedies Act, 42 U.S.C. § 11601 et seq.

82. *Domingues v. Johnson*, 323 Md. 486, 492-93, 593 A.2d 1133 (1991) (citing *Hardisty v. Salerno*, 255 Md. 436, 439, 258 A.2d 209 (1969).

CHAPTER 13

1. Md. Code Ann., Fam. Law §5-203(b) (2019 Repl. Vol.). Generally, a parent may not waive all child support and any agreement regarding child support may be disregarded by a court as being against public policy. *Stambaugh v. Child Support Enforcement*, 323 Md. 106, 591 A.2d 501, 503-04 (1991).

2. UIFSA applies to proceedings involving child support or spousal support.

3. UIFSA § 205(c).

4. 28 U.S.C. § 1738B.

5. See Md. Code Ann., Fam. Law §5-1032(b)(2) (2019 Repl. Vol.); and Md. Code Ann., Fam. Law §§ 13-101 through 13-109 (2019 Repl. Vol.).

6. 45 C.F.R. § 302.56(g).

7. Morgan, *Child Support Guidelines*, § 1.08[B], 1-22, quoting Robert Williams, *Development of Guidelines for Child Support Orders: Advisory Panel Recommendations and Final Report* (US Dept. of Health and Human Services, Office of Child Support Enforcement, 1987), II-67.

8. Md. Code Ann., Fam. Law §12-204 (2019 Repl. Vol.). Several states make an adjustment based on the age of the children by adding a percentage increase, or permitting deviation, for older children—such as age twelve and older—on the basis that it costs more to raise children at different ages.

9. Md. Code Ann., Fam. Law § 12-204(e) (2019 Repl. Vol.).

10. Morgan, *Child Support Guidelines*, § 1.08[D], 1-34–36.

11. See Md. Code Ann., Fam. Law § 12-201(b)(3) (2019 Repl. Vol.).

12. Some states do not include overtime when it's not a condition of employment.

13. See *Johnson v. Johnson*, 152 Md. App. 609, 833 A.2d 46 (2003).

14. Some states do not include income from second jobs, but only income from "regular, full-time employment, i.e., money earned during the normal work week as is appropriate to a given occupation." *Tracey v. Tracey*, 328 Md. 380, 389, 614 A.2d 590 (1992).

15. Clearly, retirement benefits in pay status constitute income. See Morgan, *Child Support Guidelines*, § 4.07[D], 4-42–4-44.

16. See Morgan, *Child Support Guidelines*, § 4.07[Q], 4-53–4-55.

17. The Texas statute that lists items that are included and excluded from gross income excludes workers' compensation benefits. Tex. Fam. Code Ann. § 8.055(a-1)(2) (2015).

18. Includes "base pay, basic allowance for housing (BAH), basic allowance for subsistence or separate rations (BAS/Sep. Rats.), supplemental subsistence allowance, cost of living adjustment, specialty pay, variable housing allowance (VHA), and pay for training and drills." Morgan, *Child Support Guidelines*, § 4.07[L], 4-73–4-75.

19. Morgan, *Child Support Guidelines*, § 4.07[I], 4-78.9–4-79.

20. The trial court may treat the value of noncash gifts as income where those gifts subsidized the parent's standard of living. *Petrini v. Petrini*, 336 Md. 453, 648 A.2d 1016 (1994).

21. See Md. Code Ann., Fam. Law, § 12-201(b)(3) (2019 Repl. Vol.).

22. *Income* generally means gross receipts minus ordinary and necessary expenses required to produce income. Md. Code Ann., Fam. Law §12-201(b)(2), and §12-201(l) (2019 Repl. Vol.). For example, net rental income may be defined as "rent after deducting operating expenses and mortgage payments, but not including noncash items such as depreciation." *Texas*: Tex. Fam. Code Ann. § 8.055(a-1)(1) (D) (2015). The burden is on the parent seeking to exclude pass-through income from actual income to persuade the court that the pass-through income is not available for child support purposes.

23. Md. Code Ann., Fam. Law, § 12-201(b)(5) (2019 Repl. Vol.).

24. Some factors: physical condition, education, any change in employment, parties' relationship before divorce proceedings, efforts to find work, efforts at any necessary retraining, history of withholding support, work history, and the job market in parent's area. *John O. v. Jane O.*, 90 Md. App. 406, 601 A.2d 149 (1992).

25. Some states take into account a parent's care of a young child. See Morgan, *Child Support Guidelines*, § 5.05[I], 5-59–5-62.

26. See Md. Rule 9-202(f) that requires each party to file a current financial statement under oath in substantially the form set forth in Rule 9-203(a) or (b (2020)).

27. 45 C.F.R. § 302.56(c)(3).

28. Morgan, *Child Support Guidelines*, § 7.01[A], Table 7-1, 7-5–7-6. In Percentage of Income Model States, one party may be required to obtain health insurance for the children without any further adjustment or apportionment of the cost. Morgan, *Child Support Guidelines*, § 7.01[A][2], 7-8 fn4.

29. Morgan, *Child Support Guidelines*, § 7.01[B], Table 7-2, 7-18–7-20. See also *FLQ* 52, no. 4 (Winter 2019), 595-99.

30. In *Bare v. Bare*, 192 Md. App. 307, 994 A.2d 487 (2010), the Maryland Court of Special Appeals held that the trial court erred by increasing Mr. Bare's child support through requiring him to pay a share of other medical expenses that do not meet the definition of "extraordinary" and that "these ordinary medical expenses are expenses that the child support calculation under §12-204(c) guidelines schedule is designed to cover."

31. Md. Code Ann., Fam. Law §§ 12-201(g)(1) and 12-204(h)(1), (2) (2019 Repl. Vol.).

32. Md. Code Ann., Fam. Law §12-201(g) (2) (2019 Repl. Vol.).

33. Morgan, Table 7-3, 7-31–7-33.

34. Morgan, *Child Support Guidelines*, § 7.02[C], 7-33–7-34.

35. Md. Code Ann., Fam. Law §12-204(g)(2)(ii) (2019 Repl. Vol.).

36. See *Witt v. Ristaino*, 118 Md. App. 155, 701 A.2d 1227 (1997).

37. The statutory list of factors to consider in determining whether a court should depart from the Guidelines is not exclusive. *Tannehill v. Tannehill*, 88 Md. App. 4, 591 A.2d 888 (1991).

38. Md. Code Ann., Fam. Law §12-202(a)(2)(iii)(2) (2019 Repl. Vol.). But the addition of half-siblings does not *per se* require departing from Guidelines. FL §12-202(a)(2)(iv) (2019 Repl. Vol.). The Court may not deviate downward on the sole basis that the father had a child from a previous relationship to support; downward deviation requires a justification that it is in the best interest of the child receiving the child support. *Beck v. Beck*, 165 Md. App. 445, 885 A.2d 887 (2005).

39. Md. Code Ann., Fam. Law §12-204(j) (2019 Repl. Vol.).

40. *Walsh v. Walsh*, 333 Md. 492, 635 A.2d 1340, 1346 (1994). See also Md. Code Ann., Fam. Law §12-202(a)(2)(v). The court's responsibility to follow the statutory scheme for deviation from child support guidelines in accepting an agreement applies to any deviation, including where parties agree to an amount of child support greater than the amount calculated under the guidelines. *Knott v. Knott*, 146 Md. App. 232, 806 A.2d 768 (2002).

41. For example, according to Morgan's research, "In Alaska, the threshold is 30% visitation; in Colorado, the threshold is 92 overnights; the District of Columbia requires 40% visitation." *Child Support Guidelines*, § 7.03[A], 7-46 fn98 (citations omitted).
42. Md. Code Ann., Fam. Law § 12-201(n) (2019 Repl. Vol.). For cases filed on or after October 1, 2020, in Maryland shared physical custody definition is when each parent keeps the children 25% (rather than 35%) of the year (at least 92 overnights), and a formula will make a "shared physical custody adjustment" increasing the obligation when the overnights are between 25%–30% (92-109) overnights of the year.
43. Morgan, *Child Support Guidelines*, § 7.03[B], Table 7-5, 7-50.1–7-52; § 7.03[B][1], 7-52.
44. *Child Support Guidelines*, § 8.07[C], Table 8-6, 8-64–8-65.
45. *Voishan v. Palma*, 327 Md. 318, 609 A.2d 319 (1992).
46. Md. Code Ann., Fam. Law §12-101(a)(1), (3) (2019 Repl. Vol.); §12-104(a) (2019 Repl. Vol.).
47. *Smith v. Freeman*, 149 Md. App. 1, 814 A.2d 65 (2002); A change is material when it meets two requirements: (1) the change must be relevant to the level of support a child is actually receiving or entitled to receive, and (2) the change must be of sufficient magnitude to justify judicial modification of the support order.
48. Md. Code Ann., Fam. Law §12-104(b) (2019 Repl. Vol.).
49. Md. Code Ann., Fam. Law §12-204(k) (2019 Repl. Vol.).
50. Md. Code Ann., Fam. Law §10-126 (2019 Repl. Vol.).
51. Md. Code Ann., Fam. Law §§10-119, 10119.3 (2019 Repl. Vol.).
52. An obligor's delinquency of sixty days or more in paying child support is available to consumer credit reporting agencies. Md. Code Ann., Fam. Law §10-108.1. The Child Support Enforcement Administration must first give the obligor notice and "reasonable opportunity to contest the accuracy of the information" before reporting a delinquency. Md. Code Ann., Fam. Law §10-108.1(c) (2019 Repl. Vol.).

CONCLUSION
1. Adams, *Marriage, Divorce and Remarriage*, 24.

About John Weaver

JOHN WEAVER is a family law attorney in Maryland, where he has practiced for forty years including six years when he presided over family law hearings as a Family Magistrate in the Circuit Court for Montgomery County. He received his J.D. from The George Washington University Law School in 1979 and his M.A. in Religion from Reformed Theological Seminary – Washington, D.C. in 2007. His thesis was "A Just Divorce: Divorce That is Right and Just and Fair." His law practice includes family law negotiation, mediation, arbitration, litigation, appellate advocacy, and expert witness services. He has regularly developed and presented Continuing Legal Education seminars, and his local bar association awarded him Section Chair of the Year (Family Law Section), Pro Bono Program Individual and Firm Awards and Service Awards, as well as President's Citation for Outstanding Service to the Bar Association three times. He also served several years in church leadership.

TO CONTACT JOHN WEAVER,
visit his website at
http://www.ajustdivorce.com
and
http://www.maryland-familylaw.com
or email him at
jweaver@ajustdivorce.com

Here's where to connect with and
follow John Weaver on social media:
FACEBOOK: https://www.facebook.com/ajustdivorce
INSTAGRAM: https://www.instagram.com/ajustdivorce
TWITTER: https://www.twitter.com/ajustdivorce

Made in the USA
Columbia, SC
11 August 2020